ALWAYS POSTPONE MEETINGS WITH TIME-WASTING MORONS

A DILBERT® BOOK

SCOTT ADAMS

LET ME GET BACK TO YOU ON THAT.

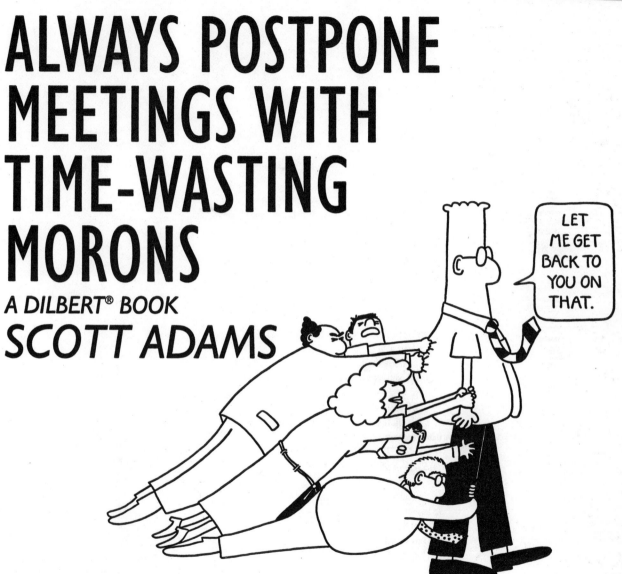

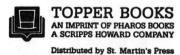

TOPPER BOOKS
AN IMPRINT OF PHAROS BOOKS
A SCRIPPS HOWARD COMPANY
Distributed by St. Martin's Press

For Pam

First published in 1992

Library of Congress Cataloging-in-Publication Data
Adams, Scott, 1957–
    [Dilbert. Selections]
    Always postpone meetings with time-wasting morons / Scott Adams.
        p.   cm. —— (A Dilbert book)
    ISBN 0-88687-688-5 (pbk.) : $7.95
    I. Title. II. Title: Dilbert. III. Series: Adams, Scott, 1957–
Dilbert book
PN6727.A3D5525   1992   92-19633
741.5'973——dc20   CIP

Topper Books
An Imprint of Pharos Books
A Scripps Howard Company
200 Park Avenue
New York, NY 10166

10 9 8 7 6 5 4 3 2 1

INTRODUCTION

Thank you for buying this book. My editor asked me to write an introduction and here it is. I don't have anything to say, but frankly, I doubt anybody will read the introduction anyway; unless you're on a long plane ride and you've already read everything else including the barf bag instructions, and you're looking desperately for something you haven't read—something to take your mind off the fact that most commercial aircraft fleets are well beyond their intended technological life, and the chances are very good that you will soon be engulfed in flames, racing toward the ground at Mach One while cursing yourself for not listening to the pre-flight safety instructions. No, you had to be nonchalant and conspicuously ignore the flight attendant, like you're some kind of big-time traveller or something. And now, because of your ego, they'll be sifting the wreckage for enough of your bony matter to fill an envelope with your name on it. And the guy sitting next to you will be interviewed on CNN saying how he watched you being devoured by flames from the comfort of his emergency asbestos suit which he knew how to get into because **he** paid attention to the flight attendant. But I digress.

The point is that I have to write this introduction. I'm almost done. I think it's going pretty well so far. Okay, I'm done.

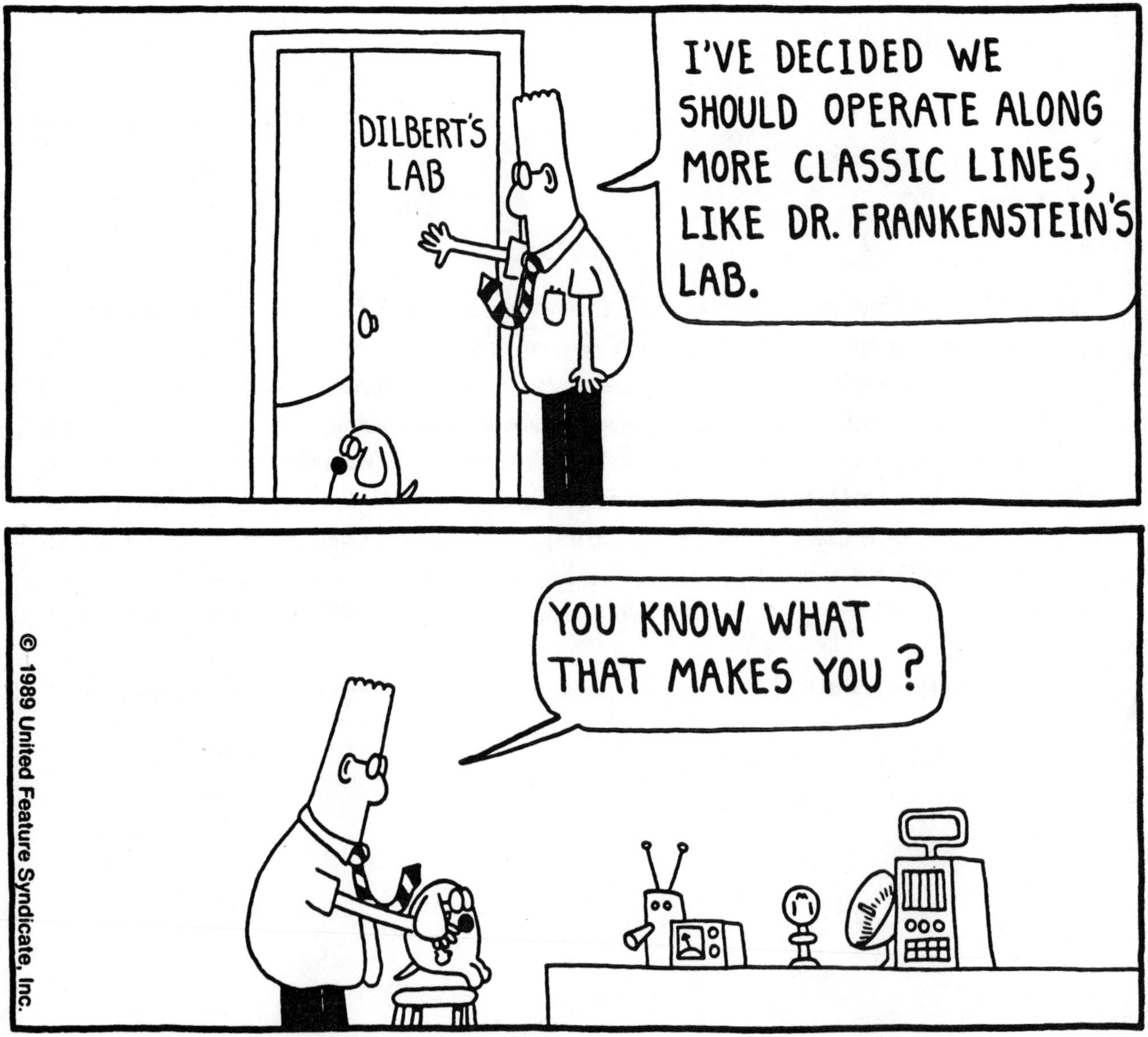
DILBERT'S LAB
I'VE DECIDED WE SHOULD OPERATE ALONG MORE CLASSIC LINES, LIKE DR. FRANKENSTEIN'S LAB.
YOU KNOW WHAT THAT MAKES YOU ?

I'VE GOT A HUNCH...
LET'S PRACTICE...
DOGBERT, FETCH ME A BRAIN!
LIKE YOUR PRESENT MODEL, OR ONE THAT WORKS?

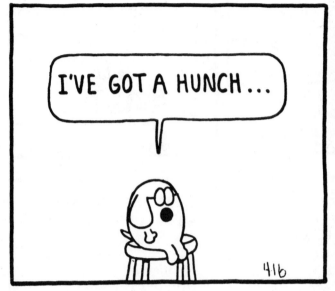

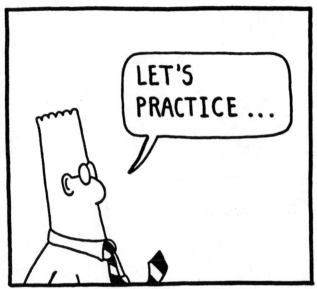

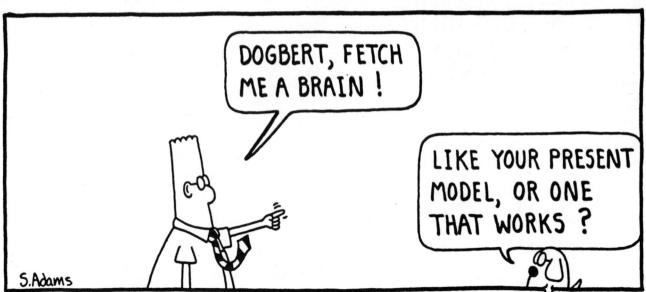

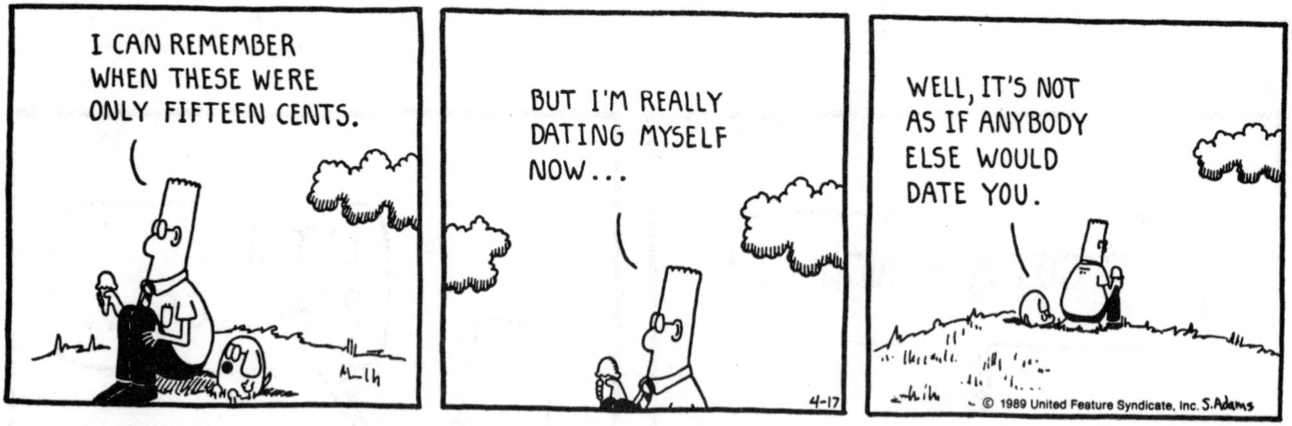
I CAN REMEMBER WHEN THESE WERE ONLY FIFTEEN CENTS.
BUT I'M REALLY DATING MYSELF NOW...
4-17
WELL, IT'S NOT AS IF ANYBODY ELSE WOULD DATE YOU.
© 1989 United Feature Syndicate, Inc. S.Adams

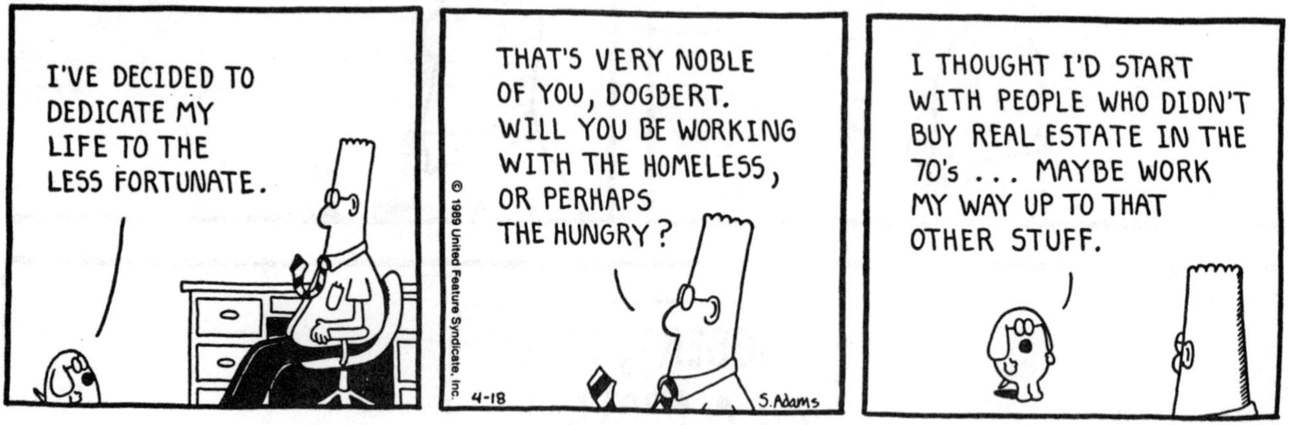
I'VE DECIDED TO DEDICATE MY LIFE TO THE LESS FORTUNATE.
© 1989 United Feature Syndicate, Inc.
4-18
THAT'S VERY NOBLE OF YOU, DOGBERT. WILL YOU BE WORKING WITH THE HOMELESS, OR PERHAPS THE HUNGRY?
S.Adams
I THOUGHT I'D START WITH PEOPLE WHO DIDN'T BUY REAL ESTATE IN THE 70's ... MAYBE WORK MY WAY UP TO THAT OTHER STUFF.

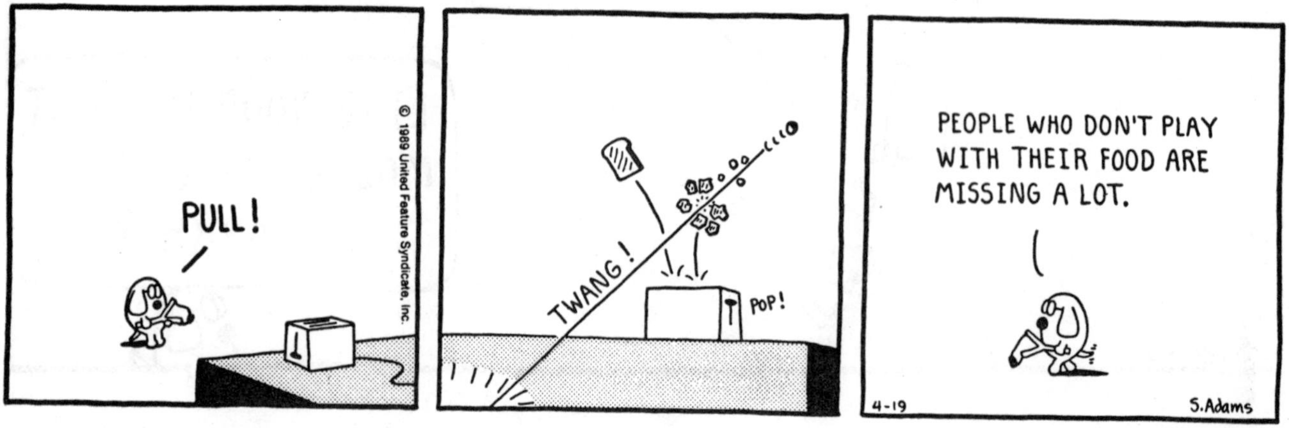
PULL!
© 1989 United Feature Syndicate, Inc.
TWANG!
POP!
PEOPLE WHO DON'T PLAY WITH THEIR FOOD ARE MISSING A LOT.
4-19
S.Adams

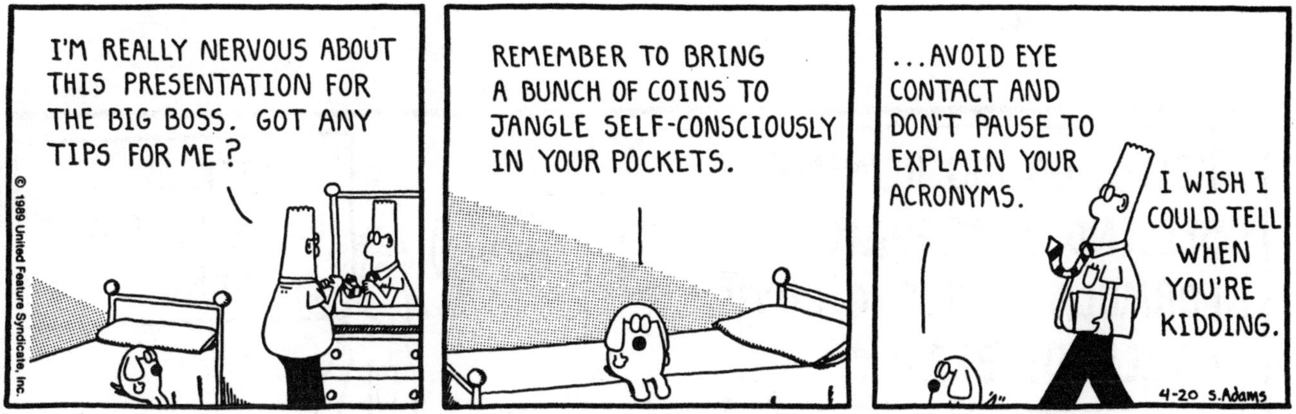
I'M REALLY NERVOUS ABOUT THIS PRESENTATION FOR THE BIG BOSS. GOT ANY TIPS FOR ME?
© 1989 United Feature Syndicate, Inc.
REMEMBER TO BRING A BUNCH OF COINS TO JANGLE SELF-CONSCIOUSLY IN YOUR POCKETS.
...AVOID EYE CONTACT AND DON'T PAUSE TO EXPLAIN YOUR ACRONYMS.
I WISH I COULD TELL WHEN YOU'RE KIDDING.
4-20 S.Adams

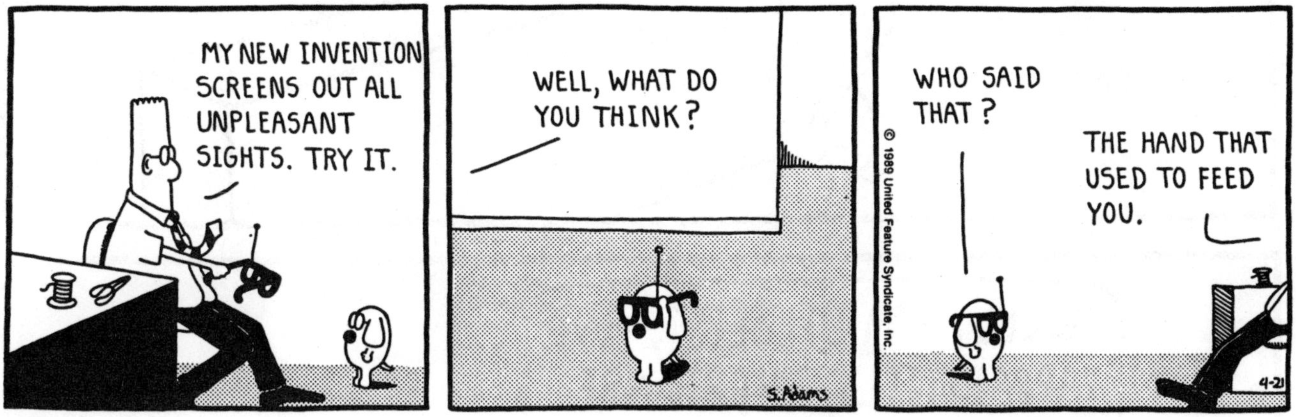
MY NEW INVENTION SCREENS OUT ALL UNPLEASANT SIGHTS. TRY IT.
WELL, WHAT DO YOU THINK?
S.Adams
© 1989 United Feature Syndicate, Inc.
WHO SAID THAT?
THE HAND THAT USED TO FEED YOU.
4-21

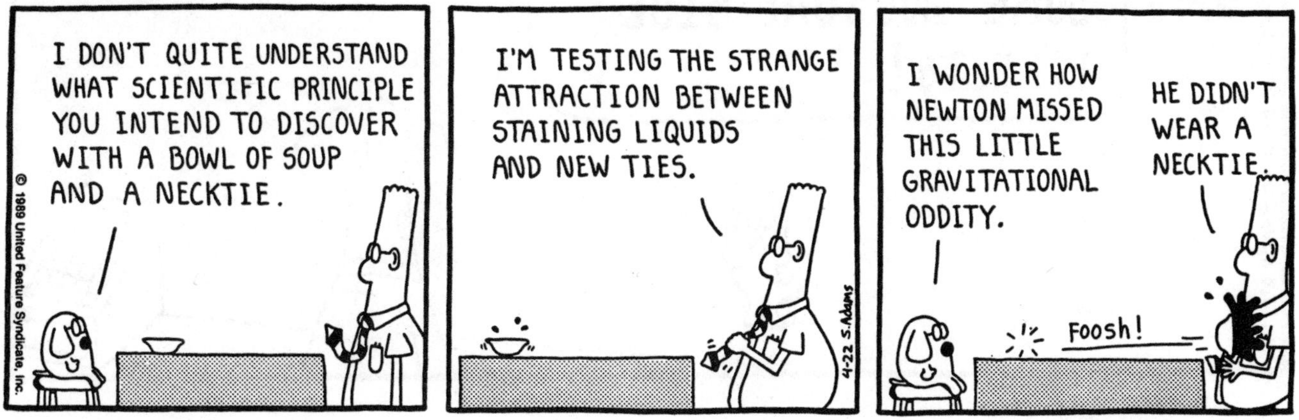
© 1989 United Feature Syndicate, Inc.
I DON'T QUITE UNDERSTAND WHAT SCIENTIFIC PRINCIPLE YOU INTEND TO DISCOVER WITH A BOWL OF SOUP AND A NECKTIE.
I'M TESTING THE STRANGE ATTRACTION BETWEEN STAINING LIQUIDS AND NEW TIES.
4-22 S.Adams
I WONDER HOW NEWTON MISSED THIS LITTLE GRAVITATIONAL ODDITY.
HE DIDN'T WEAR A NECKTIE.
FOOSH!

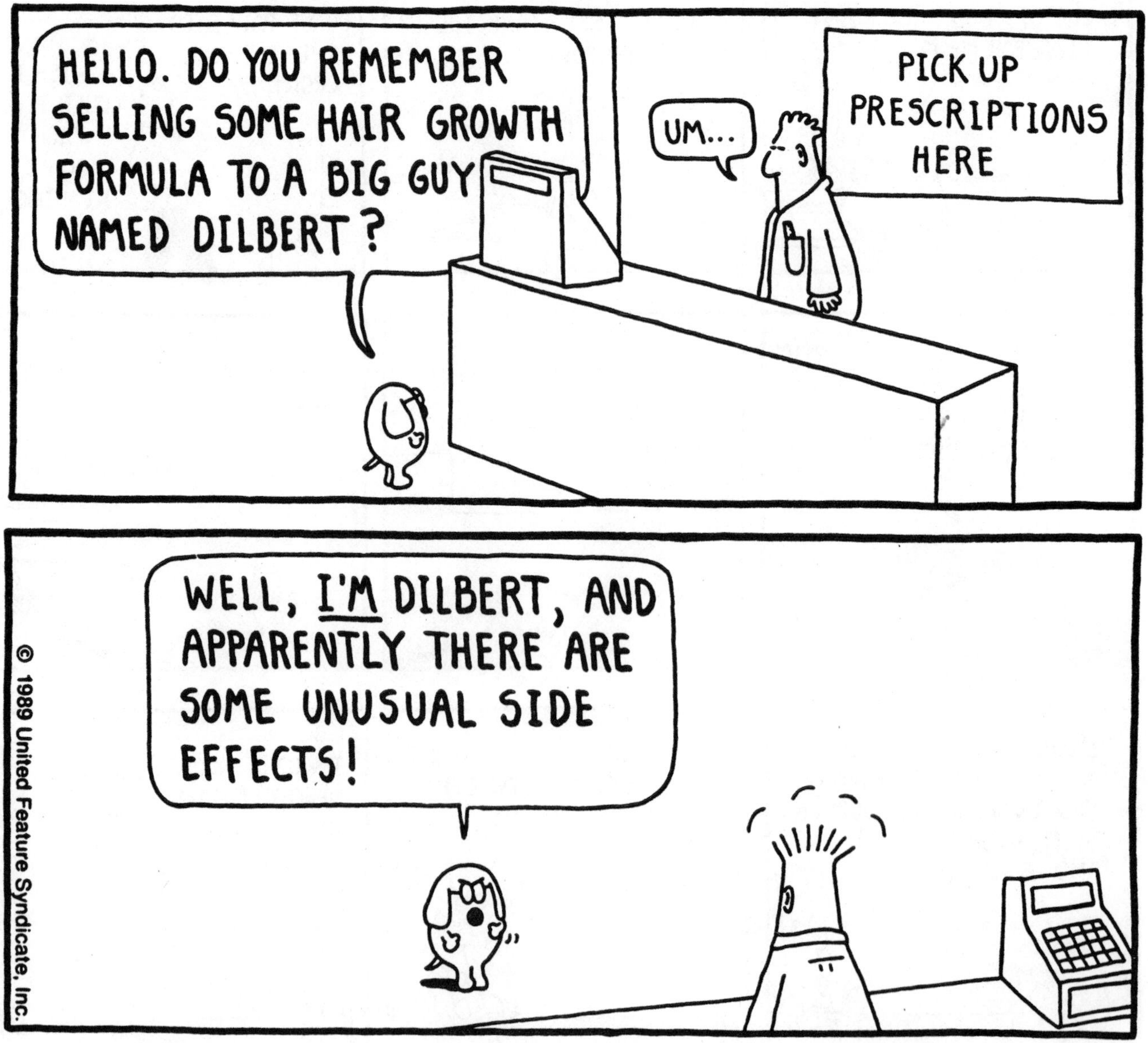
HELLO. DO YOU REMEMBER SELLING SOME HAIR GROWTH FORMULA TO A BIG GUY NAMED DILBERT?
UM...
PICK UP PRESCRIPTIONS HERE
WELL, I'M DILBERT, AND APPARENTLY THERE ARE SOME UNUSUAL SIDE EFFECTS!

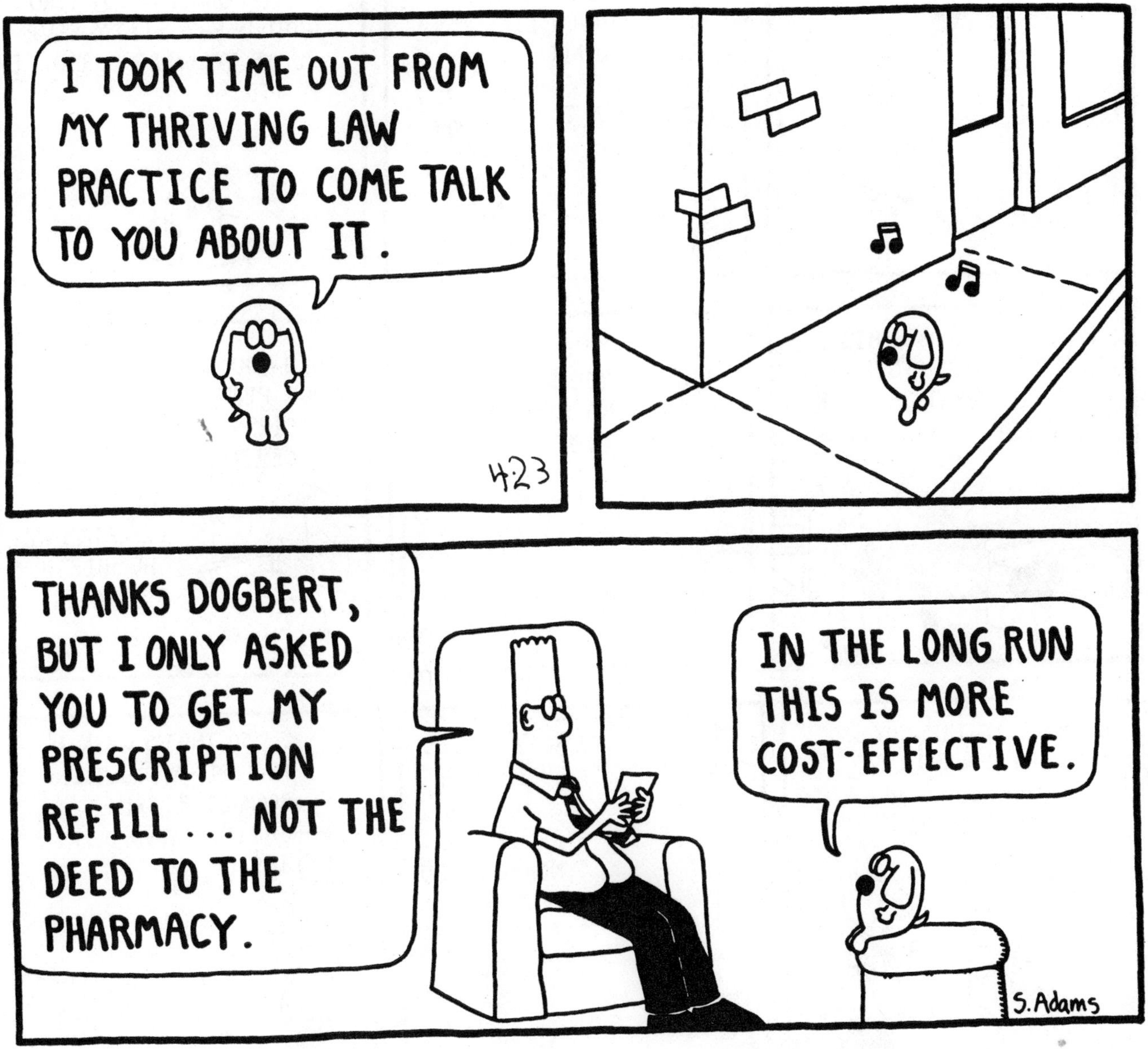
I TOOK TIME OUT FROM MY THRIVING LAW PRACTICE TO COME TALK TO YOU ABOUT IT.
4-23
THANKS DOGBERT, BUT I ONLY ASKED YOU TO GET MY PRESCRIPTION REFILL ... NOT THE DEED TO THE PHARMACY.
IN THE LONG RUN THIS IS MORE COST-EFFECTIVE.
S. Adams

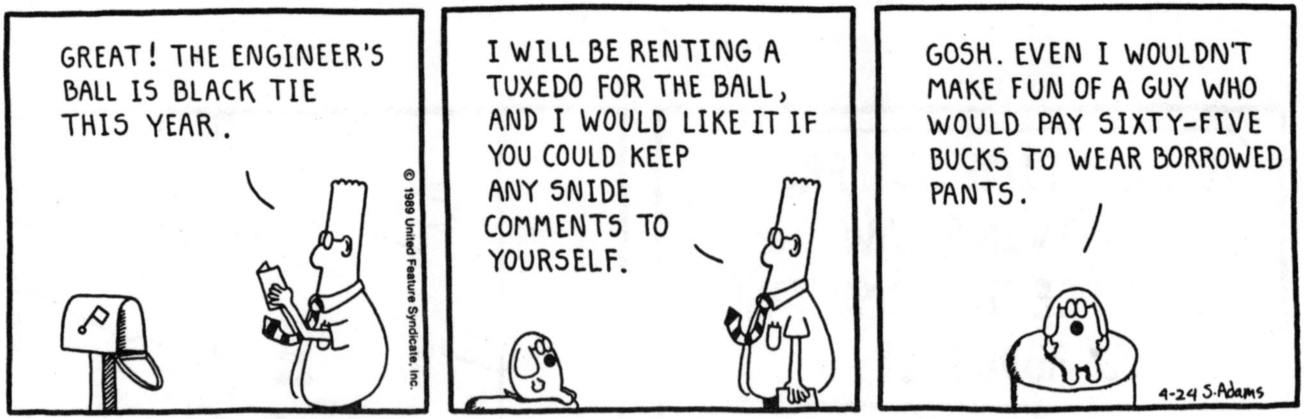
GREAT! THE ENGINEER'S BALL IS BLACK TIE THIS YEAR.
© 1989 United Feature Syndicate, Inc.
I WILL BE RENTING A TUXEDO FOR THE BALL, AND I WOULD LIKE IT IF YOU COULD KEEP ANY SNIDE COMMENTS TO YOURSELF.
GOSH. EVEN I WOULDN'T MAKE FUN OF A GUY WHO WOULD PAY SIXTY-FIVE BUCKS TO WEAR BORROWED PANTS.
4-24 S.Adams

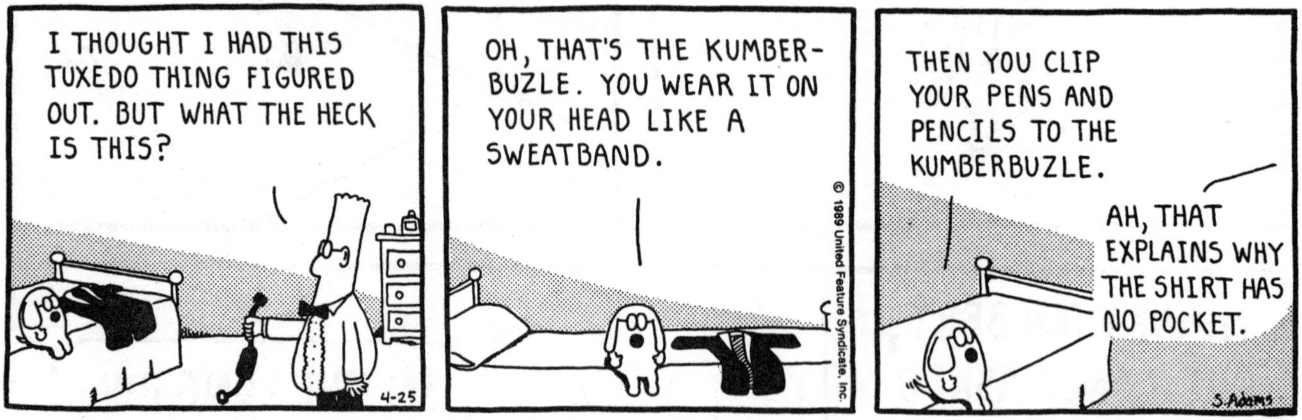
I THOUGHT I HAD THIS TUXEDO THING FIGURED OUT. BUT WHAT THE HECK IS THIS?
4-25
OH, THAT'S THE KUMBER-BUZLE. YOU WEAR IT ON YOUR HEAD LIKE A SWEATBAND.
© 1989 United Feature Syndicate, Inc.
THEN YOU CLIP YOUR PENS AND PENCILS TO THE KUMBERBUZLE.
AH, THAT EXPLAINS WHY THE SHIRT HAS NO POCKET.
S.Adams

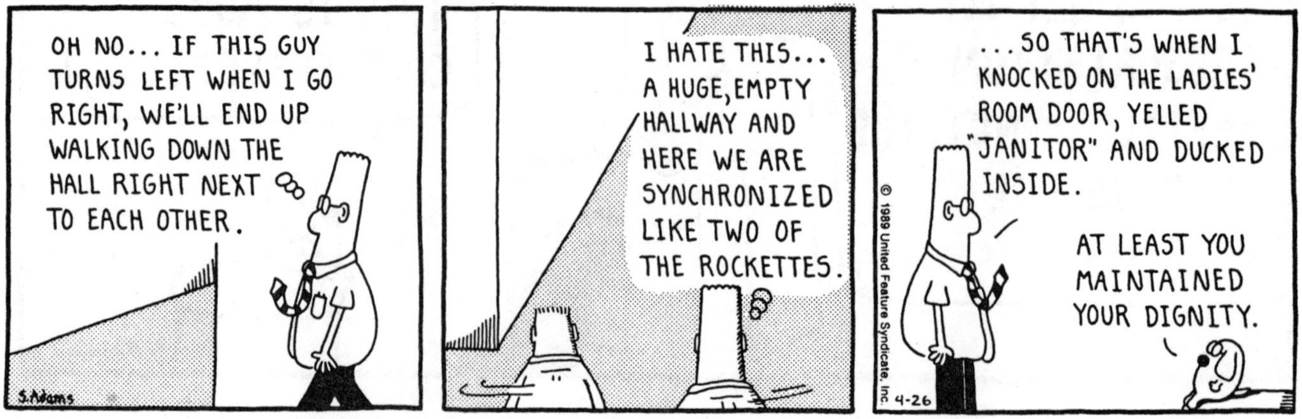
OH NO... IF THIS GUY TURNS LEFT WHEN I GO RIGHT, WE'LL END UP WALKING DOWN THE HALL RIGHT NEXT TO EACH OTHER.
S.Adams
I HATE THIS... A HUGE, EMPTY HALLWAY AND HERE WE ARE SYNCHRONIZED LIKE TWO OF THE ROCKETTES.
...SO THAT'S WHEN I KNOCKED ON THE LADIES' ROOM DOOR, YELLED "JANITOR" AND DUCKED INSIDE.
AT LEAST YOU MAINTAINED YOUR DIGNITY.
© 1989 United Feature Syndicate, Inc.
4-26

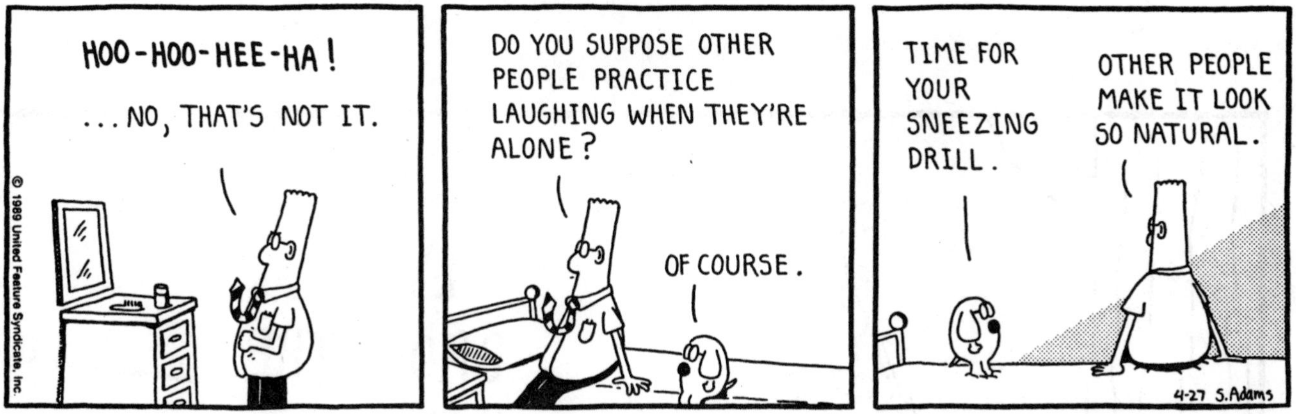
HOO-HOO-HEE-HA!
...NO, THAT'S NOT IT.
© 1989 United Feature Syndicate, Inc.
DO YOU SUPPOSE OTHER PEOPLE PRACTICE LAUGHING WHEN THEY'RE ALONE?
OF COURSE.
TIME FOR YOUR SNEEZING DRILL.
OTHER PEOPLE MAKE IT LOOK SO NATURAL.
4-27 S.Adams

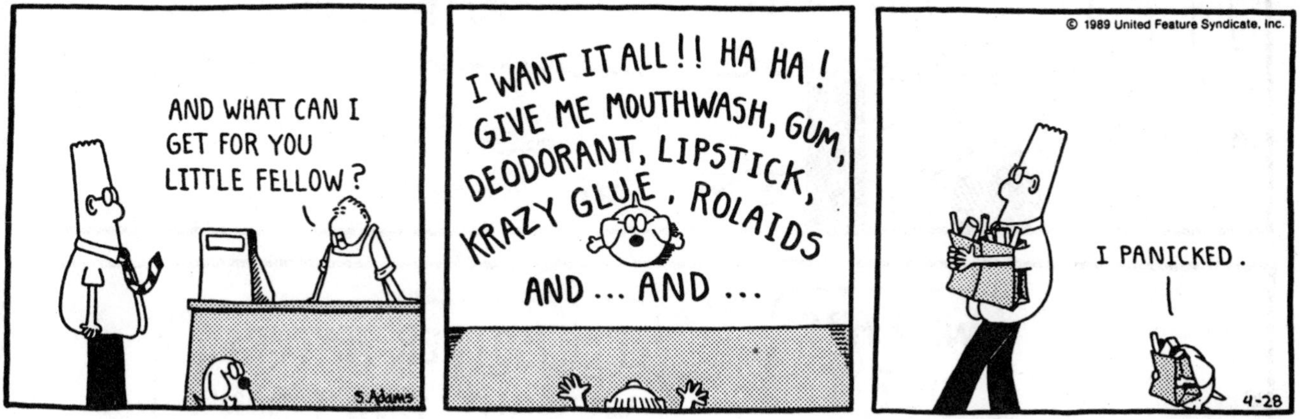
AND WHAT CAN I GET FOR YOU LITTLE FELLOW?
S.Adams
I WANT IT ALL!! HA HA!
GIVE ME MOUTHWASH, GUM, DEODORANT, LIPSTICK, KRAZY GLUE, ROLAIDS
AND... AND...
© 1989 United Feature Syndicate, Inc.
I PANICKED.
4-28

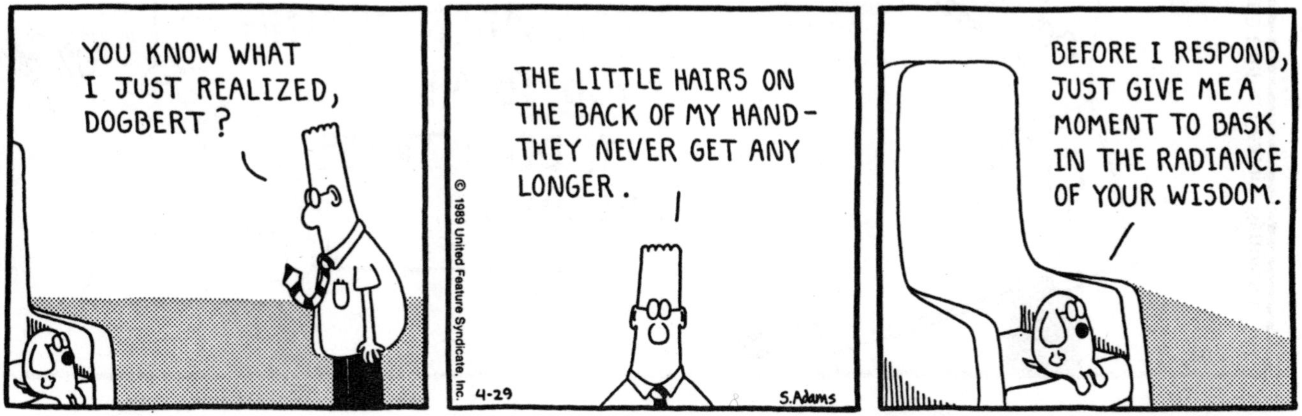
YOU KNOW WHAT I JUST REALIZED, DOGBERT?
© 1989 United Feature Syndicate, Inc.
THE LITTLE HAIRS ON THE BACK OF MY HAND-
THEY NEVER GET ANY LONGER.
4-29
S.Adams
BEFORE I RESPOND, JUST GIVE ME A MOMENT TO BASK IN THE RADIANCE OF YOUR WISDOM.

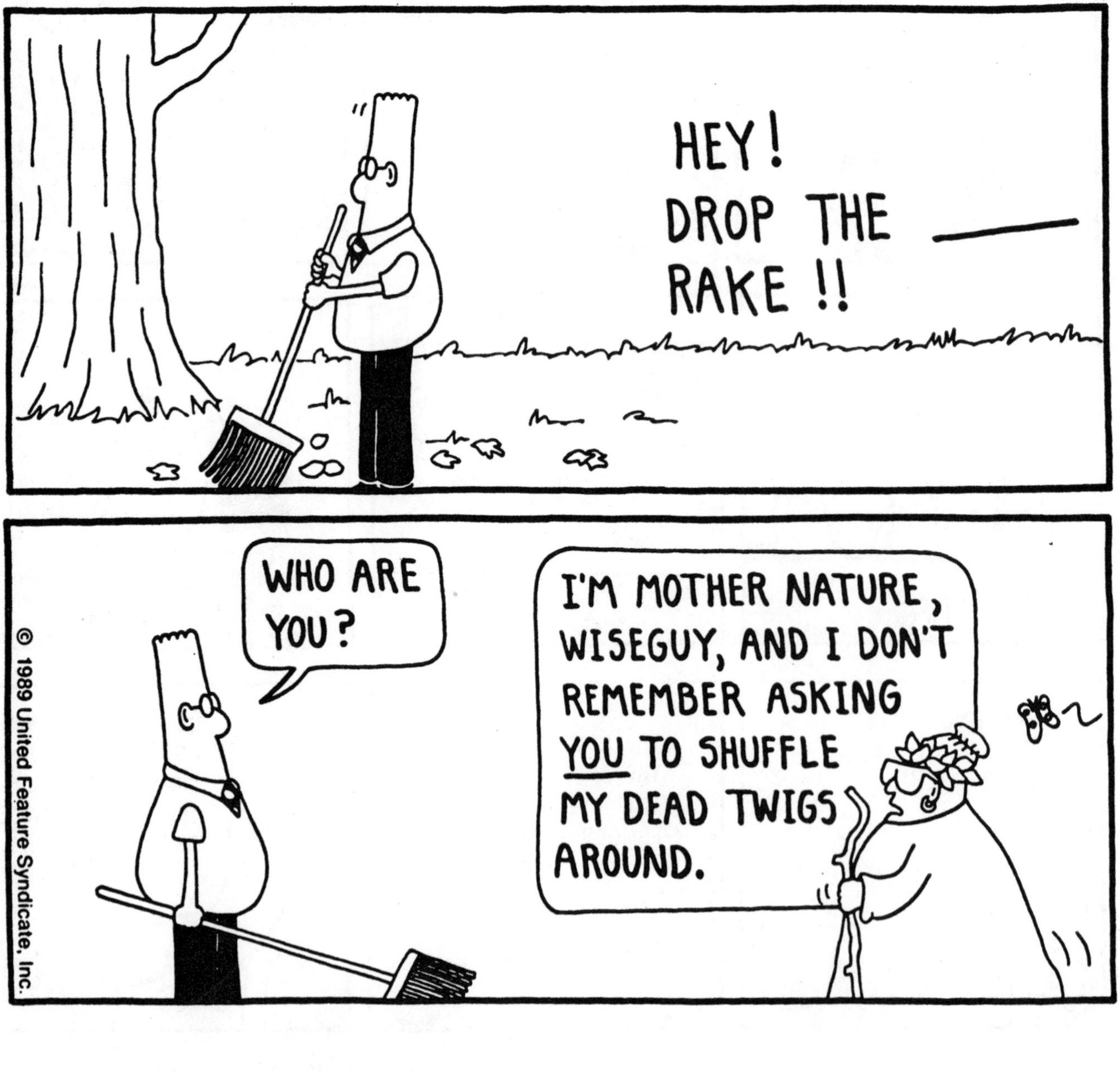
HEY! DROP THE RAKE !!
WHO ARE YOU?
I'M MOTHER NATURE, WISEGUY, AND I DON'T REMEMBER ASKING YOU TO SHUFFLE MY DEAD TWIGS AROUND.

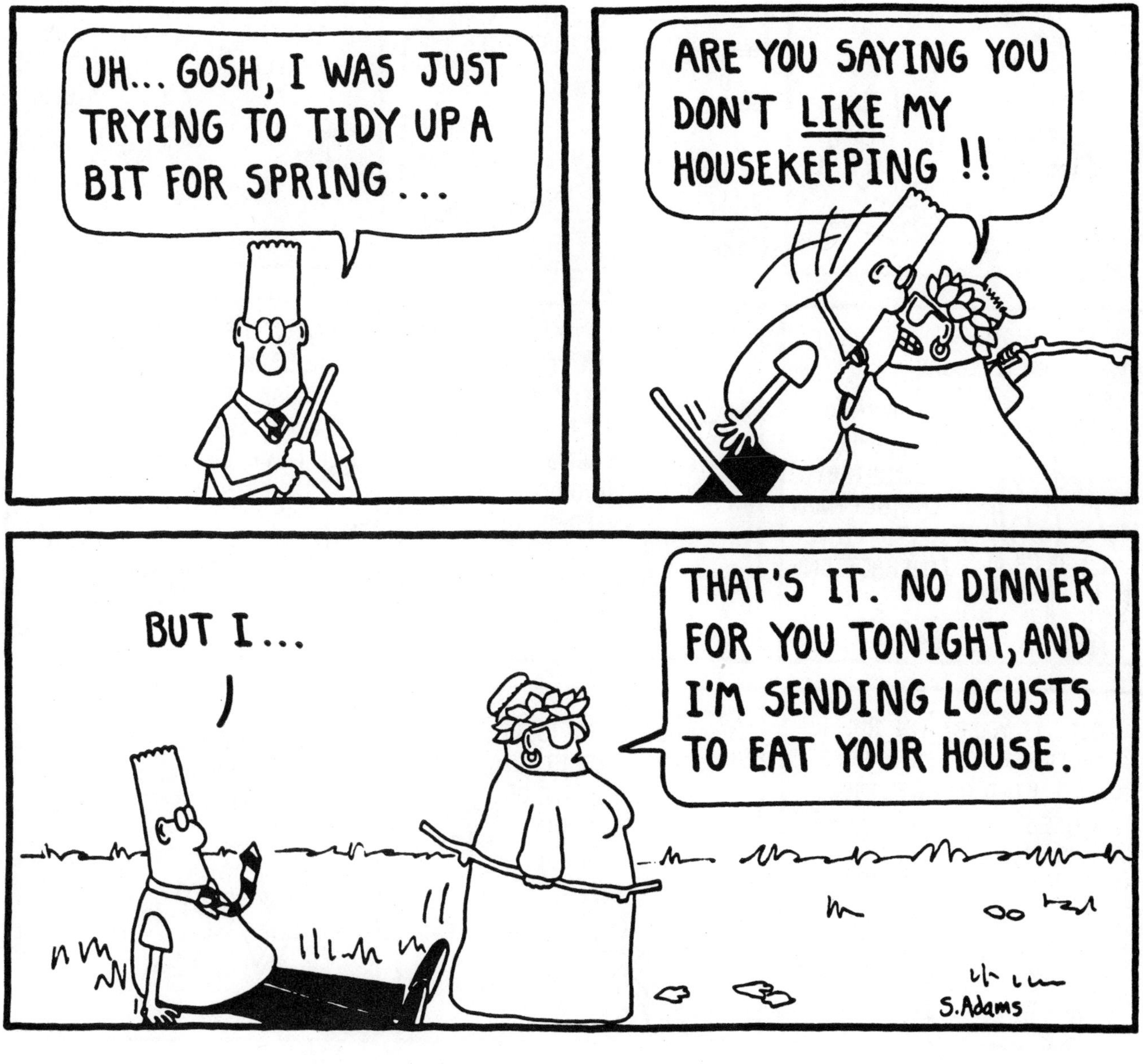
UH... GOSH, I WAS JUST TRYING TO TIDY UP A BIT FOR SPRING...
ARE YOU SAYING YOU DON'T LIKE MY HOUSEKEEPING !!
BUT I...
THAT'S IT. NO DINNER FOR YOU TONIGHT, AND I'M SENDING LOCUSTS TO EAT YOUR HOUSE.
S. Adams

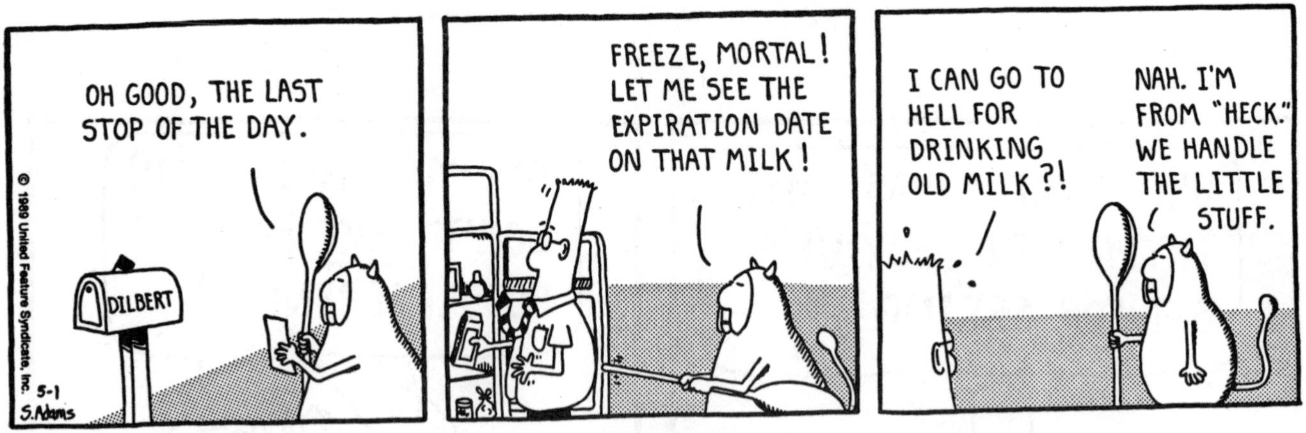
OH GOOD, THE LAST STOP OF THE DAY.
DILBERT
FREEZE, MORTAL! LET ME SEE THE EXPIRATION DATE ON THAT MILK!
I CAN GO TO HELL FOR DRINKING OLD MILK ?!
NAH. I'M FROM "HECK." WE HANDLE THE LITTLE STUFF.
© 1989 United Feature Syndicate, Inc.
5-1
S.Adams

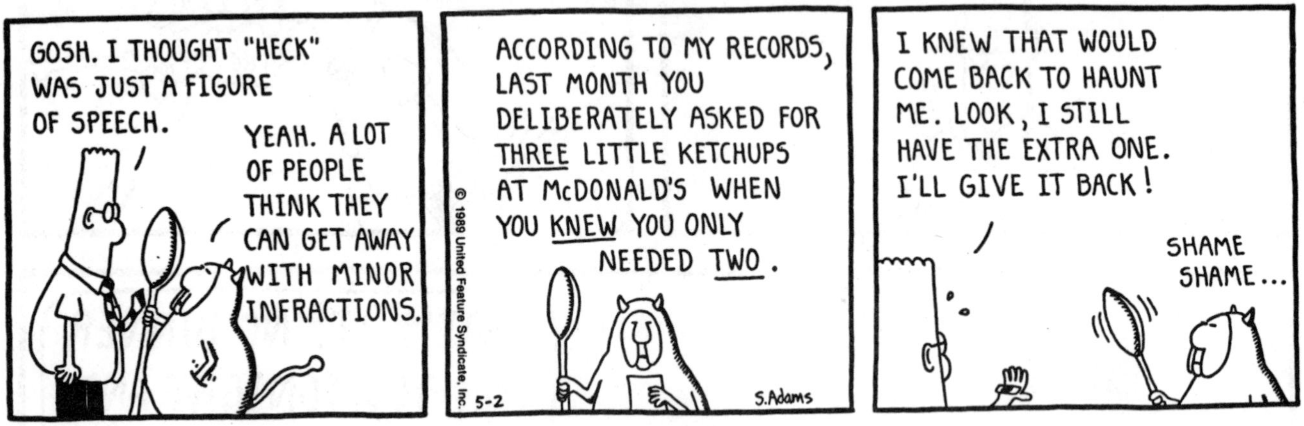
GOSH. I THOUGHT "HECK" WAS JUST A FIGURE OF SPEECH.
YEAH. A LOT OF PEOPLE THINK THEY CAN GET AWAY WITH MINOR INFRACTIONS.
ACCORDING TO MY RECORDS, LAST MONTH YOU DELIBERATELY ASKED FOR THREE LITTLE KETCHUPS AT McDONALD'S WHEN YOU KNEW YOU ONLY NEEDED TWO.
© 1989 United Feature Syndicate, Inc.
5-2
S.Adams
I KNEW THAT WOULD COME BACK TO HAUNT ME. LOOK, I STILL HAVE THE EXTRA ONE. I'LL GIVE IT BACK!
SHAME SHAME...

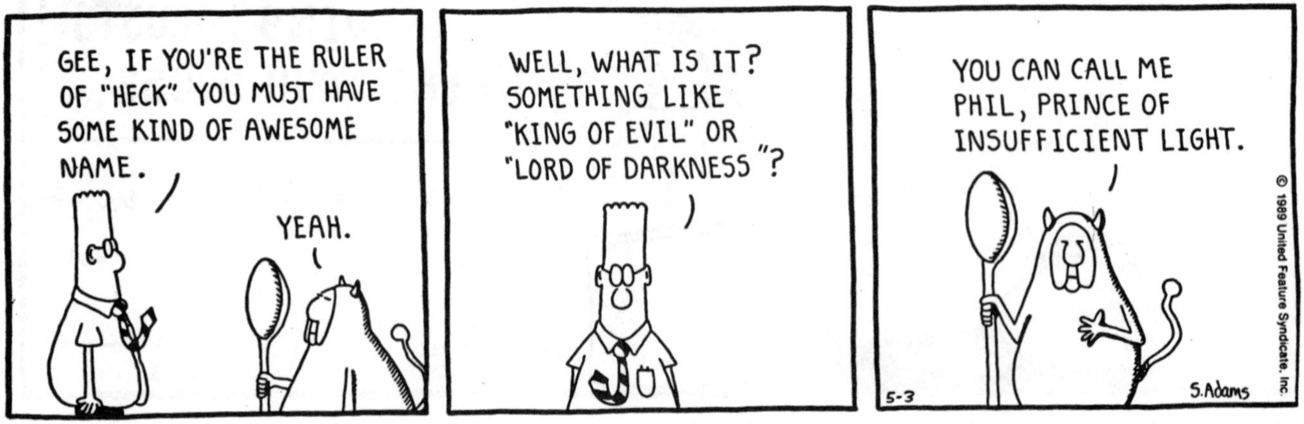
GEE, IF YOU'RE THE RULER OF "HECK" YOU MUST HAVE SOME KIND OF AWESOME NAME.
YEAH.
WELL, WHAT IS IT? SOMETHING LIKE "KING OF EVIL" OR "LORD OF DARKNESS"?
YOU CAN CALL ME PHIL, PRINCE OF INSUFFICIENT LIGHT.
© 1989 United Feature Syndicate, Inc.
5-3
S.Adams

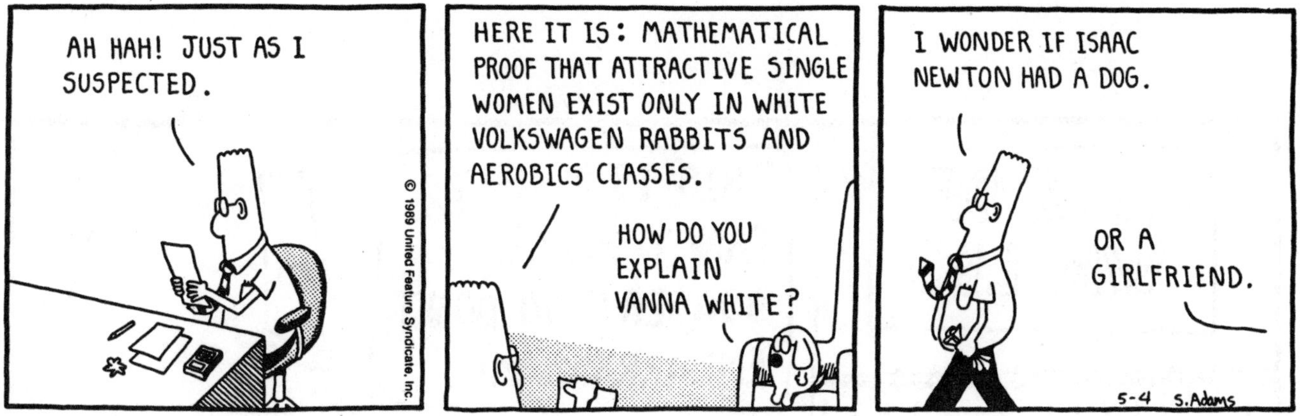
AH HAH! JUST AS I SUSPECTED.
© 1989 United Feature Syndicate, Inc.
HERE IT IS: MATHEMATICAL PROOF THAT ATTRACTIVE SINGLE WOMEN EXIST ONLY IN WHITE VOLKSWAGEN RABBITS AND AEROBICS CLASSES.
HOW DO YOU EXPLAIN VANNA WHITE?
I WONDER IF ISAAC NEWTON HAD A DOG.
OR A GIRLFRIEND.
5-4 S.Adams

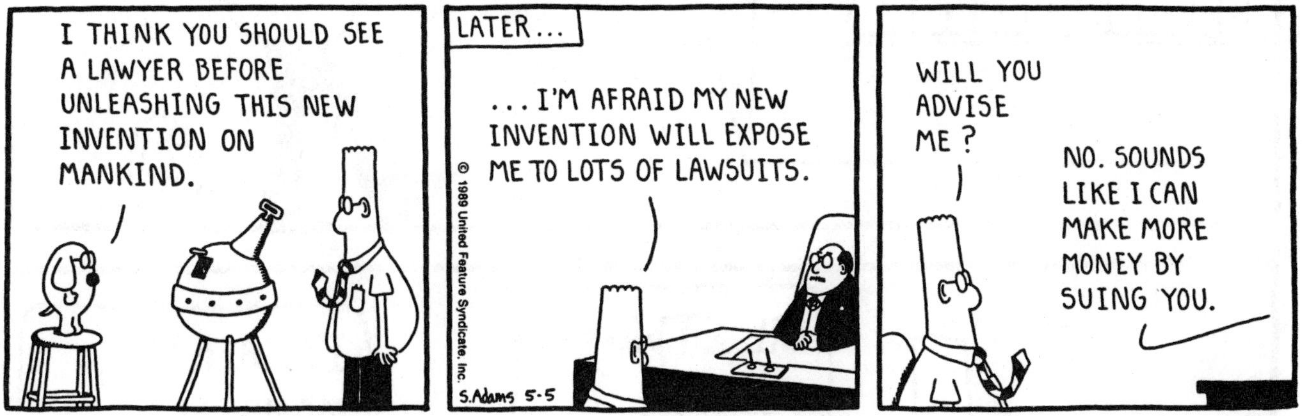
I THINK YOU SHOULD SEE A LAWYER BEFORE UNLEASHING THIS NEW INVENTION ON MANKIND.
LATER...
...I'M AFRAID MY NEW INVENTION WILL EXPOSE ME TO LOTS OF LAWSUITS.
© 1989 United Feature Syndicate, Inc.
S.Adams 5-5
WILL YOU ADVISE ME?
NO. SOUNDS LIKE I CAN MAKE MORE MONEY BY SUING YOU.

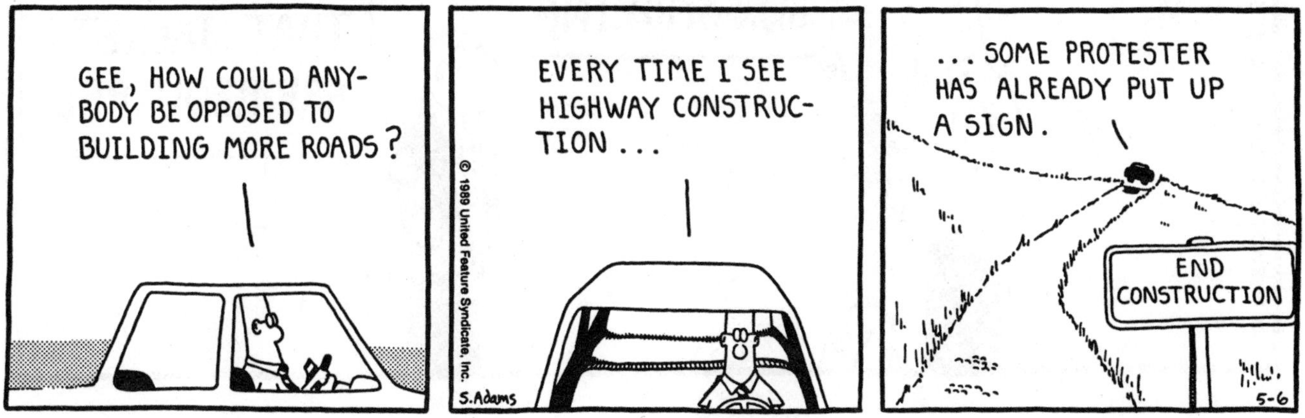
GEE, HOW COULD ANYBODY BE OPPOSED TO BUILDING MORE ROADS?
EVERY TIME I SEE HIGHWAY CONSTRUCTION...
© 1989 United Feature Syndicate, Inc.
S.Adams
...SOME PROTESTER HAS ALREADY PUT UP A SIGN.
END CONSTRUCTION
5-6

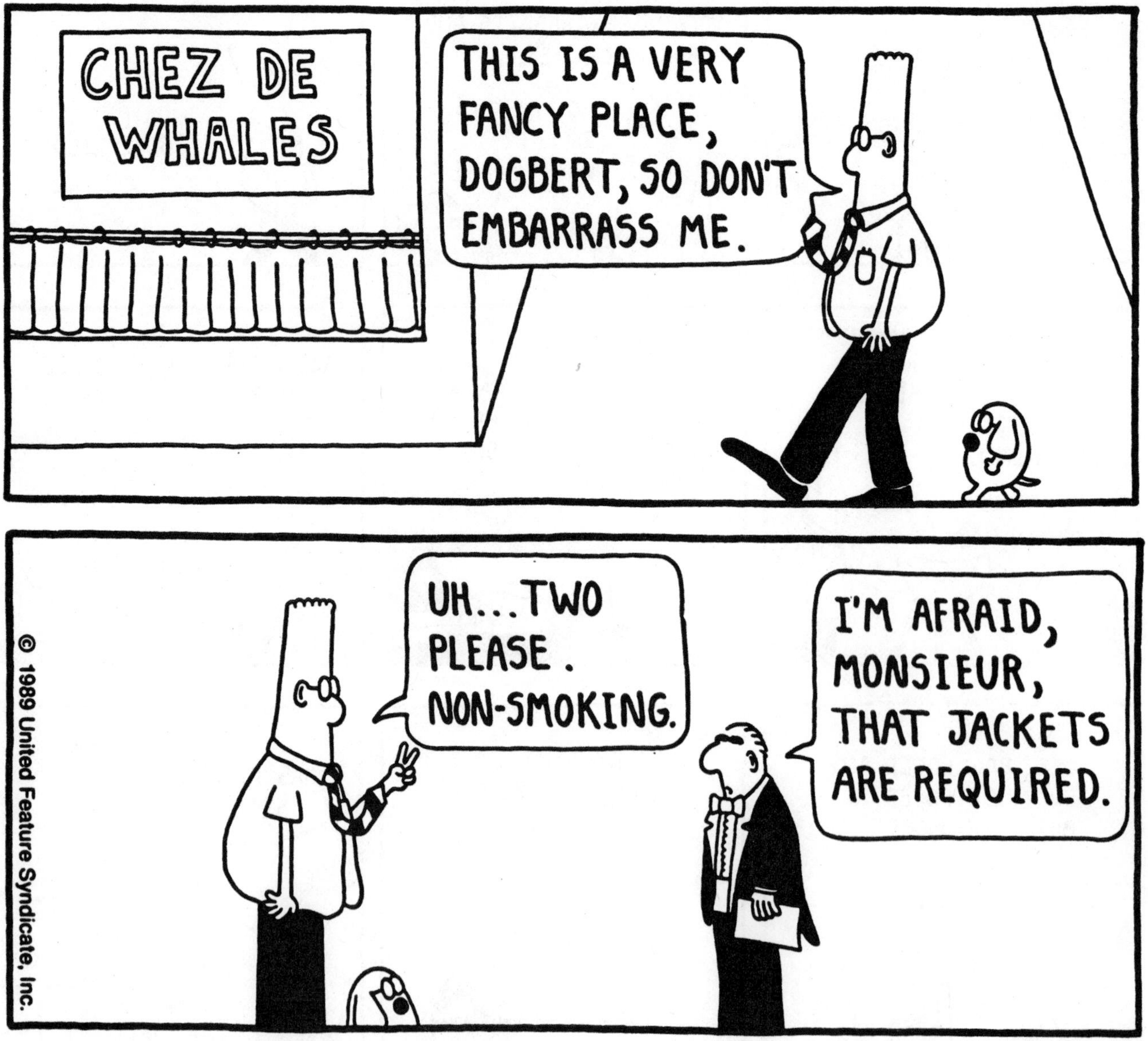
CHEZ DE WHALES
THIS IS A VERY FANCY PLACE, DOGBERT, SO DON'T EMBARRASS ME.
UH... TWO PLEASE. NON-SMOKING.
I'M AFRAID, MONSIEUR, THAT JACKETS ARE REQUIRED.© 1989 United Feature Syndicate, Inc.

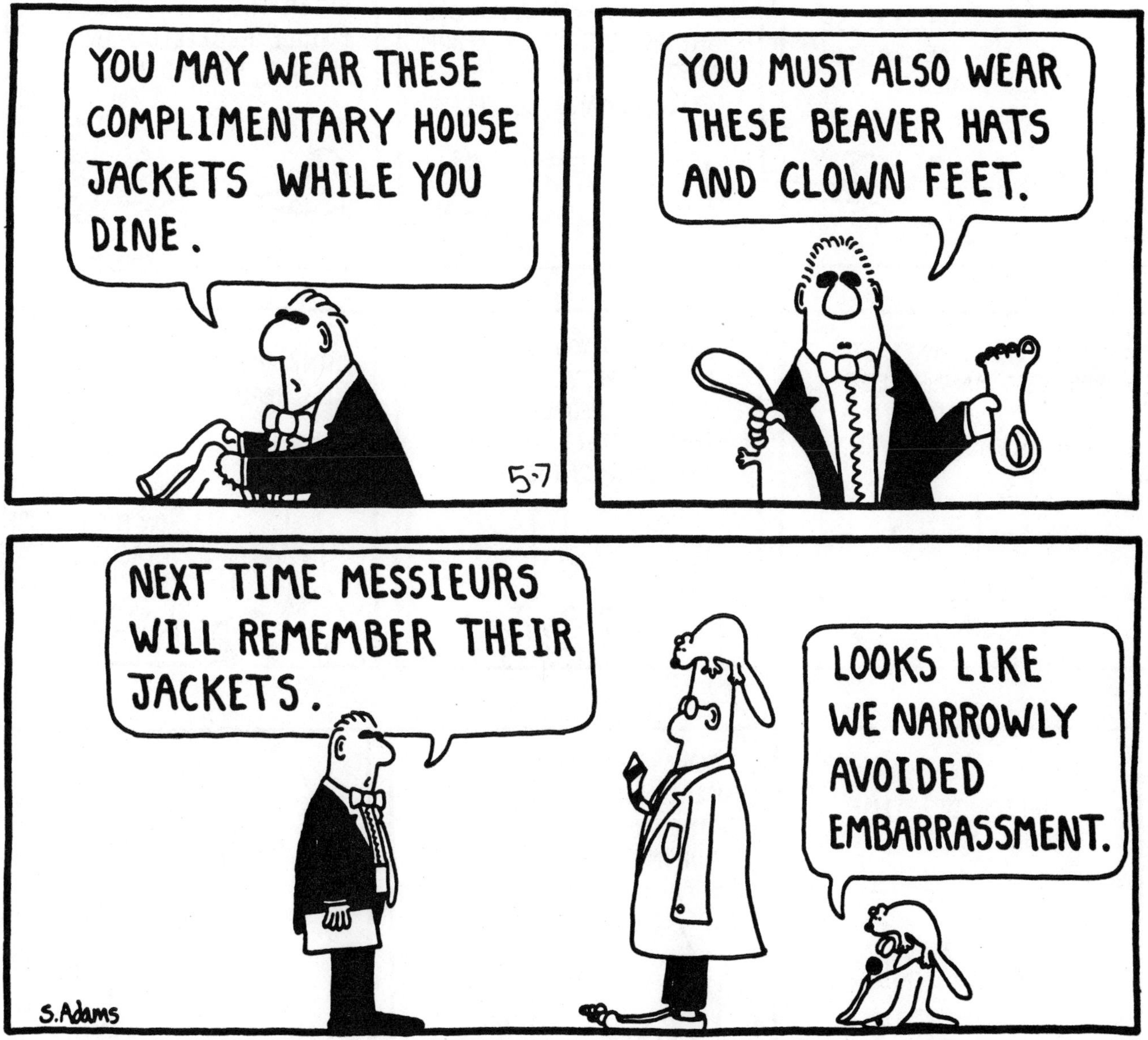
YOU MAY WEAR THESE COMPLIMENTARY HOUSE JACKETS WHILE YOU DINE.
5-7
YOU MUST ALSO WEAR THESE BEAVER HATS AND CLOWN FEET.
NEXT TIME MESSIEURS WILL REMEMBER THEIR JACKETS.
LOOKS LIKE WE NARROWLY AVOIDED EMBARRASSMENT.
S. Adams

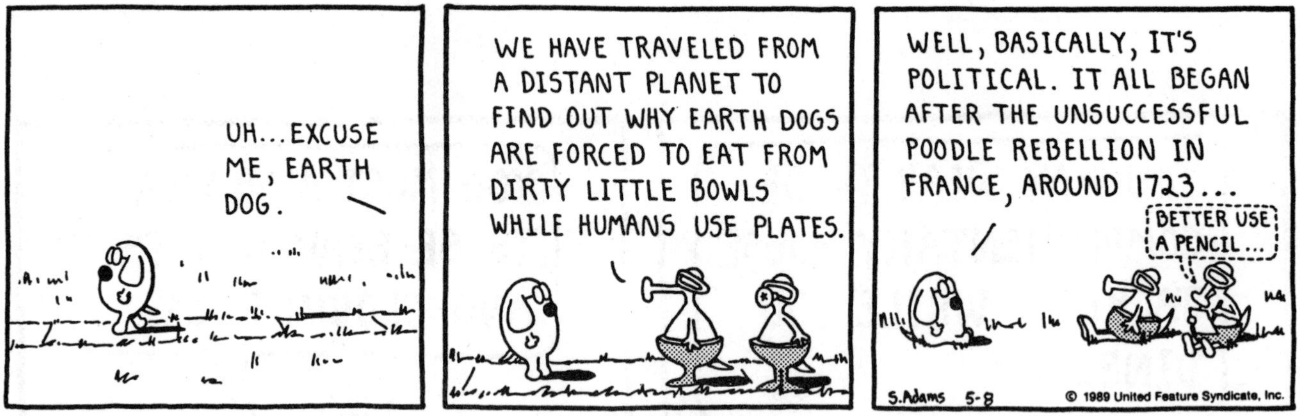
UH... EXCUSE ME, EARTH DOG.
WE HAVE TRAVELED FROM A DISTANT PLANET TO FIND OUT WHY EARTH DOGS ARE FORCED TO EAT FROM DIRTY LITTLE BOWLS WHILE HUMANS USE PLATES.
WELL, BASICALLY, IT'S POLITICAL. IT ALL BEGAN AFTER THE UNSUCCESSFUL POODLE REBELLION IN FRANCE, AROUND 1723...
BETTER USE A PENCIL...
S.Adams 5-8
© 1989 United Feature Syndicate, Inc.

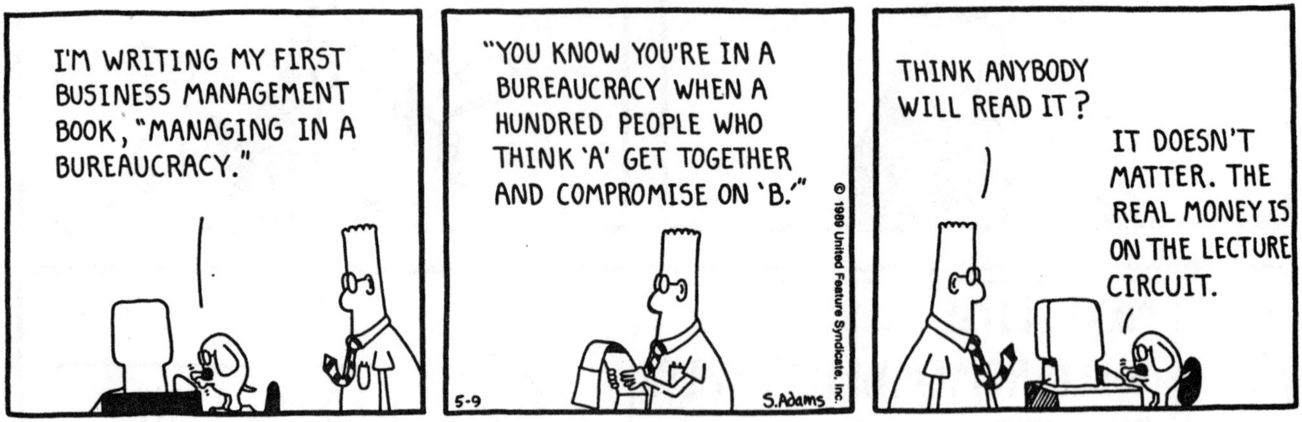
I'M WRITING MY FIRST BUSINESS MANAGEMENT BOOK, "MANAGING IN A BUREAUCRACY."
"YOU KNOW YOU'RE IN A BUREAUCRACY WHEN A HUNDRED PEOPLE WHO THINK 'A' GET TOGETHER AND COMPROMISE ON 'B.'"
THINK ANYBODY WILL READ IT?
IT DOESN'T MATTER. THE REAL MONEY IS ON THE LECTURE CIRCUIT.
5-9
S.Adams
© 1989 United Feature Syndicate, Inc.

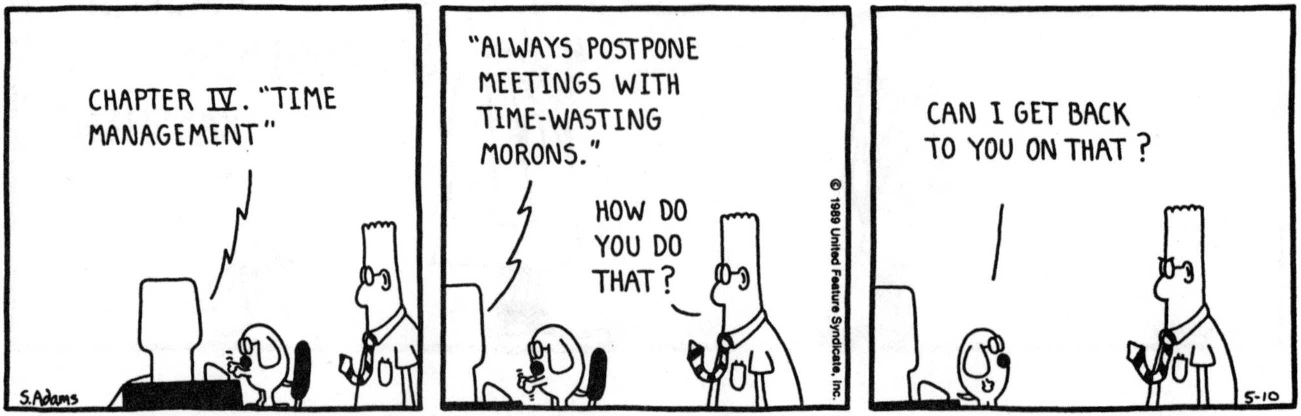
CHAPTER IV. "TIME MANAGEMENT"
"ALWAYS POSTPONE MEETINGS WITH TIME-WASTING MORONS."
HOW DO YOU DO THAT?
CAN I GET BACK TO YOU ON THAT?
S.Adams
5-10
© 1989 United Feature Syndicate, Inc.

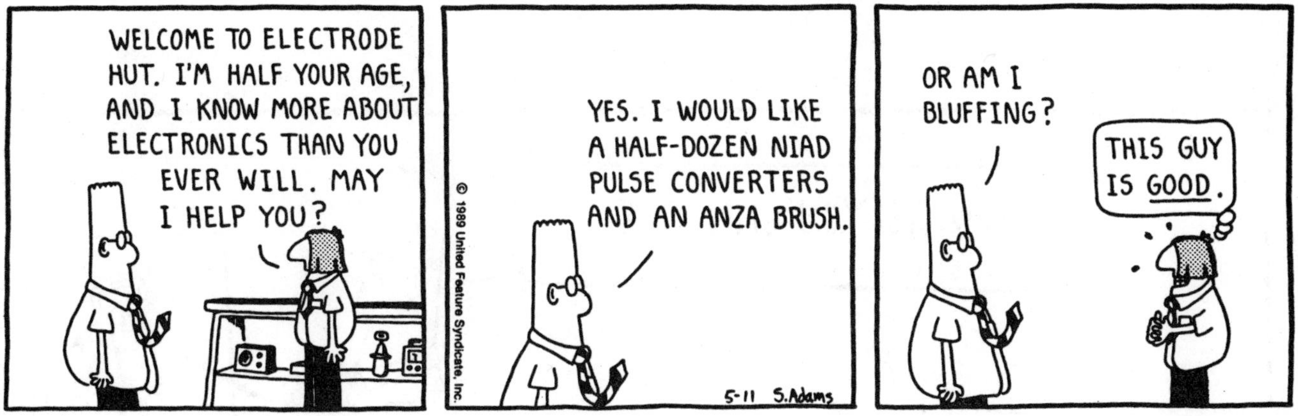
WELCOME TO ELECTRODE HUT. I'M HALF YOUR AGE, AND I KNOW MORE ABOUT ELECTRONICS THAN YOU EVER WILL. MAY I HELP YOU?
YES. I WOULD LIKE A HALF-DOZEN NIAD PULSE CONVERTERS AND AN ANZA BRUSH.
© 1989 United Feature Syndicate, Inc.
5-11 S.Adams
OR AM I BLUFFING?
THIS GUY IS GOOD.

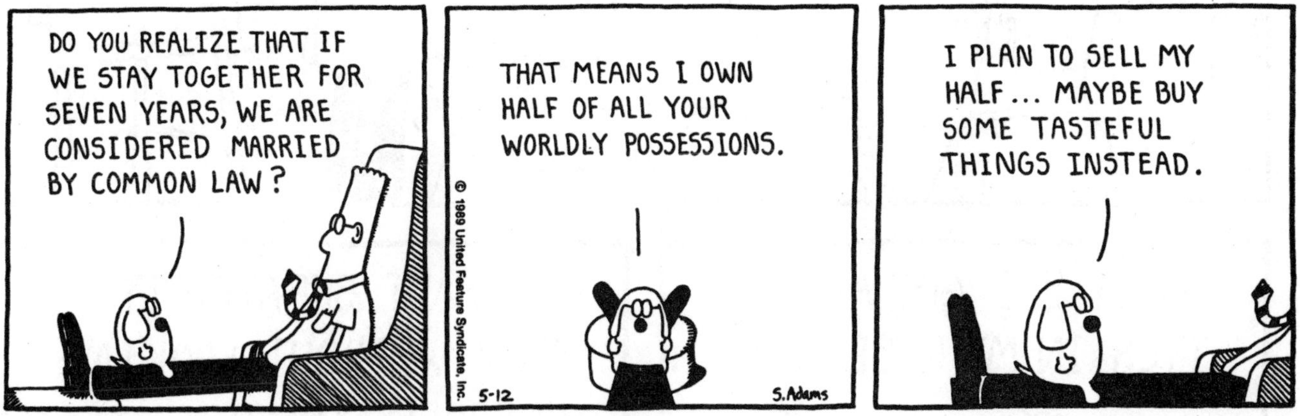
DO YOU REALIZE THAT IF WE STAY TOGETHER FOR SEVEN YEARS, WE ARE CONSIDERED MARRIED BY COMMON LAW?
THAT MEANS I OWN HALF OF ALL YOUR WORLDLY POSSESSIONS.
© 1989 United Feature Syndicate, Inc.
5-12 S.Adams
I PLAN TO SELL MY HALF... MAYBE BUY SOME TASTEFUL THINGS INSTEAD.

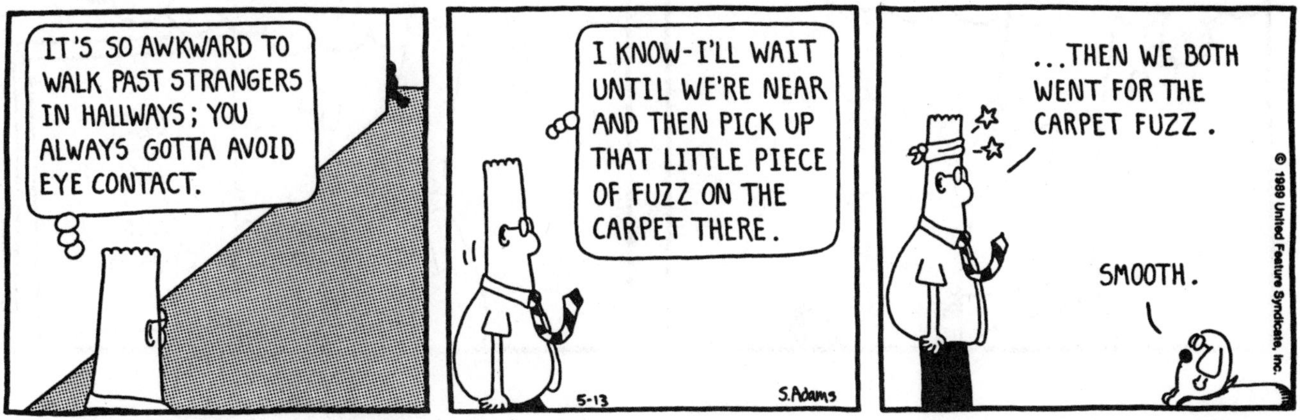
IT'S SO AWKWARD TO WALK PAST STRANGERS IN HALLWAYS; YOU ALWAYS GOTTA AVOID EYE CONTACT.
I KNOW-I'LL WAIT UNTIL WE'RE NEAR AND THEN PICK UP THAT LITTLE PIECE OF FUZZ ON THE CARPET THERE.
5-13 S.Adams
...THEN WE BOTH WENT FOR THE CARPET FUZZ.
SMOOTH.
© 1989 United Feature Syndicate, Inc.

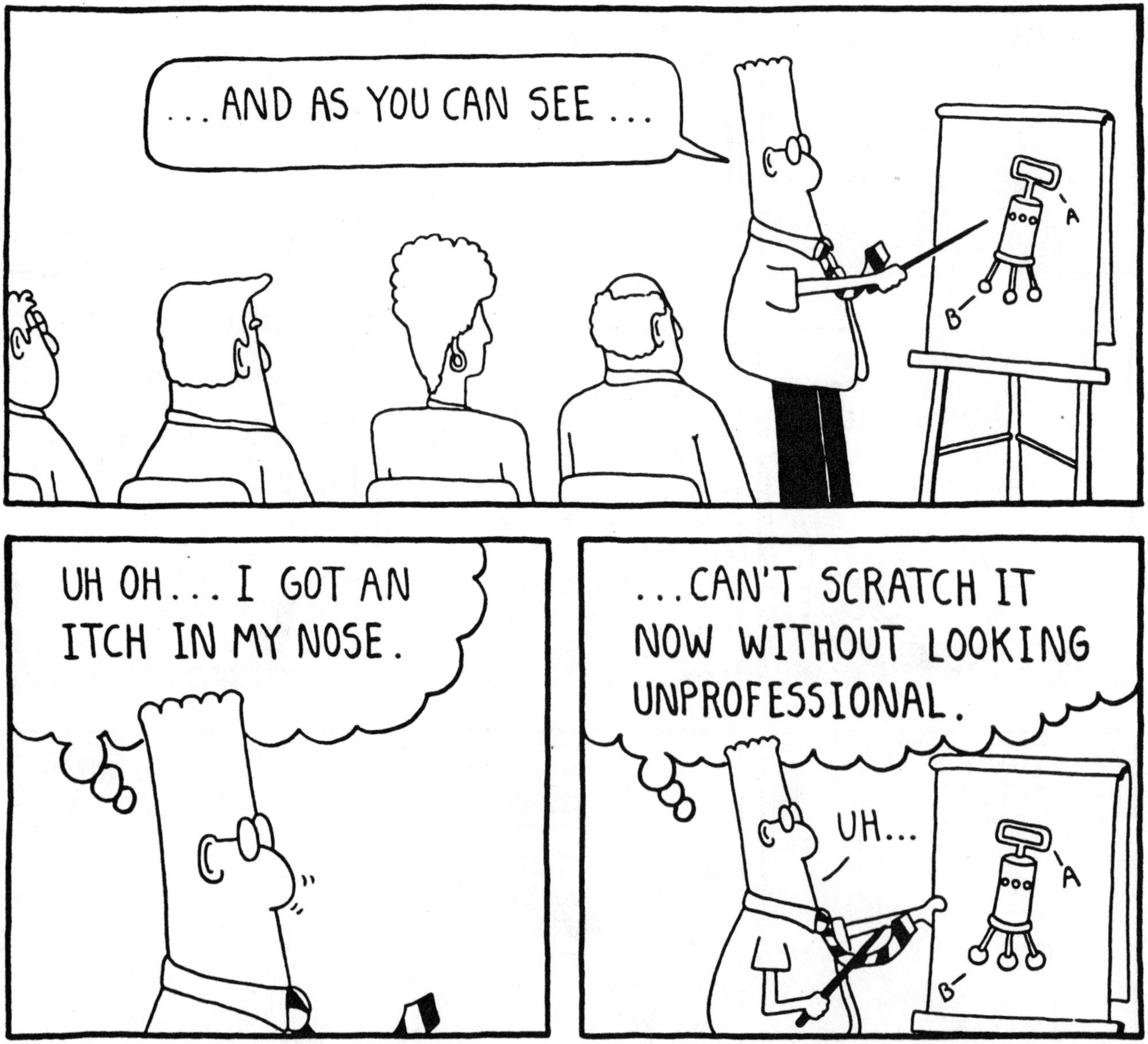
...AND AS YOU CAN SEE...
A
B
UH OH... I GOT AN ITCH IN MY NOSE.
...CAN'T SCRATCH IT NOW WITHOUT LOOKING UNPROFESSIONAL.
UH...
A
B

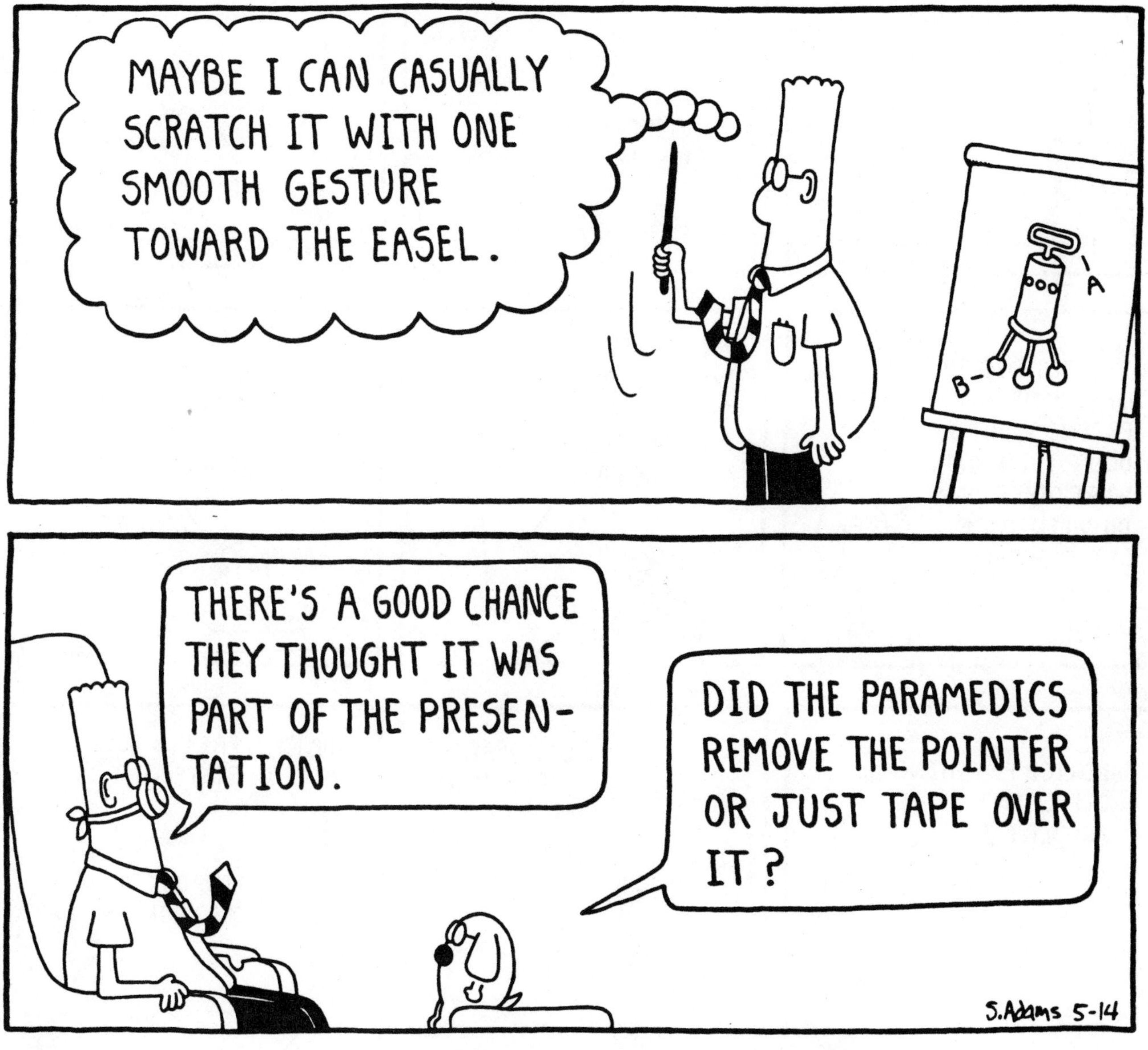
MAYBE I CAN CASUALLY SCRATCH IT WITH ONE SMOOTH GESTURE TOWARD THE EASEL.
A
B
THERE'S A GOOD CHANCE THEY THOUGHT IT WAS PART OF THE PRESEN-TATION.
DID THE PARAMEDICS REMOVE THE POINTER OR JUST TAPE OVER IT?
S.Adams 5-14

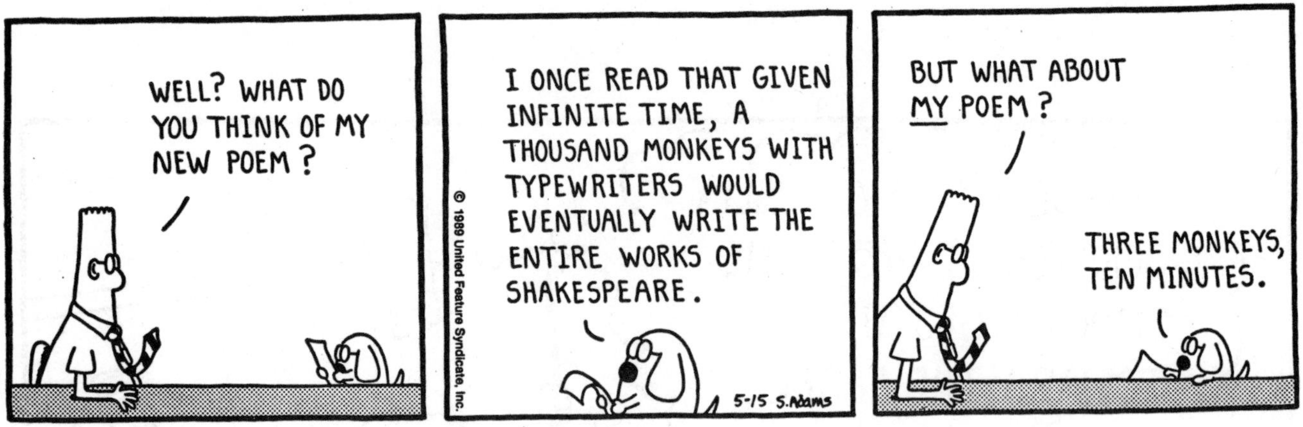

WELL? WHAT DO YOU THINK OF MY NEW POEM?
I ONCE READ THAT GIVEN INFINITE TIME, A THOUSAND MONKEYS WITH TYPEWRITERS WOULD EVENTUALLY WRITE THE ENTIRE WORKS OF SHAKESPEARE.
© 1989 United Feature Syndicate, Inc.
5-15 S.Adams
BUT WHAT ABOUT MY POEM?
THREE MONKEYS, TEN MINUTES.

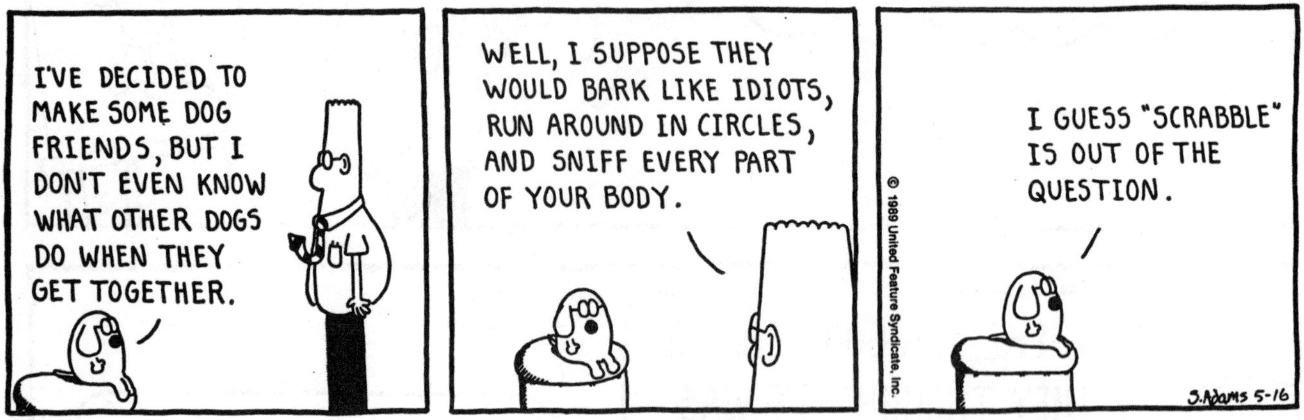

I'VE DECIDED TO MAKE SOME DOG FRIENDS, BUT I DON'T EVEN KNOW WHAT OTHER DOGS DO WHEN THEY GET TOGETHER.
WELL, I SUPPOSE THEY WOULD BARK LIKE IDIOTS, RUN AROUND IN CIRCLES, AND SNIFF EVERY PART OF YOUR BODY.
© 1989 United Feature Syndicate, Inc.
I GUESS "SCRABBLE" IS OUT OF THE QUESTION.
S.Adams 5-16

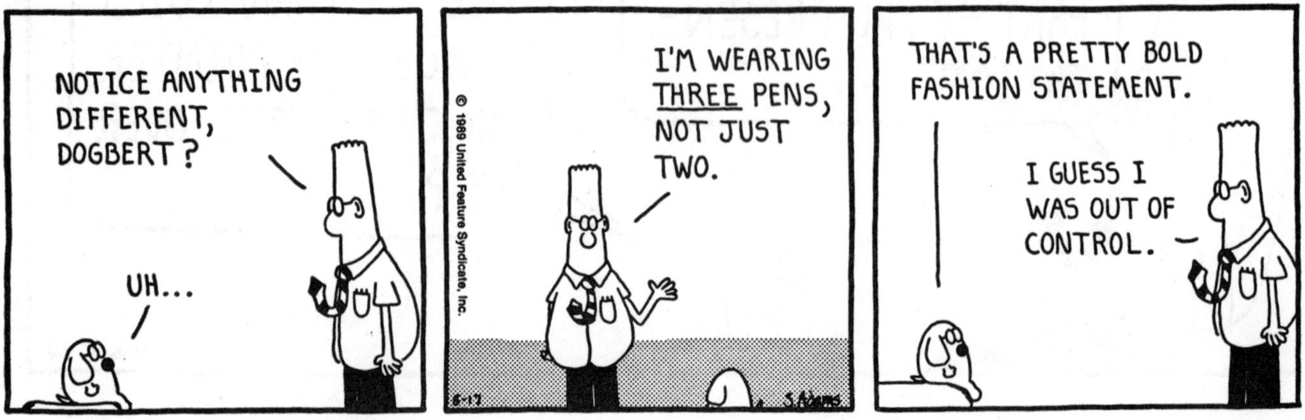

NOTICE ANYTHING DIFFERENT, DOGBERT?
UH...
© 1989 United Feature Syndicate, Inc.
I'M WEARING THREE PENS, NOT JUST TWO.
THAT'S A PRETTY BOLD FASHION STATEMENT.
I GUESS I WAS OUT OF CONTROL.

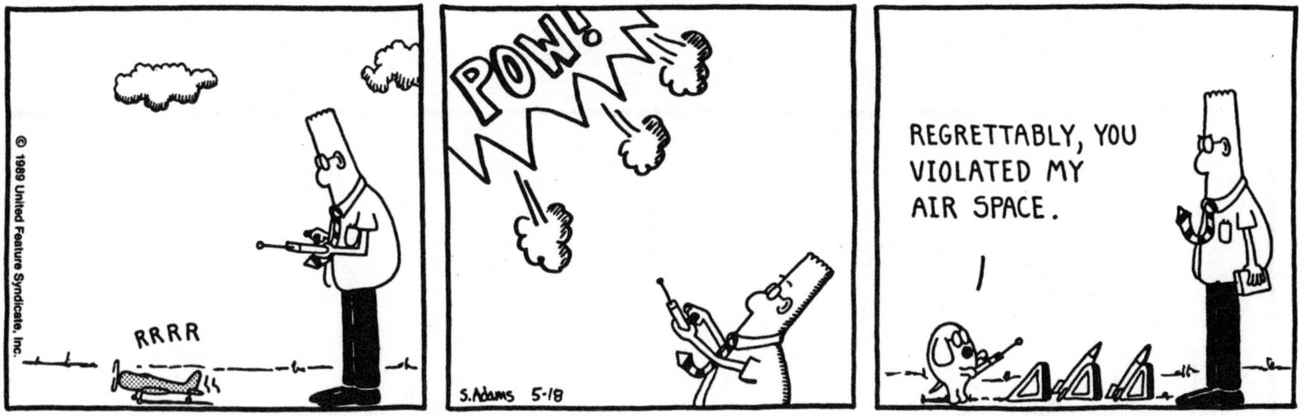
© 1989 United Feature Syndicate, Inc.
RRRR
POW!
S.Adams 5-18
REGRETTABLY, YOU VIOLATED MY AIR SPACE.

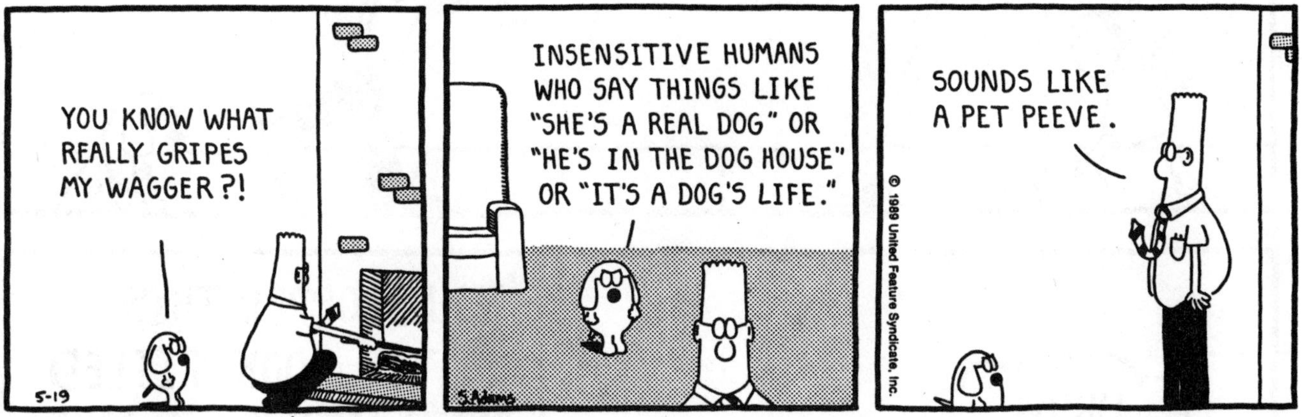
YOU KNOW WHAT REALLY GRIPES MY WAGGER?!
5-19
INSENSITIVE HUMANS WHO SAY THINGS LIKE "SHE'S A REAL DOG" OR "HE'S IN THE DOG HOUSE" OR "IT'S A DOG'S LIFE."
S.Adams
© 1989 United Feature Syndicate, Inc.
SOUNDS LIKE A PET PEEVE.

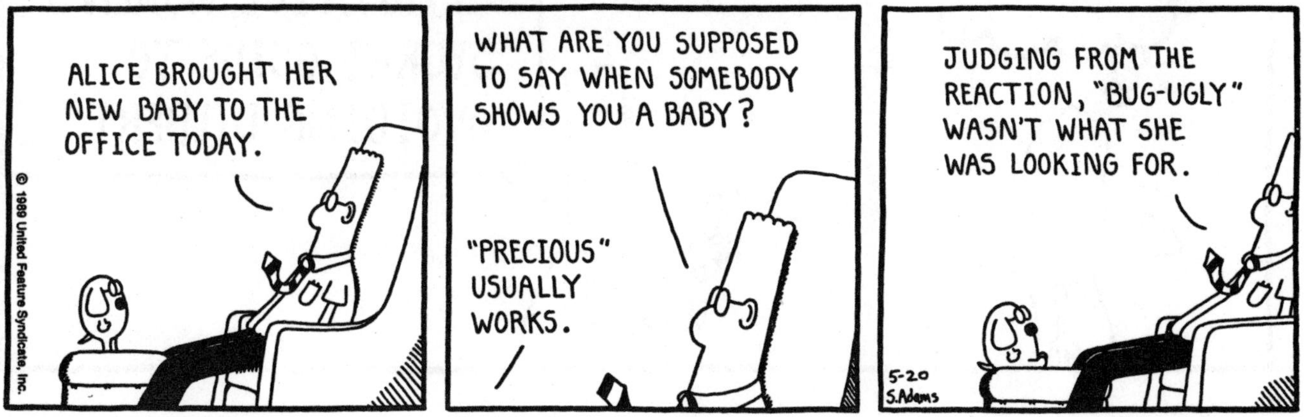
© 1989 United Feature Syndicate, Inc.
ALICE BROUGHT HER NEW BABY TO THE OFFICE TODAY.
WHAT ARE YOU SUPPOSED TO SAY WHEN SOMEBODY SHOWS YOU A BABY?
"PRECIOUS" USUALLY WORKS.
JUDGING FROM THE REACTION, "BUG-UGLY" WASN'T WHAT SHE WAS LOOKING FOR.
5-20
S.Adams

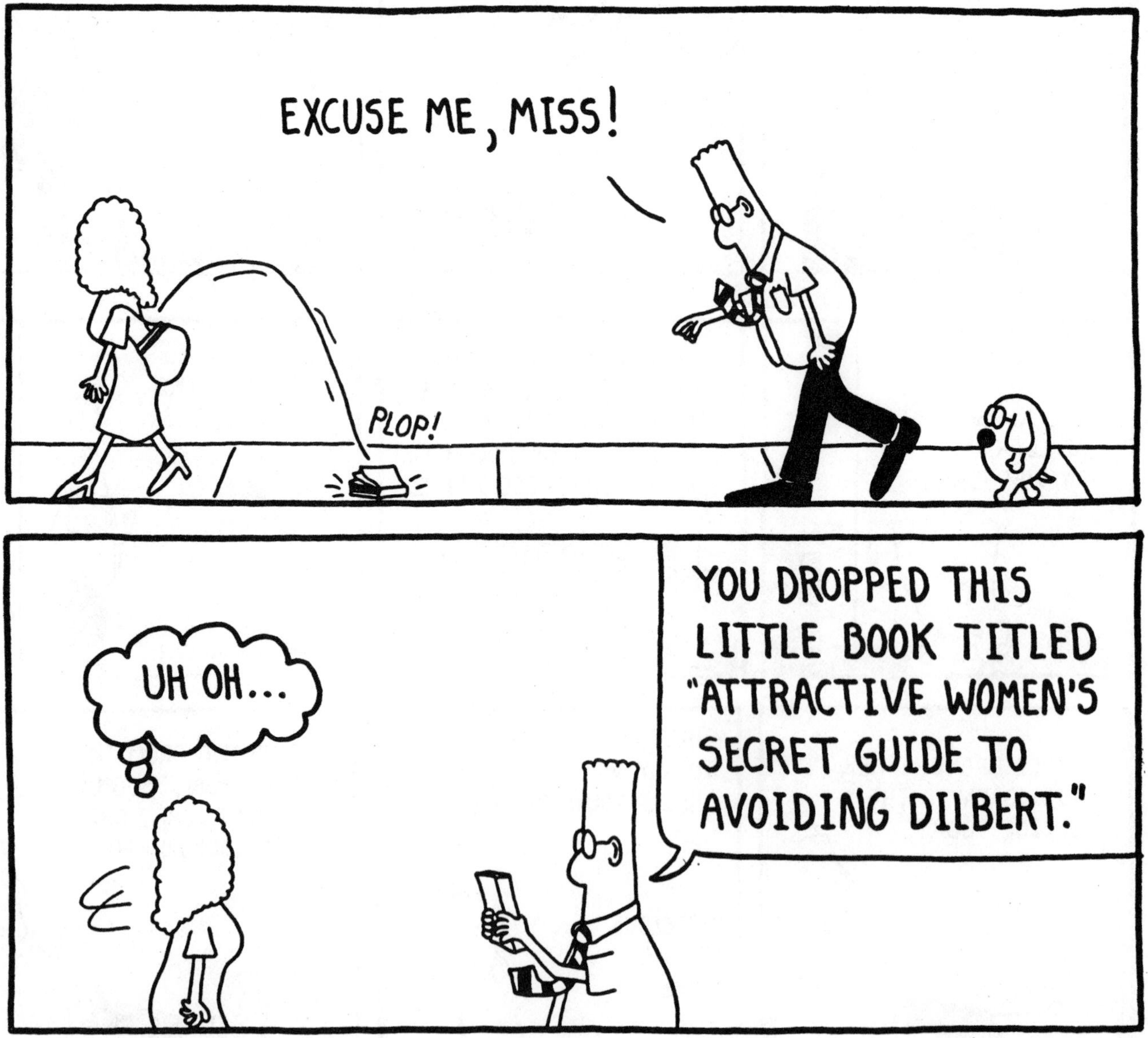
EXCUSE ME, MISS!
PLOP!
UH OH...
YOU DROPPED THIS LITTLE BOOK TITLED "ATTRACTIVE WOMEN'S SECRET GUIDE TO AVOIDING DILBERT."

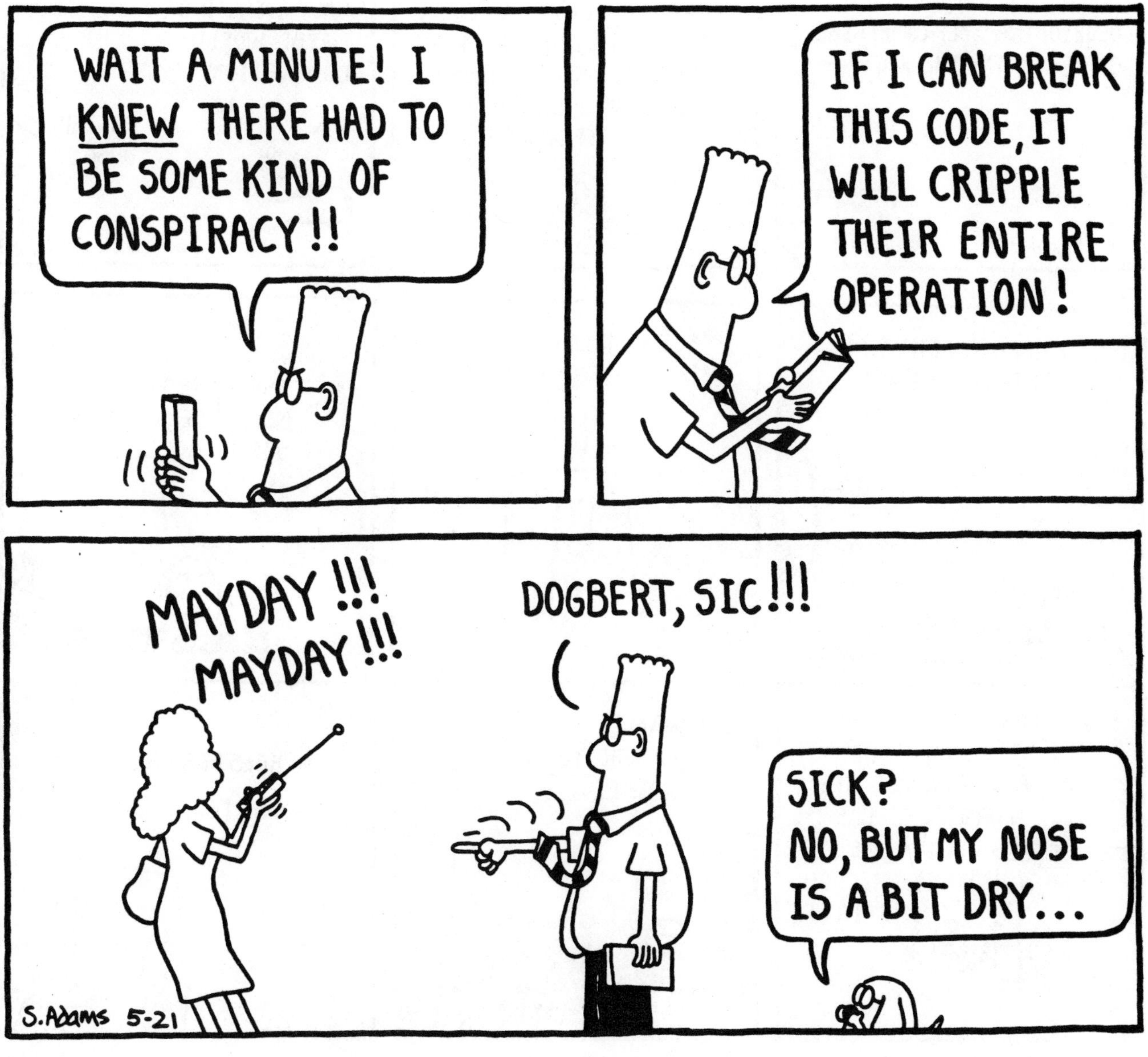
WAIT A MINUTE! I KNEW THERE HAD TO BE SOME KIND OF CONSPIRACY!!
IF I CAN BREAK THIS CODE, IT WILL CRIPPLE THEIR ENTIRE OPERATION!
MAYDAY!!! MAYDAY!!!
DOGBERT, SIC!!!
SICK? NO, BUT MY NOSE IS A BIT DRY...
S.Adams 5-21

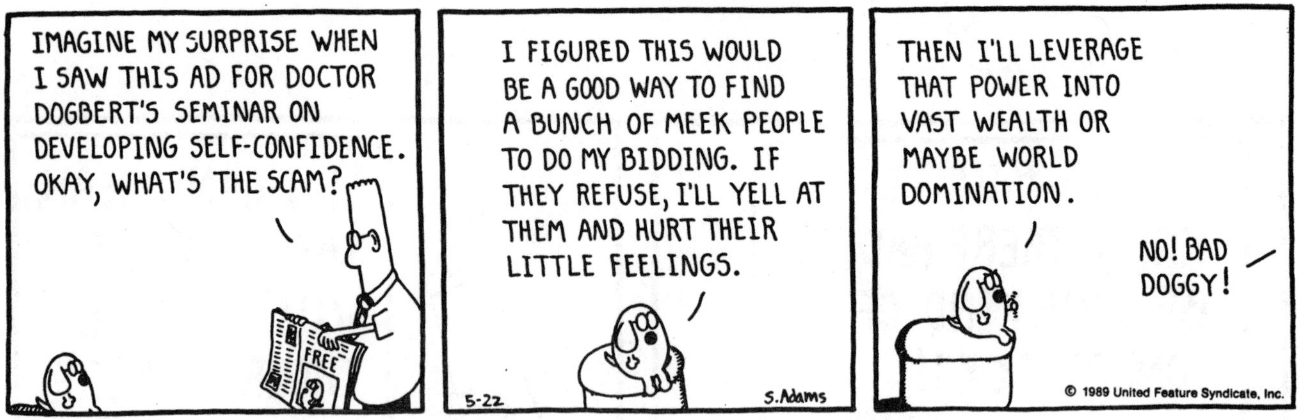
IMAGINE MY SURPRISE WHEN I SAW THIS AD FOR DOCTOR DOGBERT'S SEMINAR ON DEVELOPING SELF-CONFIDENCE. OKAY, WHAT'S THE SCAM?
FREE
I FIGURED THIS WOULD BE A GOOD WAY TO FIND A BUNCH OF MEEK PEOPLE TO DO MY BIDDING. IF THEY REFUSE, I'LL YELL AT THEM AND HURT THEIR LITTLE FEELINGS.
5-22
S. Adams
THEN I'LL LEVERAGE THAT POWER INTO VAST WEALTH OR MAYBE WORLD DOMINATION.
NO! BAD DOGGY!
© 1989 United Feature Syndicate, Inc.

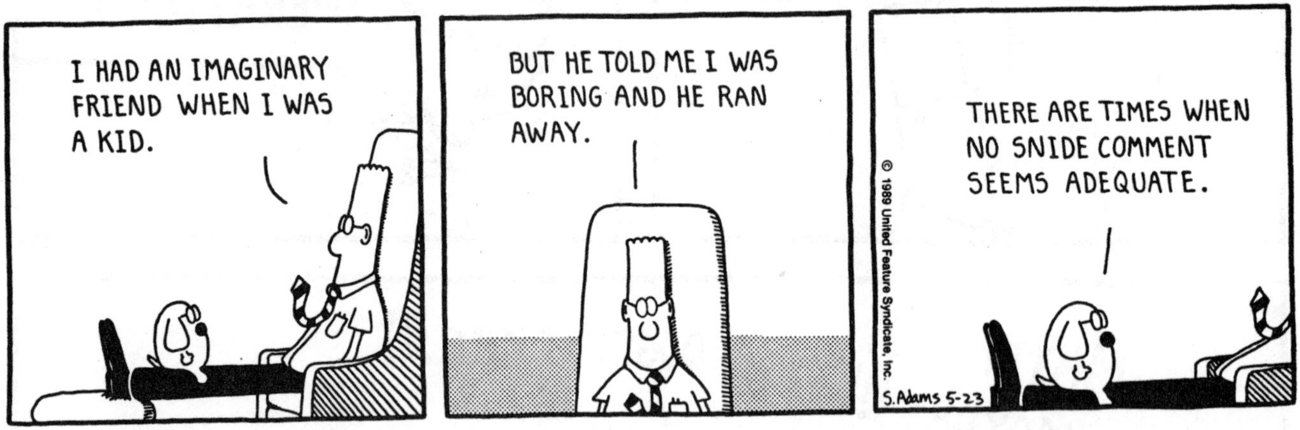
I HAD AN IMAGINARY FRIEND WHEN I WAS A KID.
BUT HE TOLD ME I WAS BORING AND HE RAN AWAY.
© 1989 United Feature Syndicate, Inc.
THERE ARE TIMES WHEN NO SNIDE COMMENT SEEMS ADEQUATE.
S. Adams 5-23

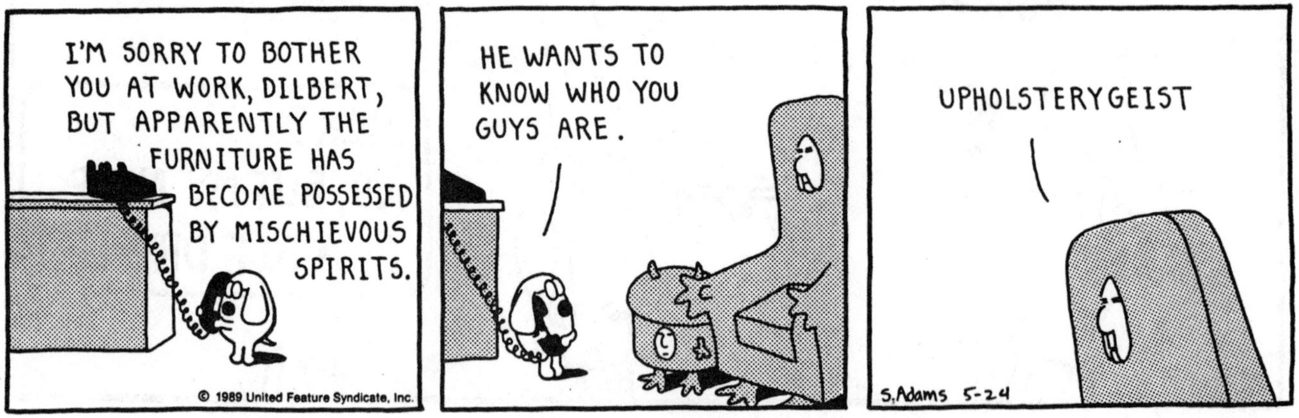
I'M SORRY TO BOTHER YOU AT WORK, DILBERT, BUT APPARENTLY THE FURNITURE HAS BECOME POSSESSED BY MISCHIEVOUS SPIRITS.
© 1989 United Feature Syndicate, Inc.
HE WANTS TO KNOW WHO YOU GUYS ARE.
UPHOLSTERYGEIST
S. Adams 5-24

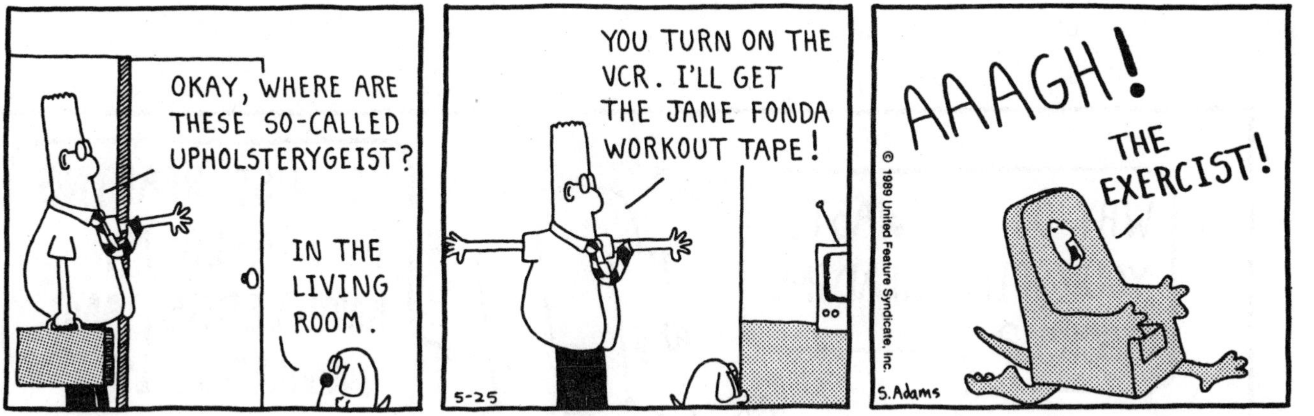
OKAY, WHERE ARE THESE SO-CALLED UPHOLSTERYGEIST?
IN THE LIVING ROOM.
YOU TURN ON THE VCR. I'LL GET THE JANE FONDA WORKOUT TAPE!
5-25
AAAGH!
THE EXERCIST!
© 1989 United Feature Syndicate, Inc.
S. Adams

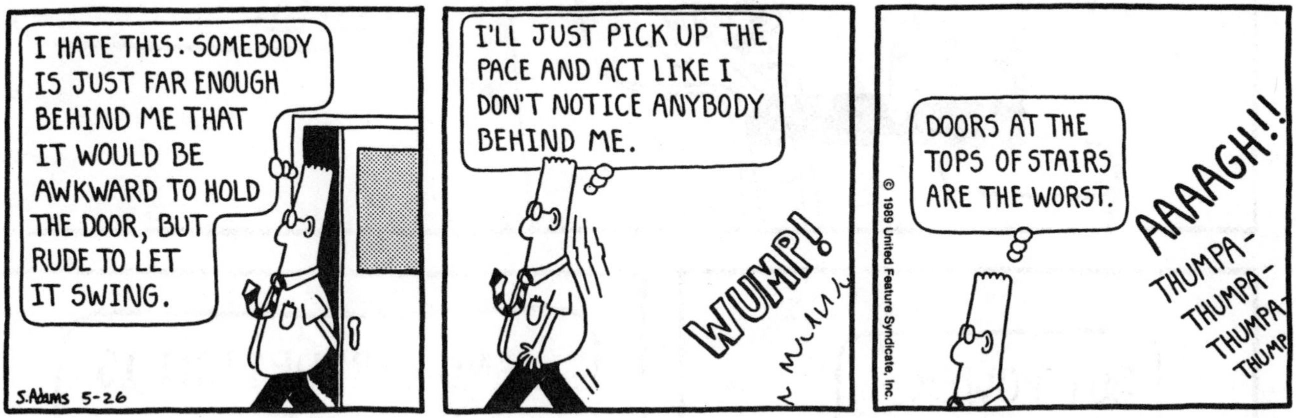
I HATE THIS: SOMEBODY IS JUST FAR ENOUGH BEHIND ME THAT IT WOULD BE AWKWARD TO HOLD THE DOOR, BUT RUDE TO LET IT SWING.
S. Adams 5-26
I'LL JUST PICK UP THE PACE AND ACT LIKE I DON'T NOTICE ANYBODY BEHIND ME.
WUMP!
DOORS AT THE TOPS OF STAIRS ARE THE WORST.
AAAAGH!!
THUMPA-
THUMPA-
THUMPA-
THUMP
© 1989 United Feature Syndicate, Inc.

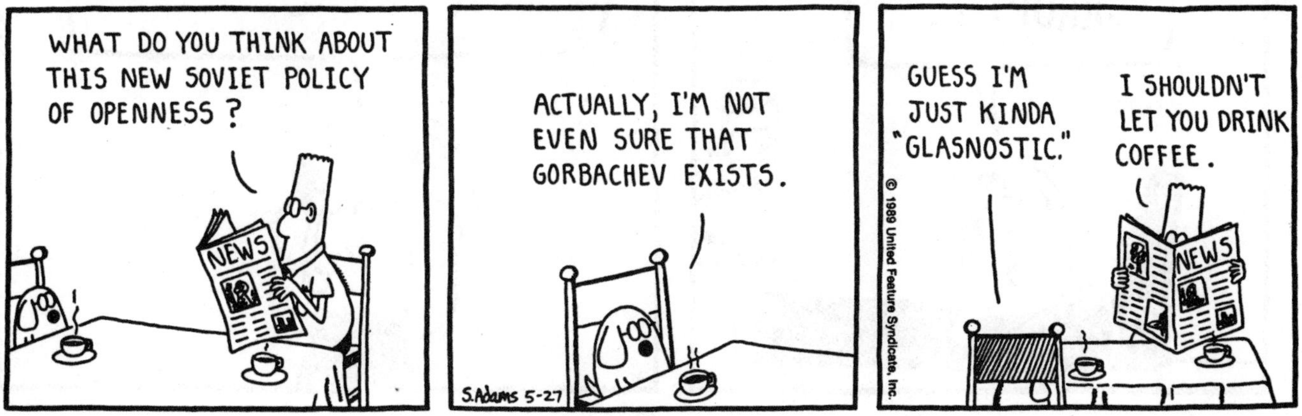
WHAT DO YOU THINK ABOUT THIS NEW SOVIET POLICY OF OPENNESS?
NEWS
ACTUALLY, I'M NOT EVEN SURE THAT GORBACHEV EXISTS.
S. Adams 5-27
GUESS I'M JUST KINDA "GLASNOSTIC."
I SHOULDN'T LET YOU DRINK COFFEE.
NEWS
© 1989 United Feature Syndicate, Inc.

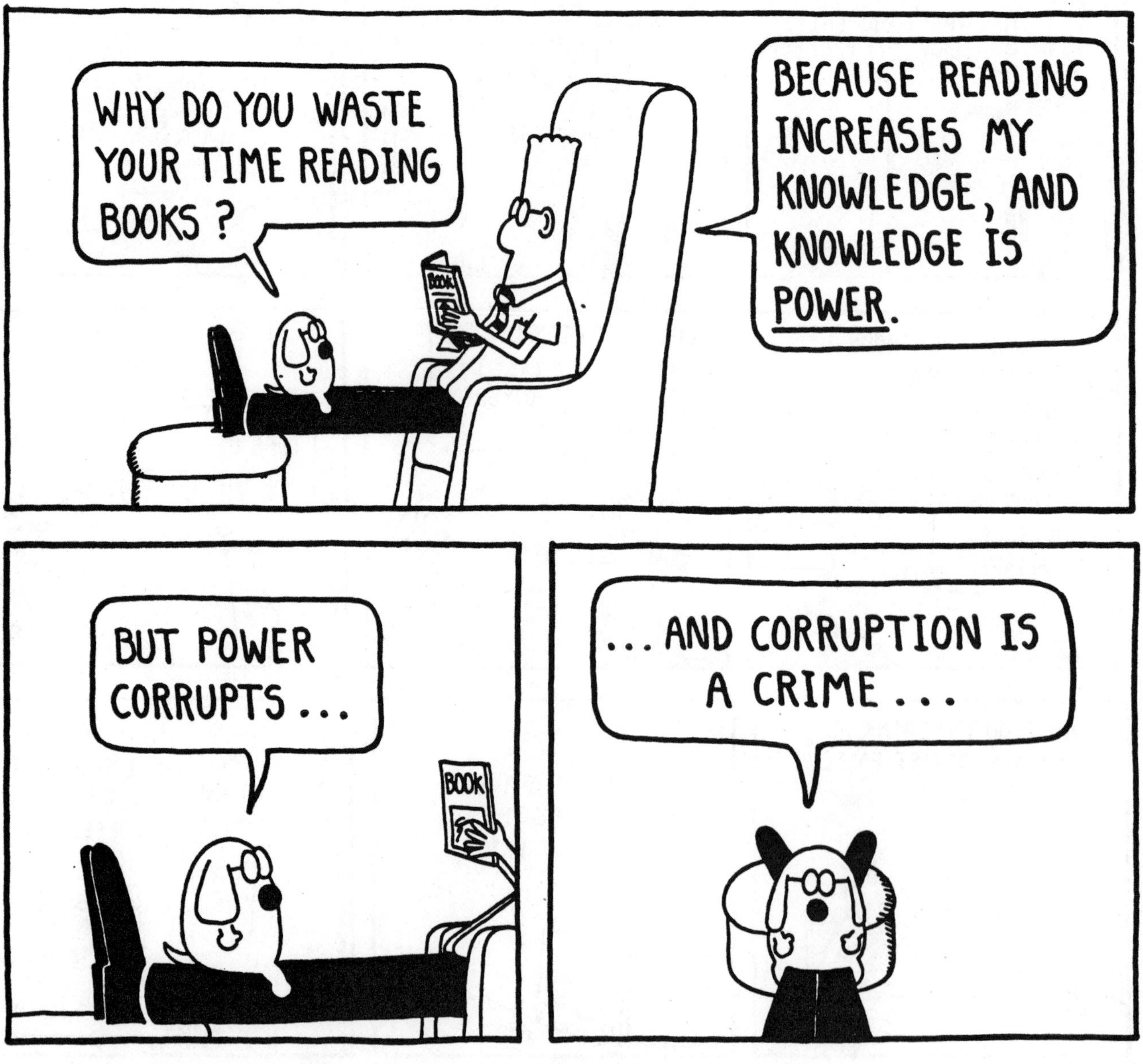
WHY DO YOU WASTE YOUR TIME READING BOOKS ?
BECAUSE READING INCREASES MY KNOWLEDGE, AND KNOWLEDGE IS POWER.
BOOK
BUT POWER CORRUPTS . . .
BOOK
. . . AND CORRUPTION IS A CRIME . . .

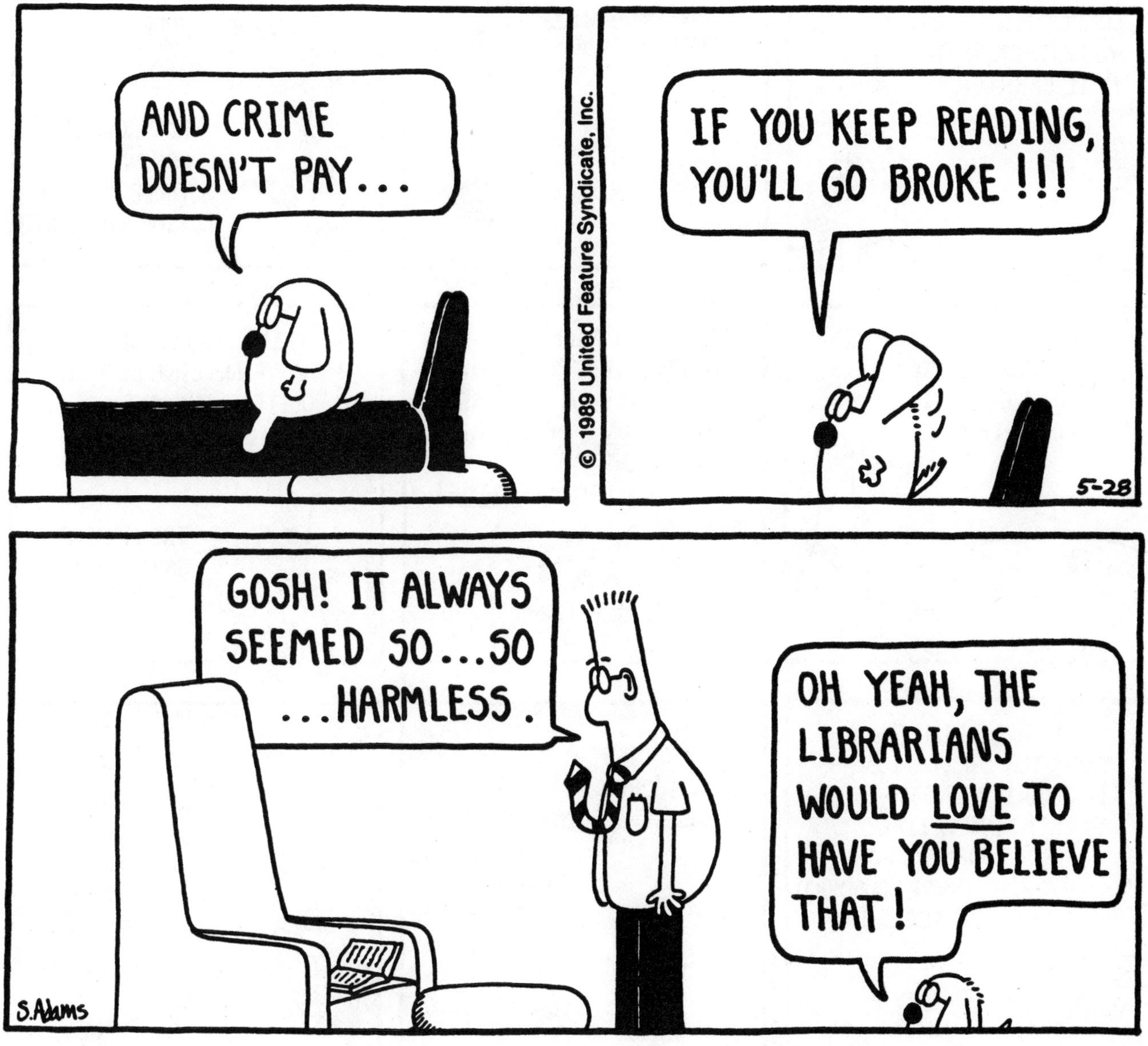
AND CRIME DOESN'T PAY...
© 1989 United Feature Syndicate, Inc.
IF YOU KEEP READING, YOU'LL GO BROKE !!!
5-28
GOSH! IT ALWAYS SEEMED SO...SO ...HARMLESS.
OH YEAH, THE LIBRARIANS WOULD LOVE TO HAVE YOU BELIEVE THAT!
S.Adams

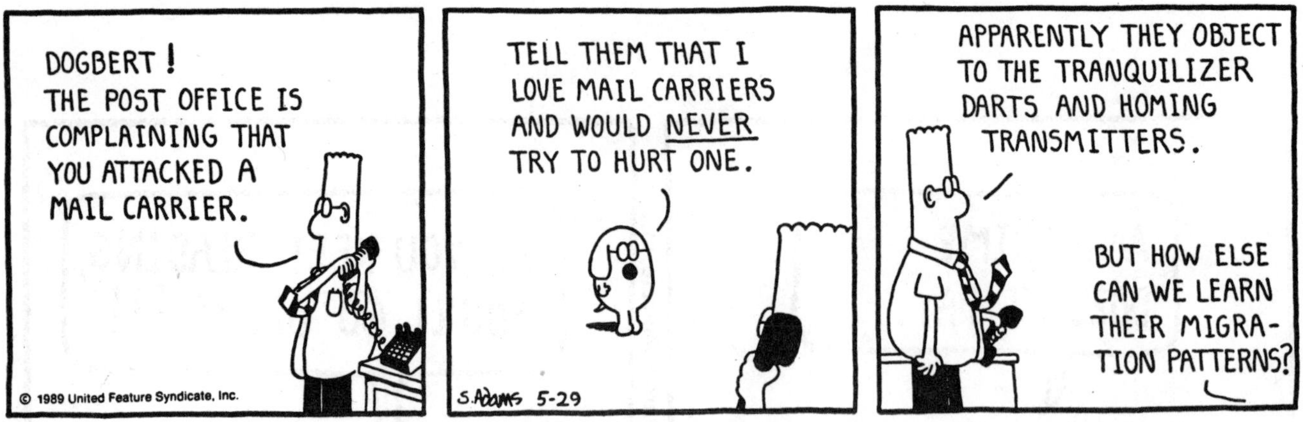
DOGBERT! THE POST OFFICE IS COMPLAINING THAT YOU ATTACKED A MAIL CARRIER.
© 1989 United Feature Syndicate, Inc.
TELL THEM THAT I LOVE MAIL CARRIERS AND WOULD NEVER TRY TO HURT ONE.
S.Adams 5-29
APPARENTLY THEY OBJECT TO THE TRANQUILIZER DARTS AND HOMING TRANSMITTERS.
BUT HOW ELSE CAN WE LEARN THEIR MIGRATION PATTERNS?

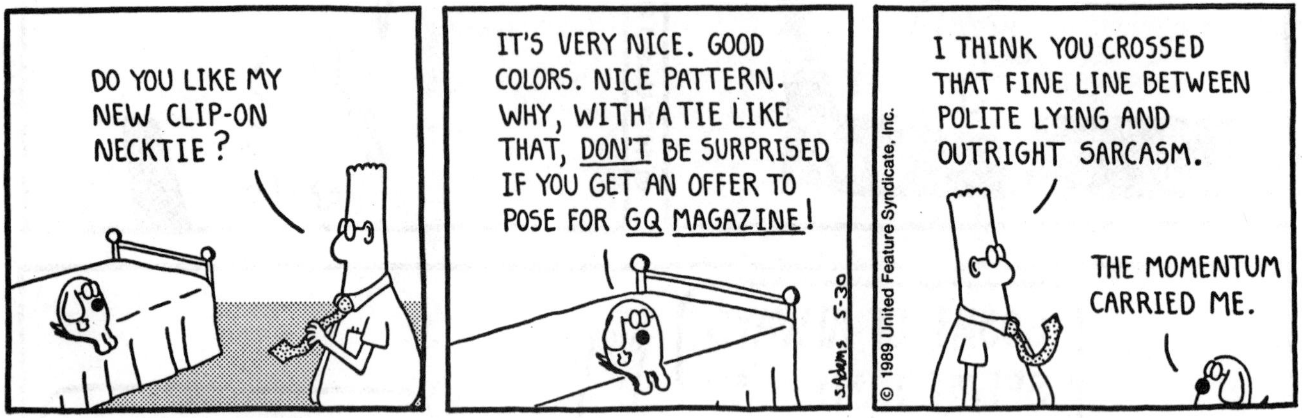
DO YOU LIKE MY NEW CLIP-ON NECKTIE?
IT'S VERY NICE. GOOD COLORS. NICE PATTERN. WHY, WITH A TIE LIKE THAT, DON'T BE SURPRISED IF YOU GET AN OFFER TO POSE FOR GQ MAGAZINE!
S.Adams 5-30
© 1989 United Feature Syndicate, Inc.
I THINK YOU CROSSED THAT FINE LINE BETWEEN POLITE LYING AND OUTRIGHT SARCASM.
THE MOMENTUM CARRIED ME.

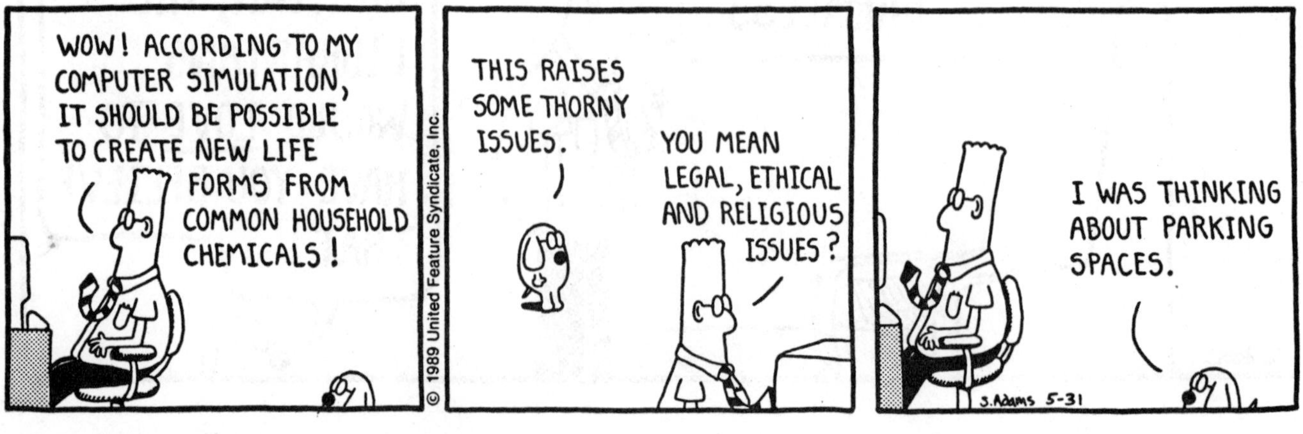
WOW! ACCORDING TO MY COMPUTER SIMULATION, IT SHOULD BE POSSIBLE TO CREATE NEW LIFE FORMS FROM COMMON HOUSEHOLD CHEMICALS!
© 1989 United Feature Syndicate, Inc.
THIS RAISES SOME THORNY ISSUES.
YOU MEAN LEGAL, ETHICAL AND RELIGIOUS ISSUES?
I WAS THINKING ABOUT PARKING SPACES.
S.Adams 5-31

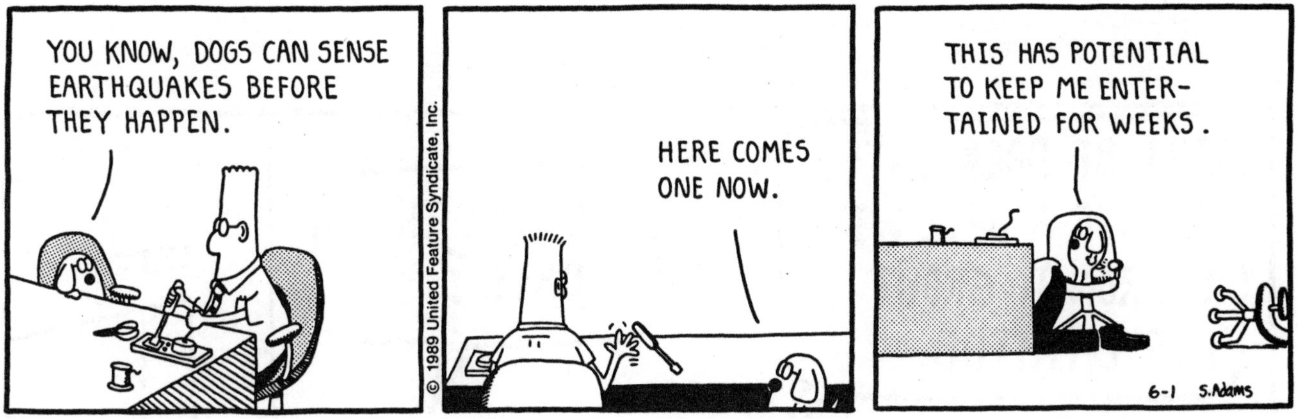
YOU KNOW, DOGS CAN SENSE EARTHQUAKES BEFORE THEY HAPPEN.
© 1989 United Feature Syndicate, Inc.
HERE COMES ONE NOW.
THIS HAS POTENTIAL TO KEEP ME ENTER-TAINED FOR WEEKS.
6-1 S.Adams

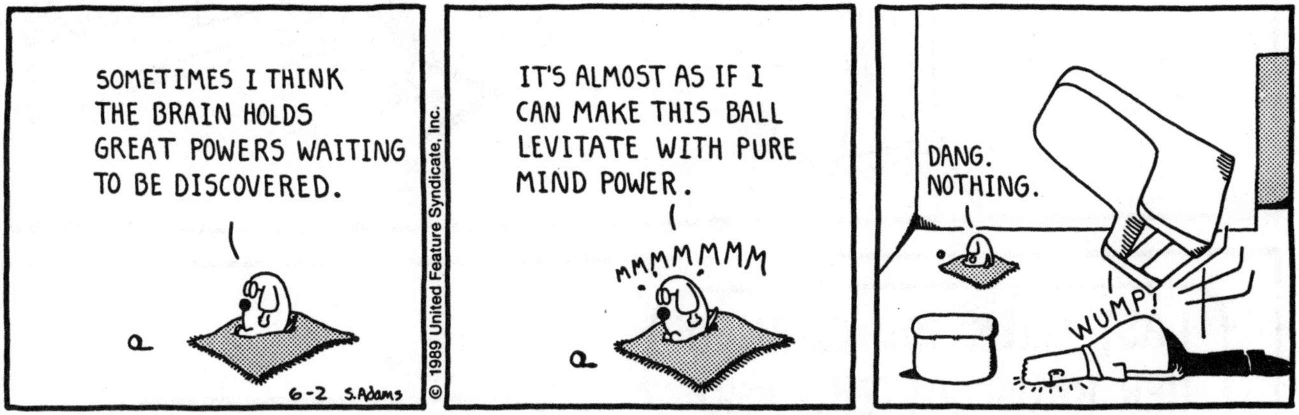
SOMETIMES I THINK THE BRAIN HOLDS GREAT POWERS WAITING TO BE DISCOVERED.
6-2 S.Adams
© 1989 United Feature Syndicate, Inc.
IT'S ALMOST AS IF I CAN MAKE THIS BALL LEVITATE WITH PURE MIND POWER.
MMMMMMM
DANG. NOTHING.
WUMP!

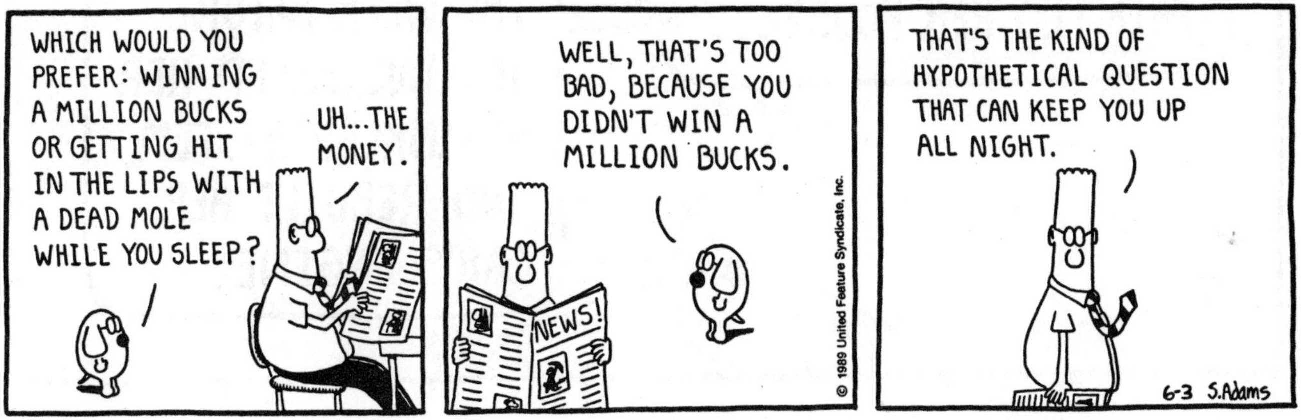
WHICH WOULD YOU PREFER: WINNING A MILLION BUCKS OR GETTING HIT IN THE LIPS WITH A DEAD MOLE WHILE YOU SLEEP?
UH...THE MONEY.
WELL, THAT'S TOO BAD, BECAUSE YOU DIDN'T WIN A MILLION BUCKS.
NEWS!
© 1989 United Feature Syndicate, Inc.
THAT'S THE KIND OF HYPOTHETICAL QUESTION THAT CAN KEEP YOU UP ALL NIGHT.
6-3 S.Adams

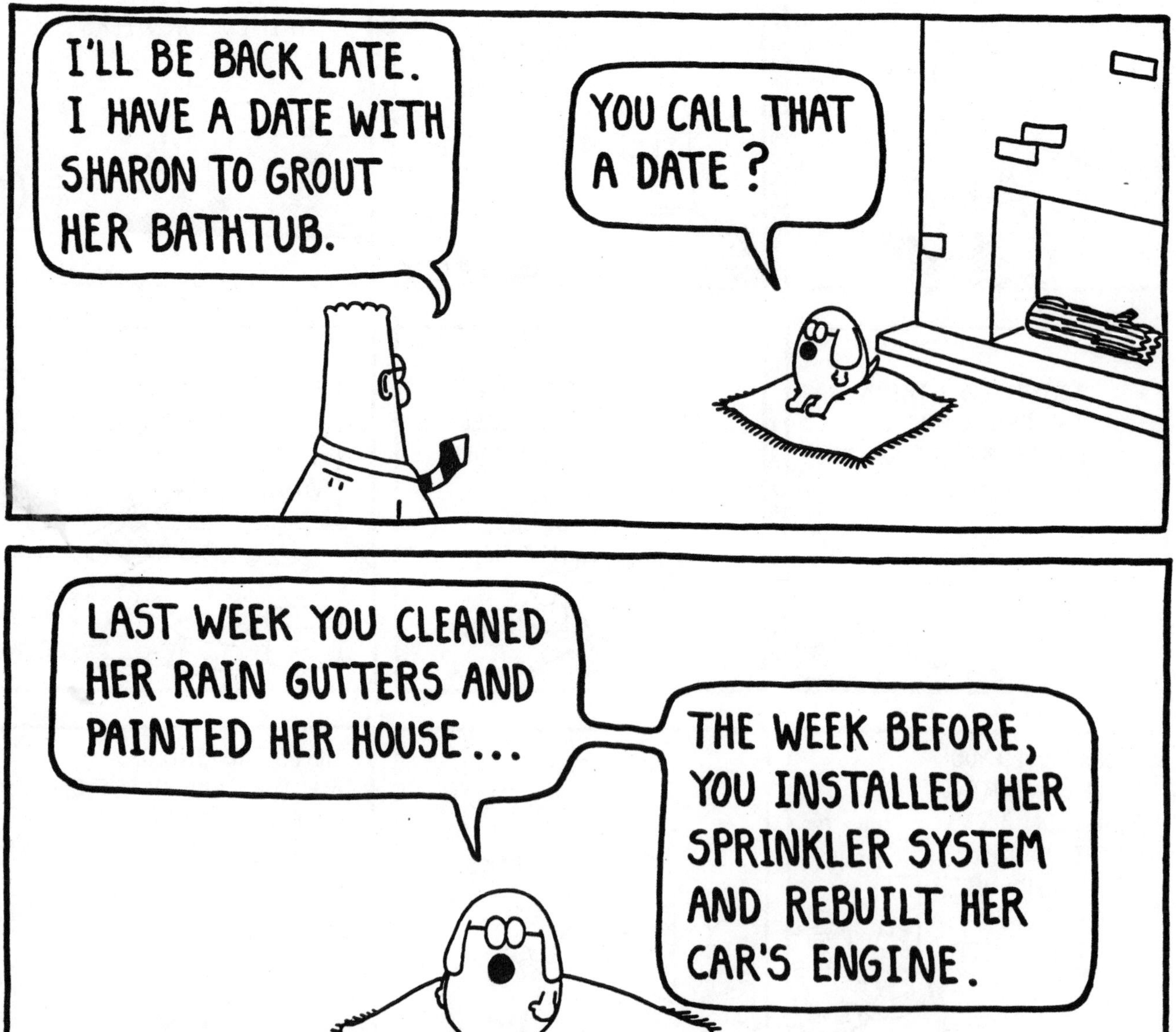
I'LL BE BACK LATE. I HAVE A DATE WITH SHARON TO GROUT HER BATHTUB.
YOU CALL THAT A DATE?
LAST WEEK YOU CLEANED HER RAIN GUTTERS AND PAINTED HER HOUSE...
THE WEEK BEFORE, YOU INSTALLED HER SPRINKLER SYSTEM AND REBUILT HER CAR'S ENGINE.

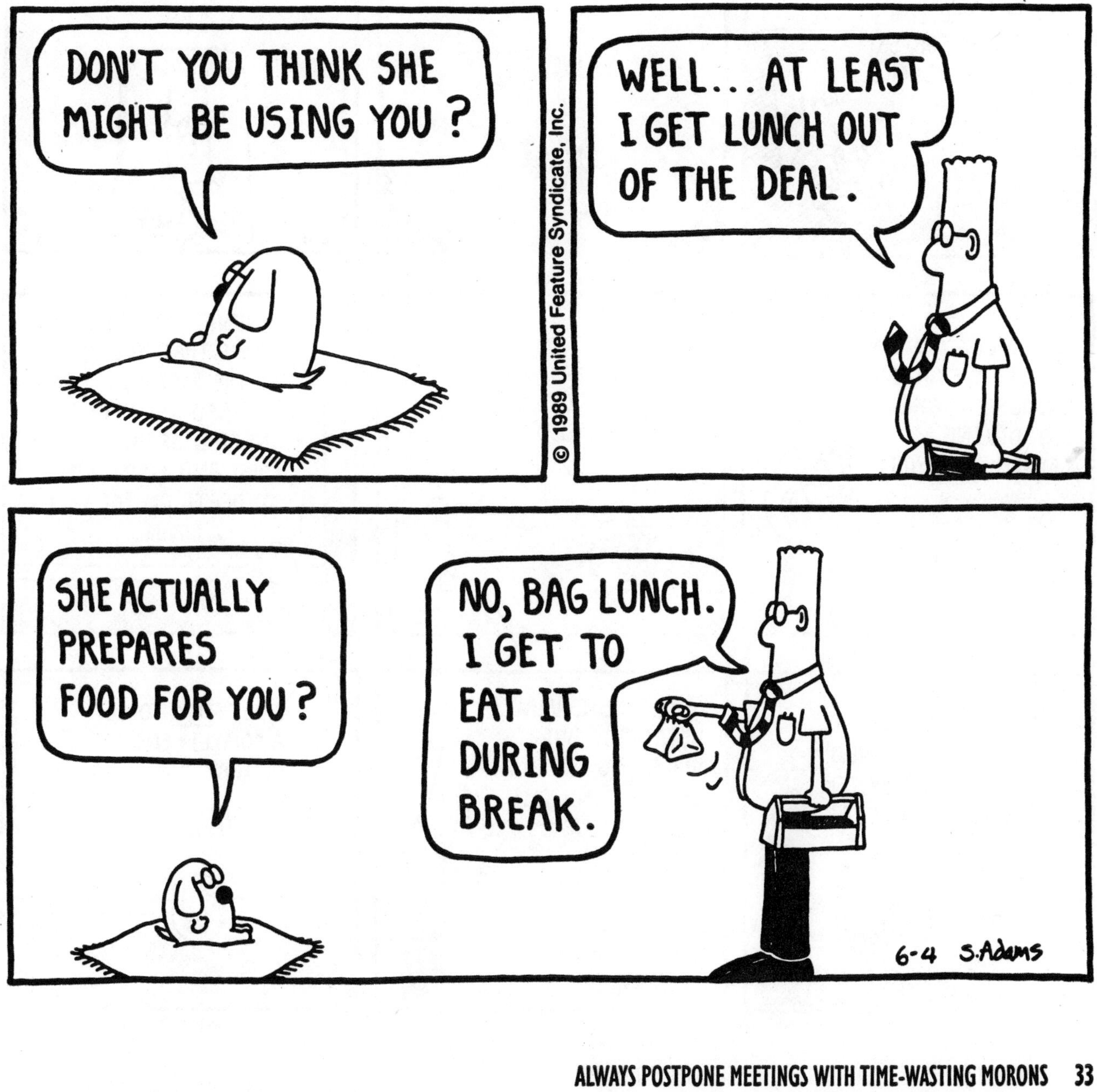
DON'T YOU THINK SHE MIGHT BE USING YOU?
© 1989 United Feature Syndicate, Inc.
WELL... AT LEAST I GET LUNCH OUT OF THE DEAL.
SHE ACTUALLY PREPARES FOOD FOR YOU?
NO, BAG LUNCH. I GET TO EAT IT DURING BREAK.
6-4 S.Adams

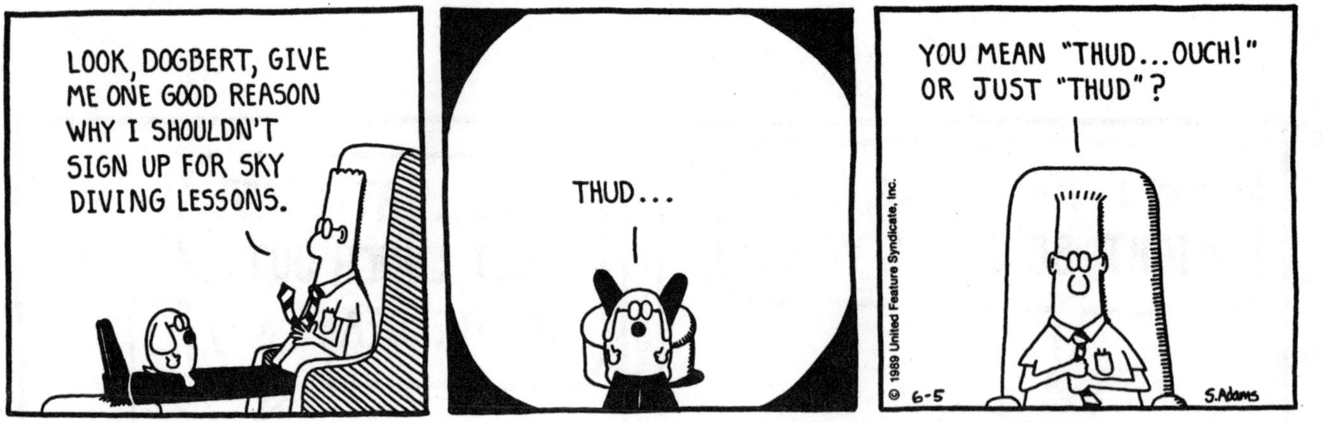
LOOK, DOGBERT, GIVE ME ONE GOOD REASON WHY I SHOULDN'T SIGN UP FOR SKY DIVING LESSONS.
THUD...
YOU MEAN "THUD...OUCH!" OR JUST "THUD"?
© 1989 United Feature Syndicate, Inc.
6-5
S.Adams

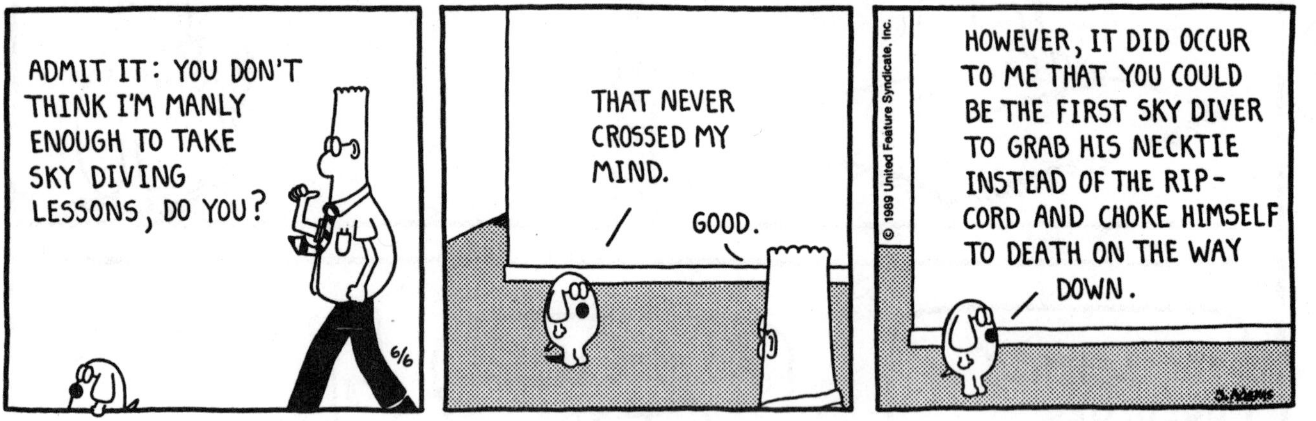
ADMIT IT: YOU DON'T THINK I'M MANLY ENOUGH TO TAKE SKY DIVING LESSONS, DO YOU?
6/6
THAT NEVER CROSSED MY MIND.
GOOD.
© 1989 United Feature Syndicate, Inc.
HOWEVER, IT DID OCCUR TO ME THAT YOU COULD BE THE FIRST SKY DIVER TO GRAB HIS NECKTIE INSTEAD OF THE RIP-CORD AND CHOKE HIMSELF TO DEATH ON THE WAY DOWN.
S.Adams

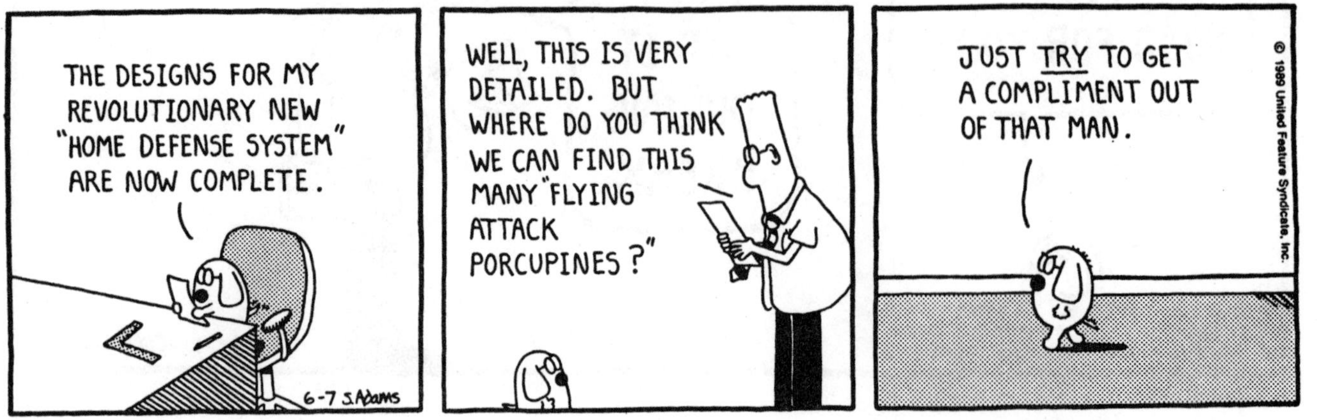
THE DESIGNS FOR MY REVOLUTIONARY NEW "HOME DEFENSE SYSTEM" ARE NOW COMPLETE.
6-7 S.Adams
WELL, THIS IS VERY DETAILED. BUT WHERE DO YOU THINK WE CAN FIND THIS MANY "FLYING ATTACK PORCUPINES?"
JUST TRY TO GET A COMPLIMENT OUT OF THAT MAN.
© 1989 United Feature Syndicate, Inc.

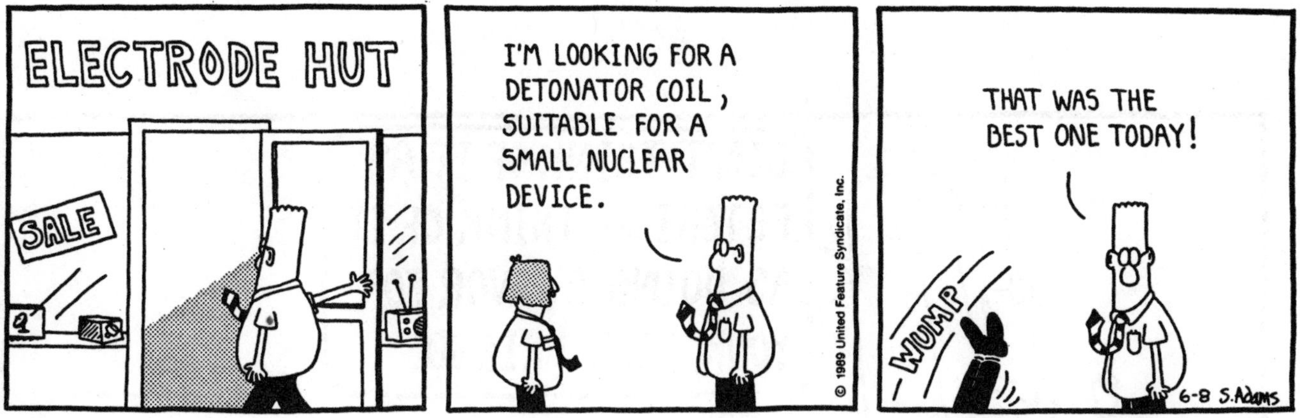
ELECTRODE HUT
SALE
I'M LOOKING FOR A DETONATOR COIL, SUITABLE FOR A SMALL NUCLEAR DEVICE.
© 1989 United Feature Syndicate, Inc.
WUMP
THAT WAS THE BEST ONE TODAY!
6-8 S.Adams

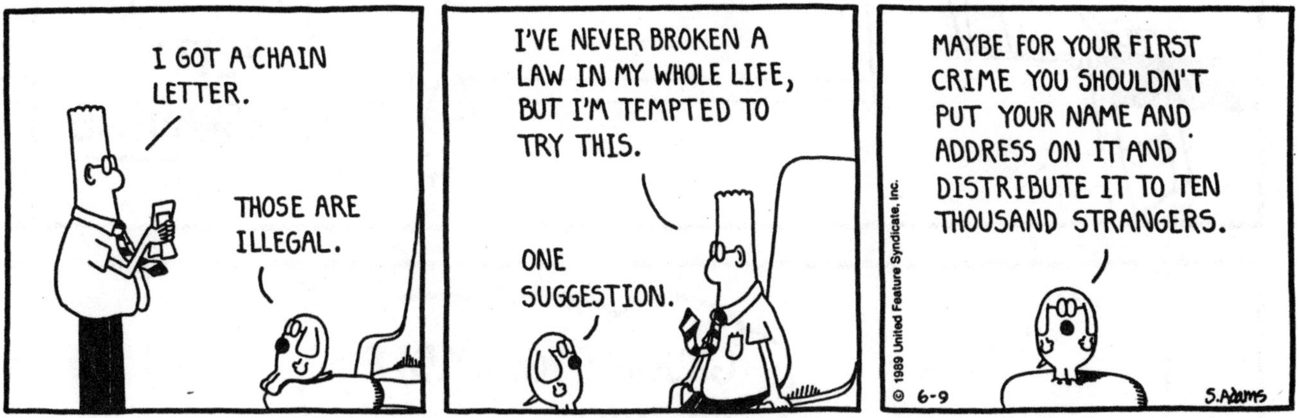
I GOT A CHAIN LETTER.
THOSE ARE ILLEGAL.
I'VE NEVER BROKEN A LAW IN MY WHOLE LIFE, BUT I'M TEMPTED TO TRY THIS.
ONE SUGGESTION.
© 1989 United Feature Syndicate, Inc.
MAYBE FOR YOUR FIRST CRIME YOU SHOULDN'T PUT YOUR NAME AND ADDRESS ON IT AND DISTRIBUTE IT TO TEN THOUSAND STRANGERS.
6-9
S.Adams

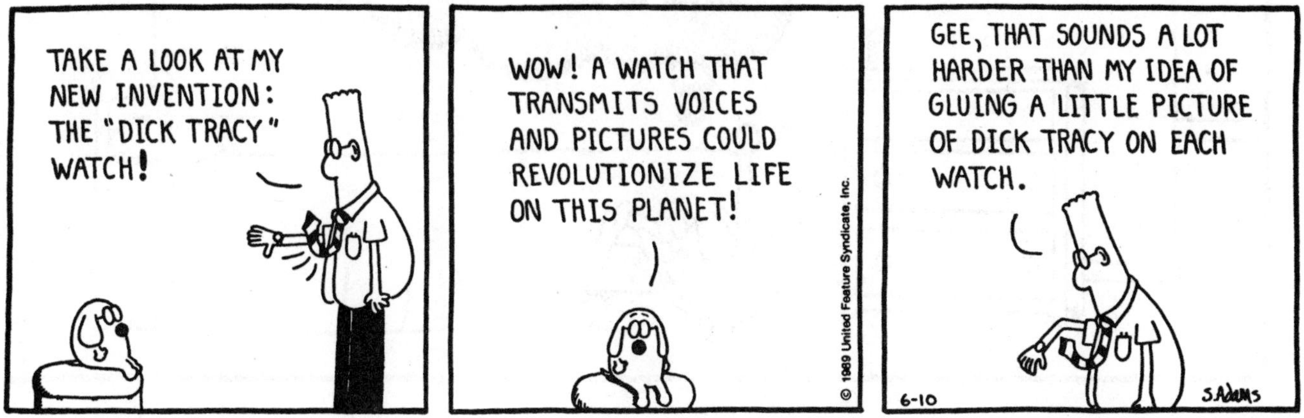
TAKE A LOOK AT MY NEW INVENTION: THE "DICK TRACY" WATCH!
WOW! A WATCH THAT TRANSMITS VOICES AND PICTURES COULD REVOLUTIONIZE LIFE ON THIS PLANET!
© 1989 United Feature Syndicate, Inc.
GEE, THAT SOUNDS A LOT HARDER THAN MY IDEA OF GLUING A LITTLE PICTURE OF DICK TRACY ON EACH WATCH.
6-10
S.Adams

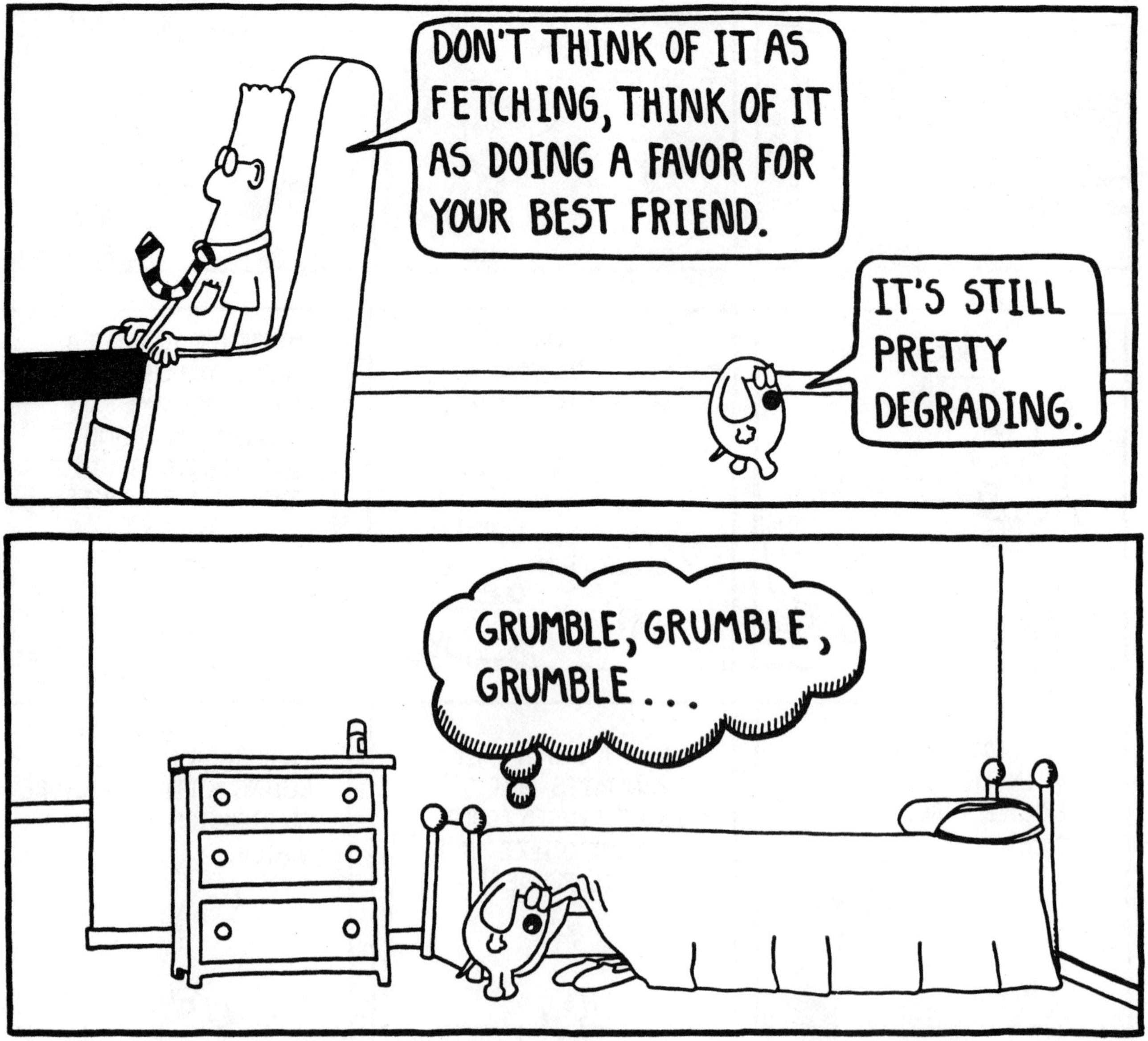
DON'T THINK OF IT AS FETCHING, THINK OF IT AS DOING A FAVOR FOR YOUR BEST FRIEND.
IT'S STILL PRETTY DEGRADING.
GRUMBLE, GRUMBLE, GRUMBLE...

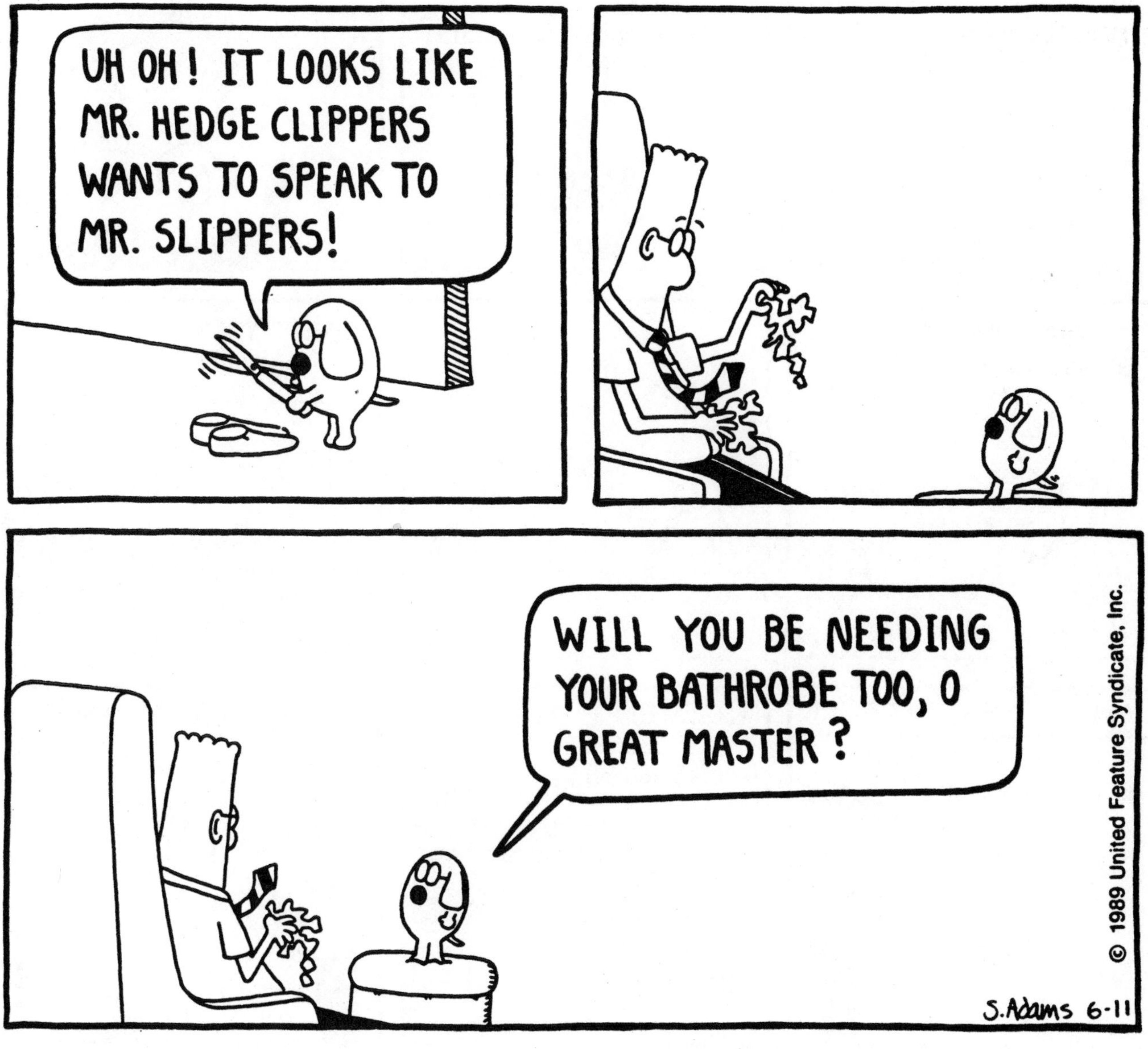
UH OH! IT LOOKS LIKE MR. HEDGE CLIPPERS WANTS TO SPEAK TO MR. SLIPPERS!
WILL YOU BE NEEDING YOUR BATHROBE TOO, O GREAT MASTER?
© 1989 United Feature Syndicate, Inc.
S. Adams 6-11

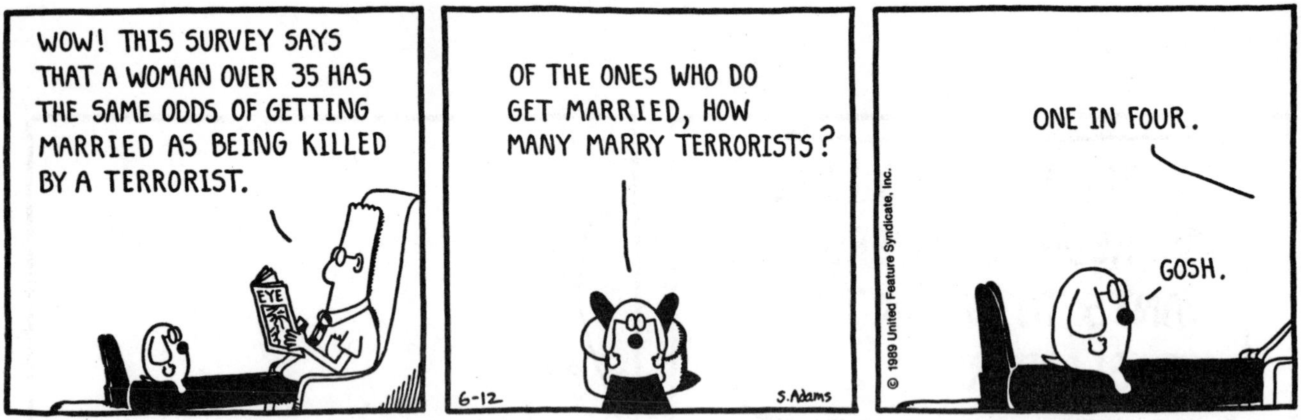
WOW! THIS SURVEY SAYS THAT A WOMAN OVER 35 HAS THE SAME ODDS OF GETTING MARRIED AS BEING KILLED BY A TERRORIST.
EYE
OF THE ONES WHO DO GET MARRIED, HOW MANY MARRY TERRORISTS?
6-12
S. Adams
© 1989 United Feature Syndicate, Inc.
ONE IN FOUR.
GOSH.

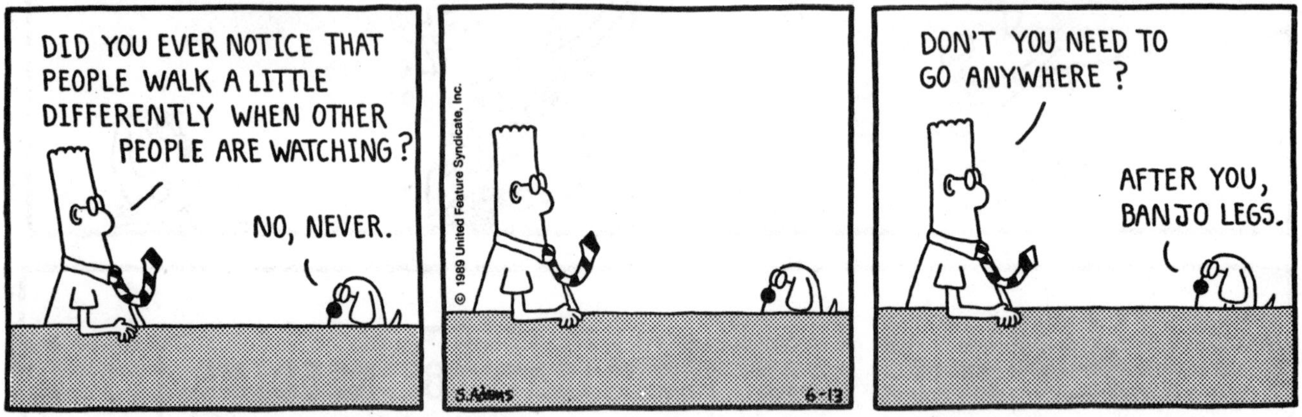
DID YOU EVER NOTICE THAT PEOPLE WALK A LITTLE DIFFERENTLY WHEN OTHER PEOPLE ARE WATCHING?
NO, NEVER.
© 1989 United Feature Syndicate, Inc.
S. Adams
6-13
DON'T YOU NEED TO GO ANYWHERE?
AFTER YOU, BANJO LEGS.

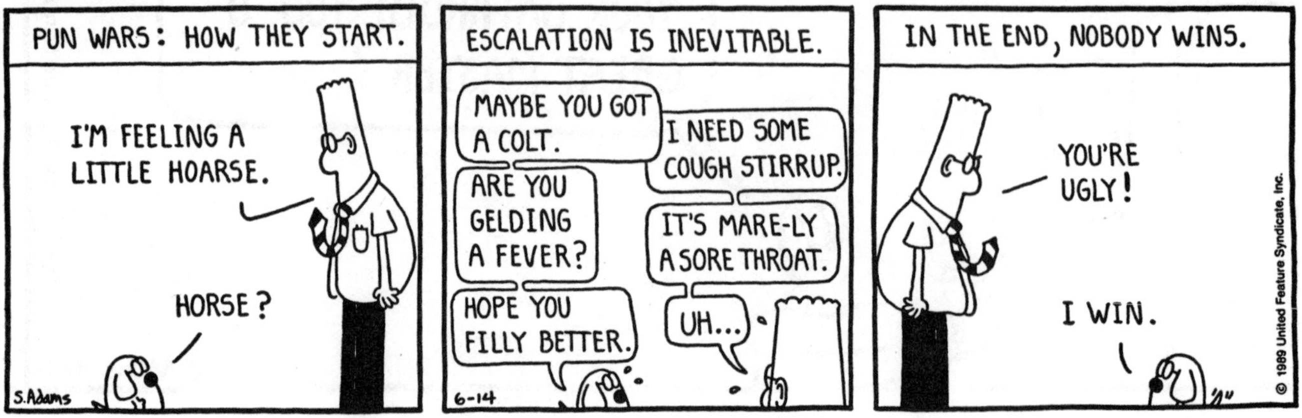
PUN WARS: HOW THEY START.
I'M FEELING A LITTLE HOARSE.
HORSE?
S. Adams
ESCALATION IS INEVITABLE.
MAYBE YOU GOT A COLT.
I NEED SOME COUGH STIRRUP.
ARE YOU GELDING A FEVER?
IT'S MARE-LY A SORE THROAT.
HOPE YOU FILLY BETTER.
UH...
6-14
IN THE END, NOBODY WINS.
YOU'RE UGLY!
I WIN.
© 1989 United Feature Syndicate, Inc.

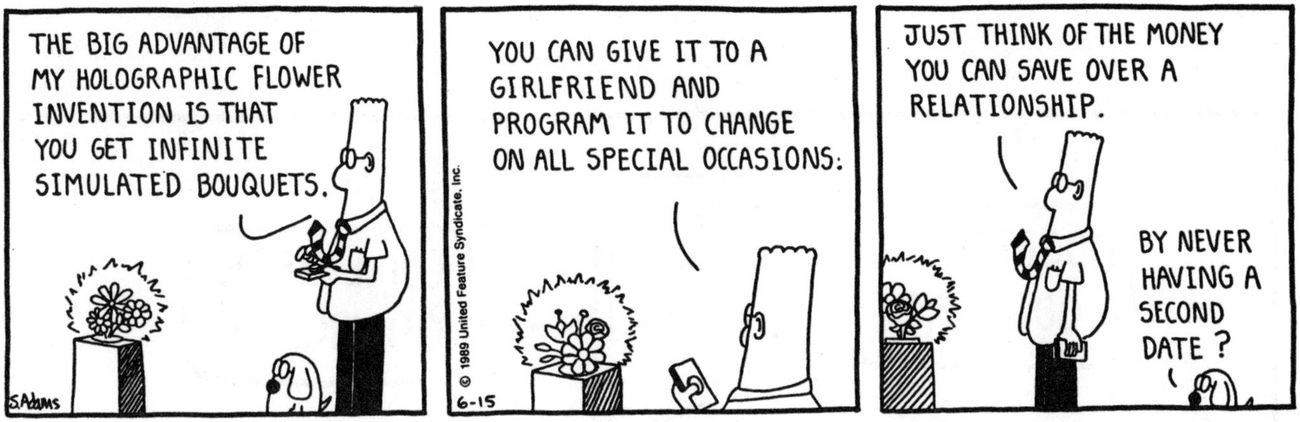
THE BIG ADVANTAGE OF MY HOLOGRAPHIC FLOWER INVENTION IS THAT YOU GET INFINITE SIMULATED BOUQUETS.
S.Adams
YOU CAN GIVE IT TO A GIRLFRIEND AND PROGRAM IT TO CHANGE ON ALL SPECIAL OCCASIONS.
© 1989 United Feature Syndicate, Inc.
6-15
JUST THINK OF THE MONEY YOU CAN SAVE OVER A RELATIONSHIP.
BY NEVER HAVING A SECOND DATE ?

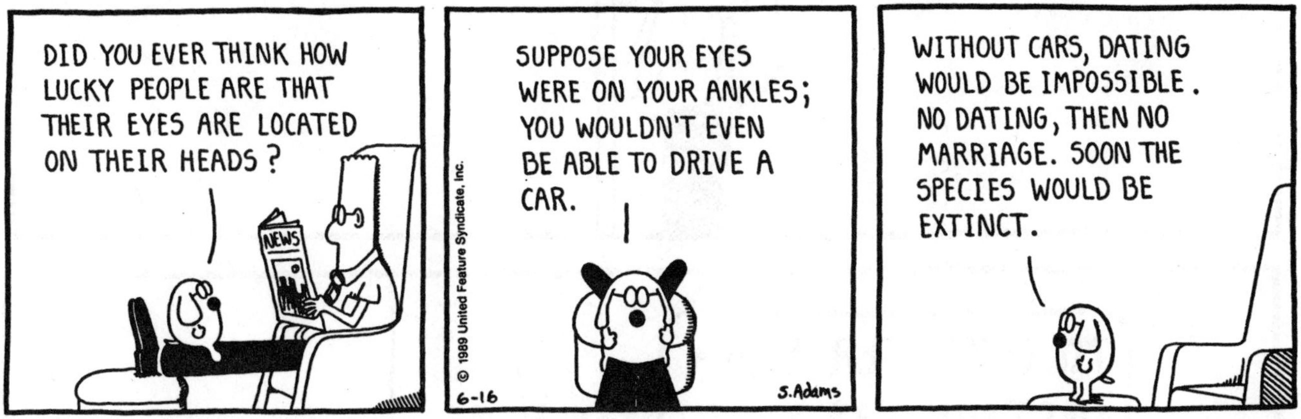
DID YOU EVER THINK HOW LUCKY PEOPLE ARE THAT THEIR EYES ARE LOCATED ON THEIR HEADS ?
NEWS
SUPPOSE YOUR EYES WERE ON YOUR ANKLES; YOU WOULDN'T EVEN BE ABLE TO DRIVE A CAR.
© 1989 United Feature Syndicate, Inc.
6-16
S.Adams
WITHOUT CARS, DATING WOULD BE IMPOSSIBLE. NO DATING, THEN NO MARRIAGE. SOON THE SPECIES WOULD BE EXTINCT.

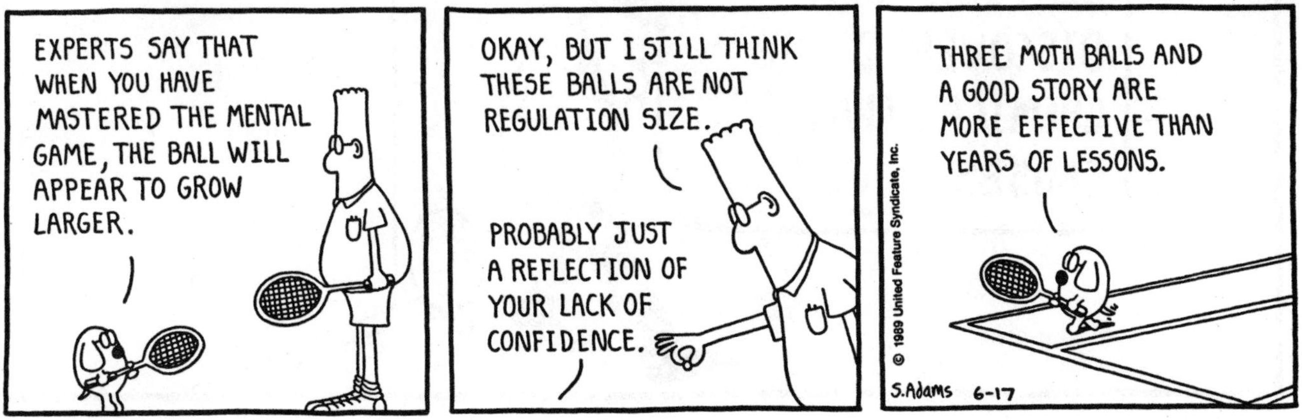
EXPERTS SAY THAT WHEN YOU HAVE MASTERED THE MENTAL GAME, THE BALL WILL APPEAR TO GROW LARGER.
OKAY, BUT I STILL THINK THESE BALLS ARE NOT REGULATION SIZE.
PROBABLY JUST A REFLECTION OF YOUR LACK OF CONFIDENCE.
THREE MOTH BALLS AND A GOOD STORY ARE MORE EFFECTIVE THAN YEARS OF LESSONS.
© 1989 United Feature Syndicate, Inc.
S.Adams 6-17

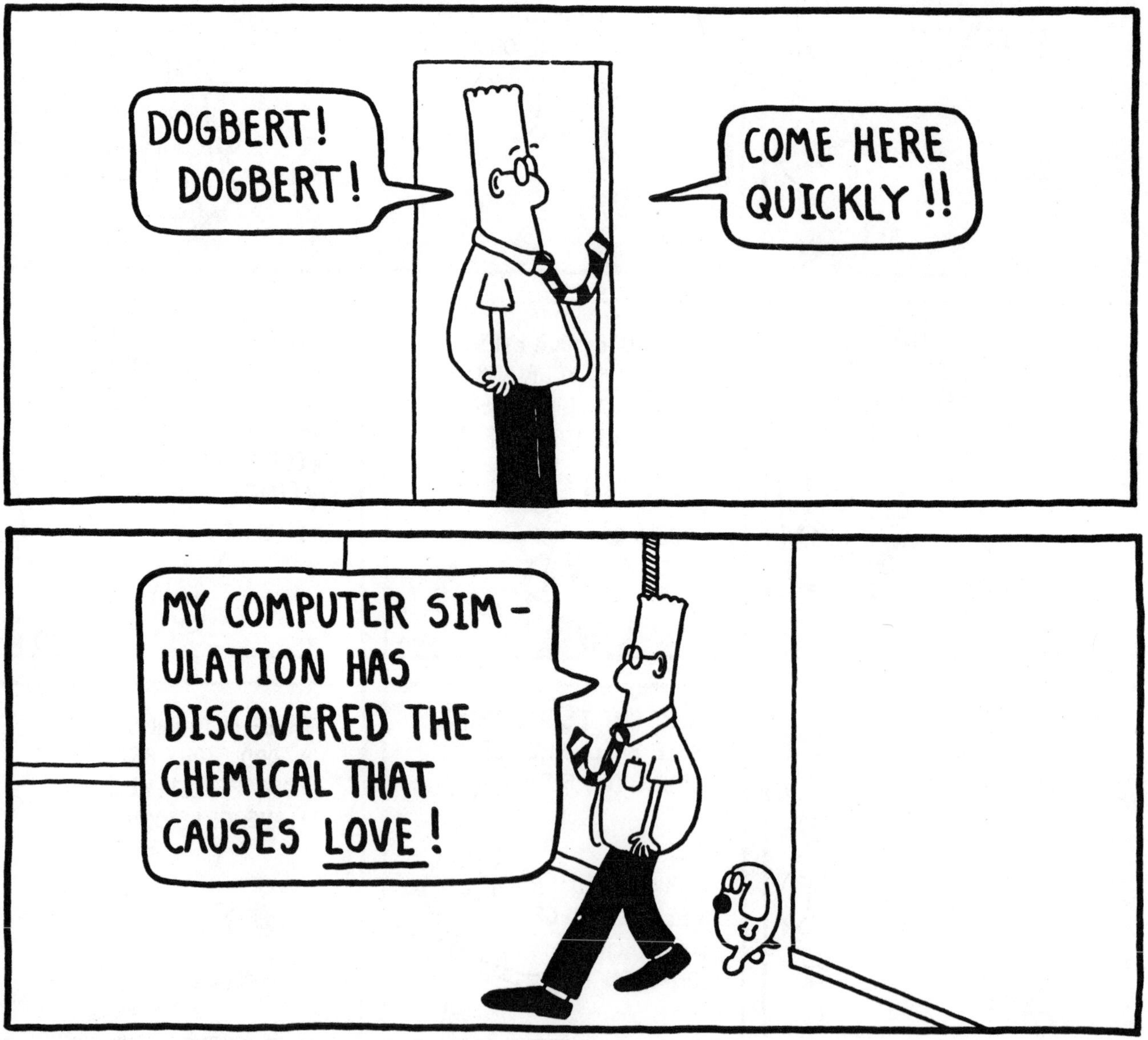
DOGBERT! DOGBERT!
COME HERE QUICKLY !!
MY COMPUTER SIM-ULATION HAS DISCOVERED THE CHEMICAL THAT CAUSES LOVE !

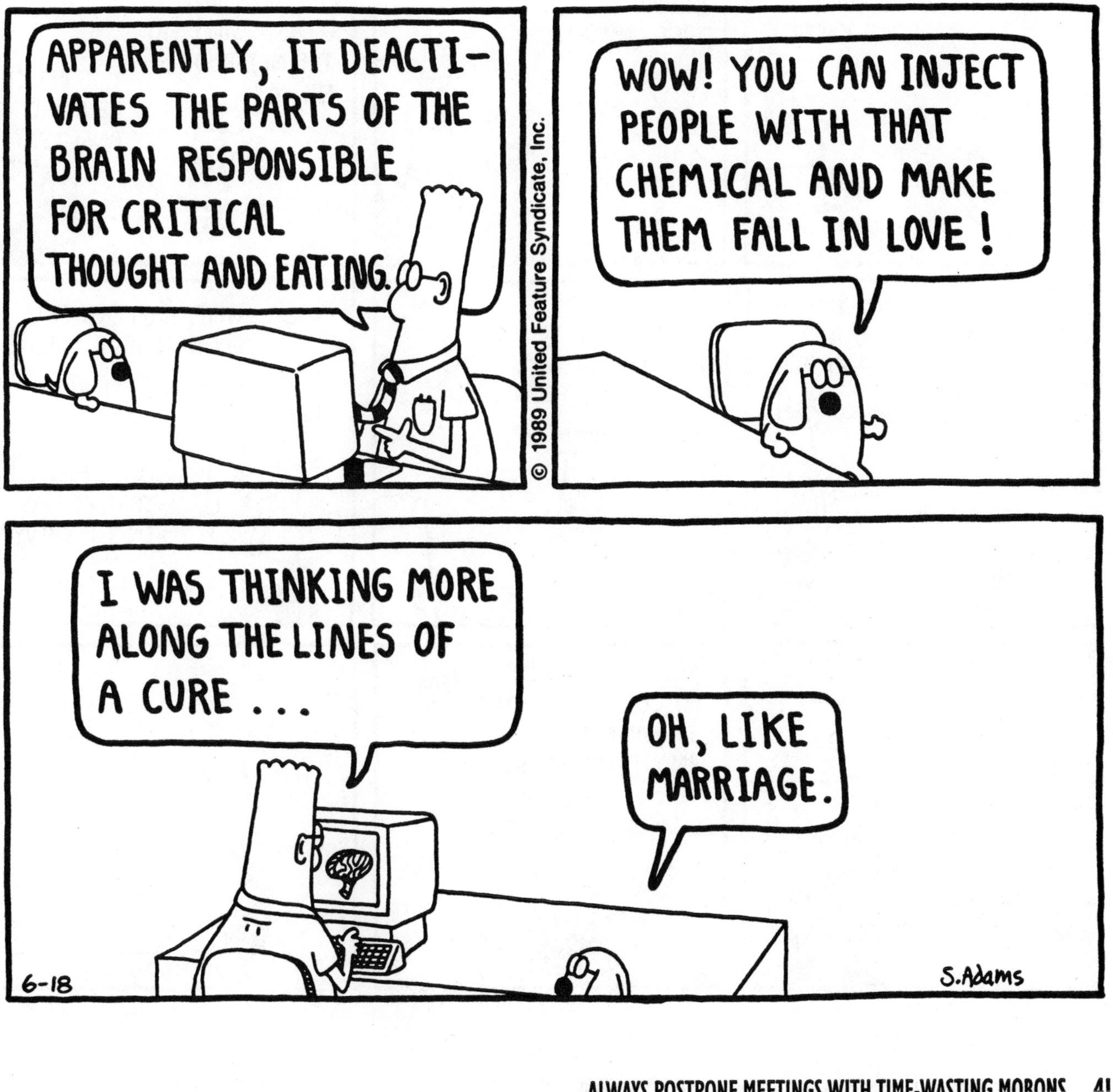
APPARENTLY, IT DEACTIVATES THE PARTS OF THE BRAIN RESPONSIBLE FOR CRITICAL THOUGHT AND EATING.
© 1989 United Feature Syndicate, Inc.
WOW! YOU CAN INJECT PEOPLE WITH THAT CHEMICAL AND MAKE THEM FALL IN LOVE!
I WAS THINKING MORE ALONG THE LINES OF A CURE ...
OH, LIKE MARRIAGE.
6-18
S. Adams

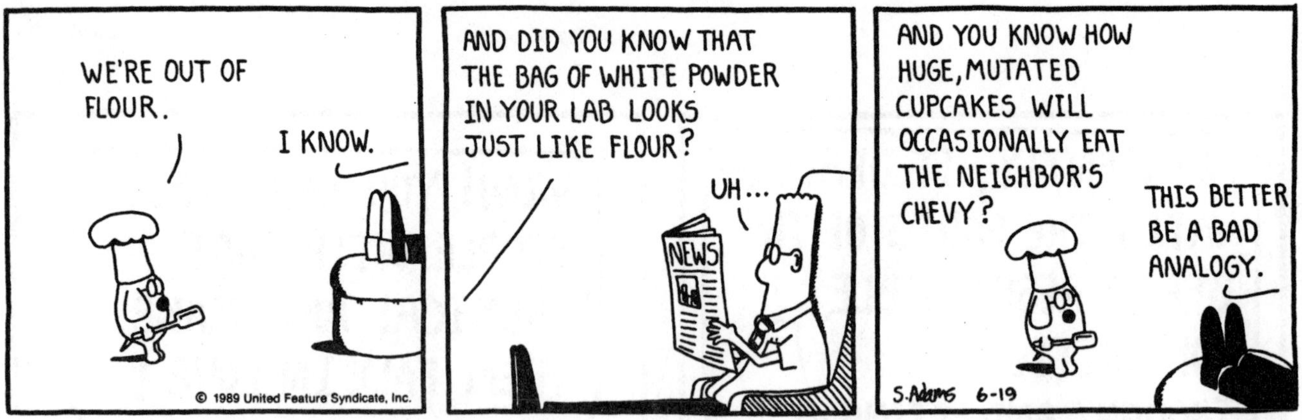
WE'RE OUT OF FLOUR.
I KNOW.
© 1989 United Feature Syndicate, Inc.
AND DID YOU KNOW THAT THE BAG OF WHITE POWDER IN YOUR LAB LOOKS JUST LIKE FLOUR?
UH...
NEWS
AND YOU KNOW HOW HUGE, MUTATED CUPCAKES WILL OCCASIONALLY EAT THE NEIGHBOR'S CHEVY?
THIS BETTER BE A BAD ANALOGY.
S. Adams 6-19

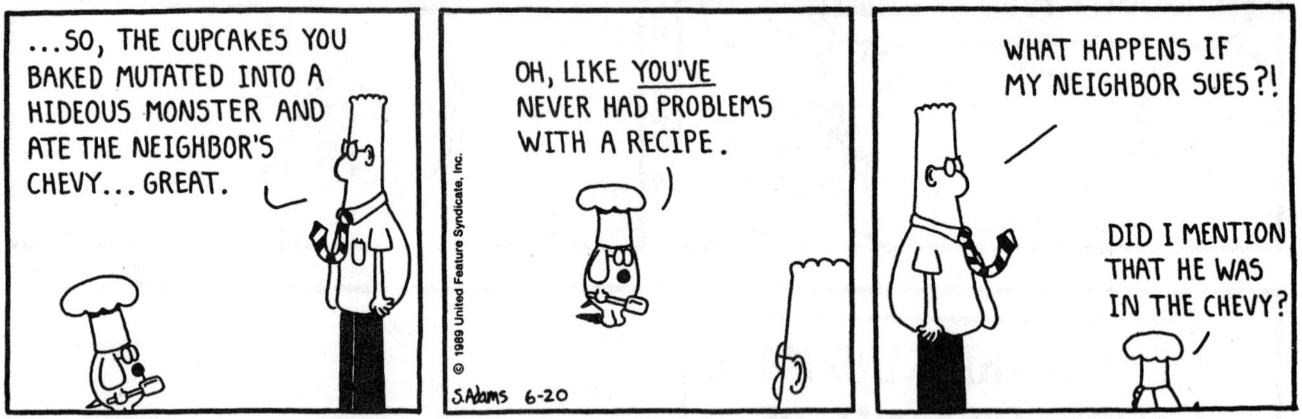
...SO, THE CUPCAKES YOU BAKED MUTATED INTO A HIDEOUS MONSTER AND ATE THE NEIGHBOR'S CHEVY... GREAT.
OH, LIKE YOU'VE NEVER HAD PROBLEMS WITH A RECIPE.
© 1989 United Feature Syndicate, Inc.
S. Adams 6-20
WHAT HAPPENS IF MY NEIGHBOR SUES?!
DID I MENTION THAT HE WAS IN THE CHEVY?

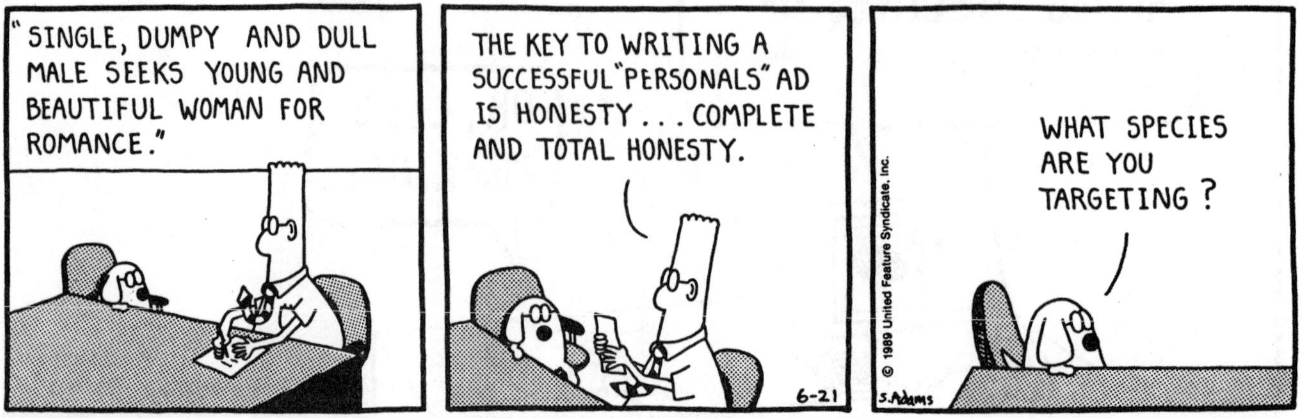
"SINGLE, DUMPY AND DULL MALE SEEKS YOUNG AND BEAUTIFUL WOMAN FOR ROMANCE."
THE KEY TO WRITING A SUCCESSFUL "PERSONALS" AD IS HONESTY . . . COMPLETE AND TOTAL HONESTY.
6-21
© 1989 United Feature Syndicate, Inc.
WHAT SPECIES ARE YOU TARGETING?
S. Adams

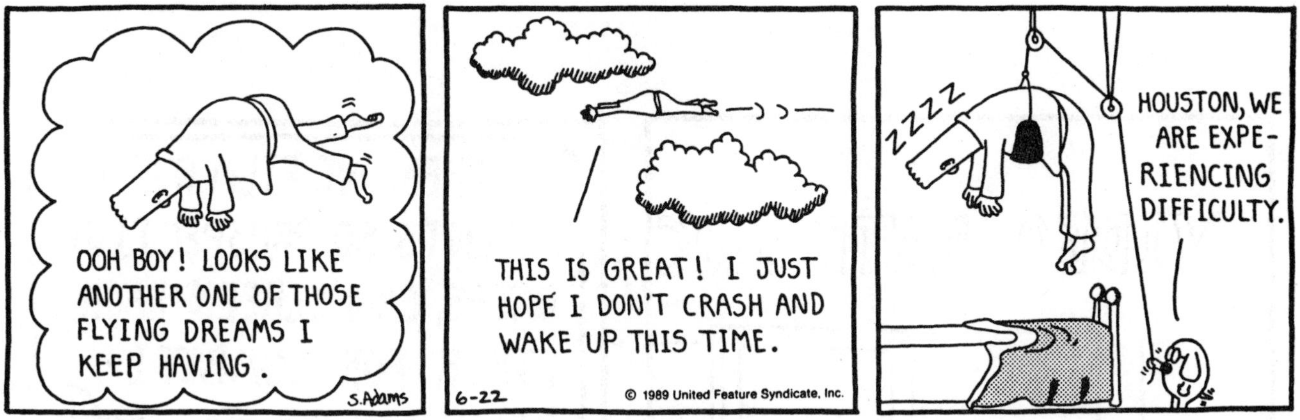
OOH BOY! LOOKS LIKE ANOTHER ONE OF THOSE FLYING DREAMS I KEEP HAVING.
S.Adams
THIS IS GREAT! I JUST HOPE I DON'T CRASH AND WAKE UP THIS TIME.
6-22
© 1989 United Feature Syndicate, Inc.
ZZZZ
HOUSTON, WE ARE EXPE-RIENCING DIFFICULTY.

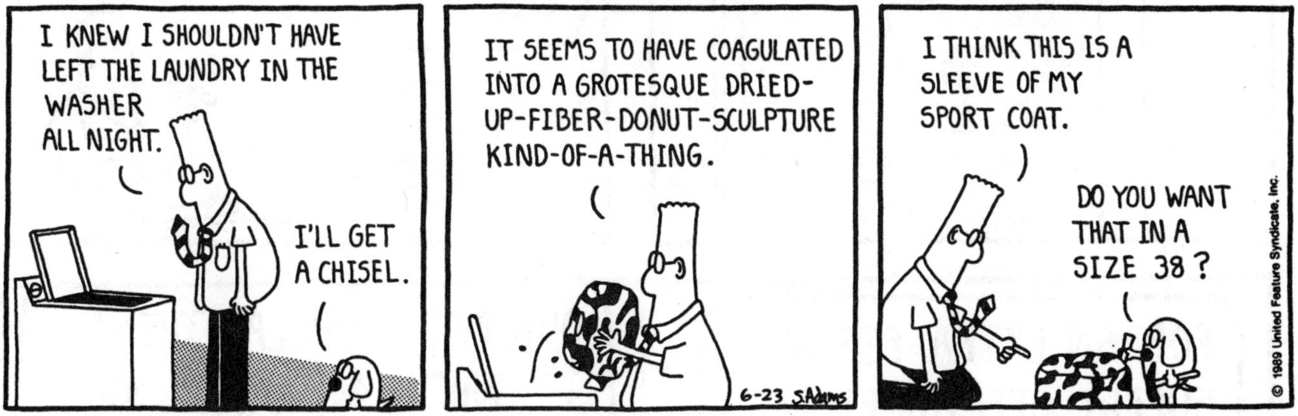
I KNEW I SHOULDN'T HAVE LEFT THE LAUNDRY IN THE WASHER ALL NIGHT.
I'LL GET A CHISEL.
IT SEEMS TO HAVE COAGULATED INTO A GROTESQUE DRIED-UP-FIBER-DONUT-SCULPTURE KIND-OF-A-THING.
6-23 S.Adams
I THINK THIS IS A SLEEVE OF MY SPORT COAT.
DO YOU WANT THAT IN A SIZE 38?
© 1989 United Feature Syndicate, Inc.

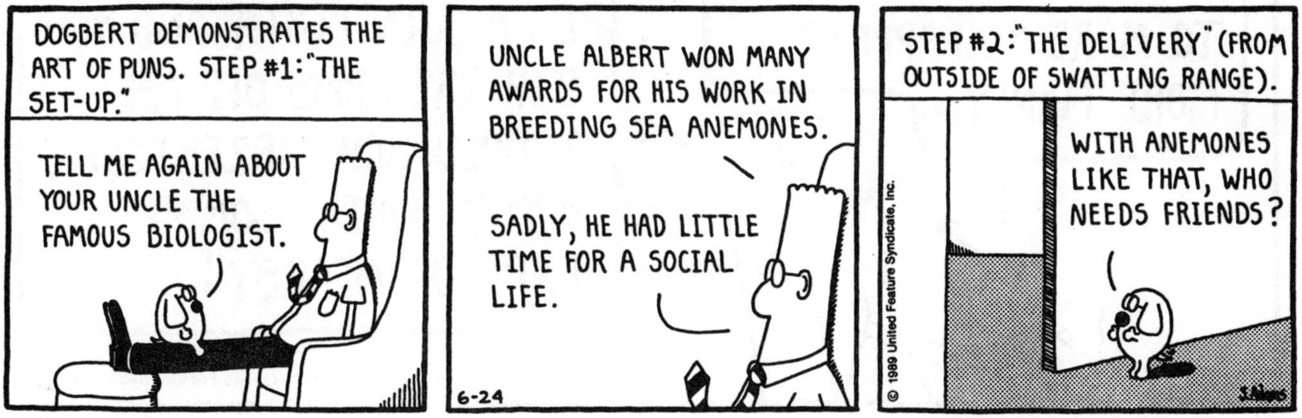
DOGBERT DEMONSTRATES THE ART OF PUNS. STEP #1: "THE SET-UP."
TELL ME AGAIN ABOUT YOUR UNCLE THE FAMOUS BIOLOGIST.
UNCLE ALBERT WON MANY AWARDS FOR HIS WORK IN BREEDING SEA ANEMONES.
SADLY, HE HAD LITTLE TIME FOR A SOCIAL LIFE.
6-24
© 1989 United Feature Syndicate, Inc.
STEP #2: "THE DELIVERY" (FROM OUTSIDE OF SWATTING RANGE).
WITH ANEMONES LIKE THAT, WHO NEEDS FRIENDS?
S.Adams

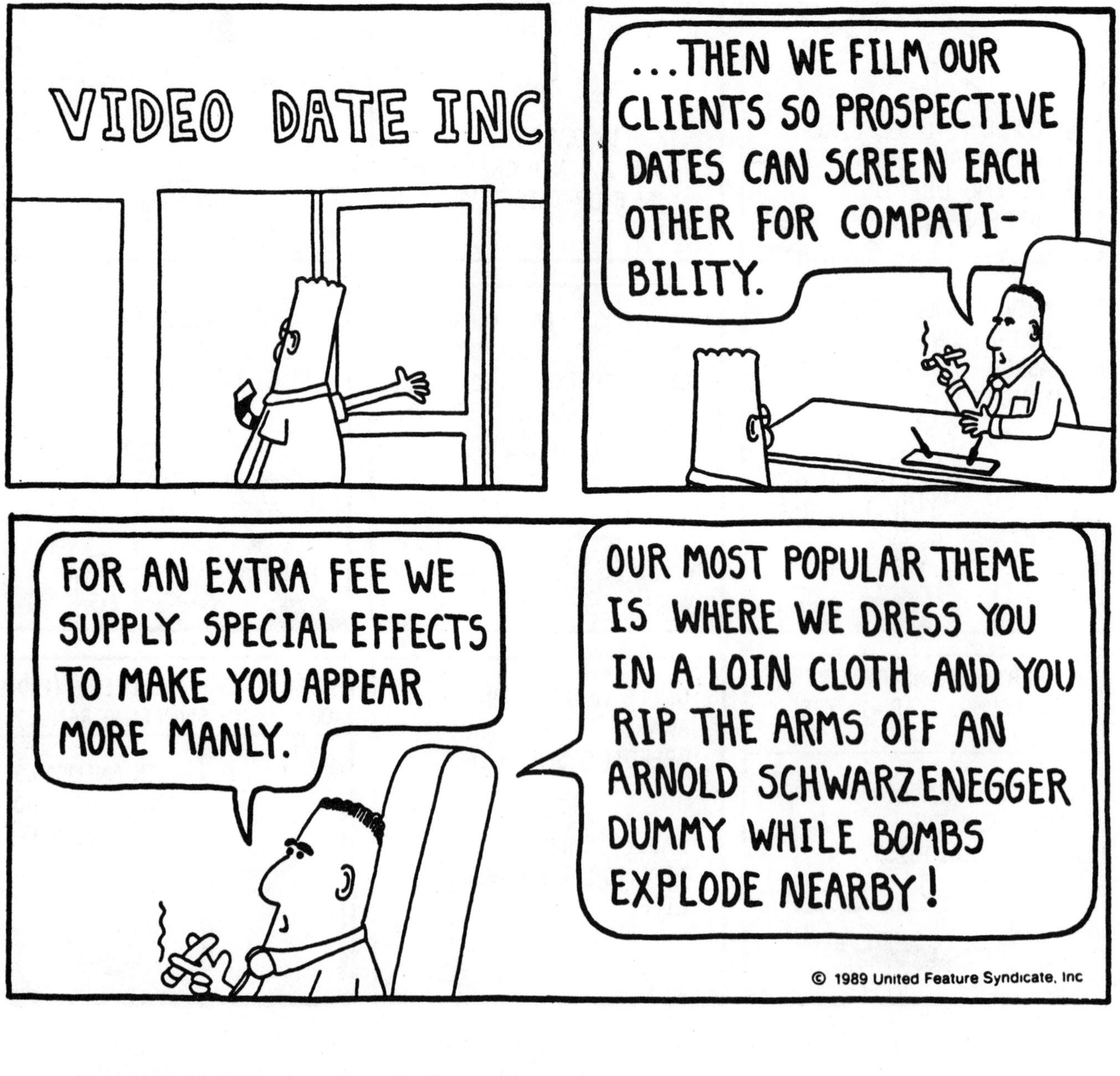
VIDEO DATE INC
...THEN WE FILM OUR CLIENTS SO PROSPECTIVE DATES CAN SCREEN EACH OTHER FOR COMPATI-BILITY.
FOR AN EXTRA FEE WE SUPPLY SPECIAL EFFECTS TO MAKE YOU APPEAR MORE MANLY.
OUR MOST POPULAR THEME IS WHERE WE DRESS YOU IN A LOIN CLOTH AND YOU RIP THE ARMS OFF AN ARNOLD SCHWARZENEGGER DUMMY WHILE BOMBS EXPLODE NEARBY!
© 1989 United Feature Syndicate, Inc

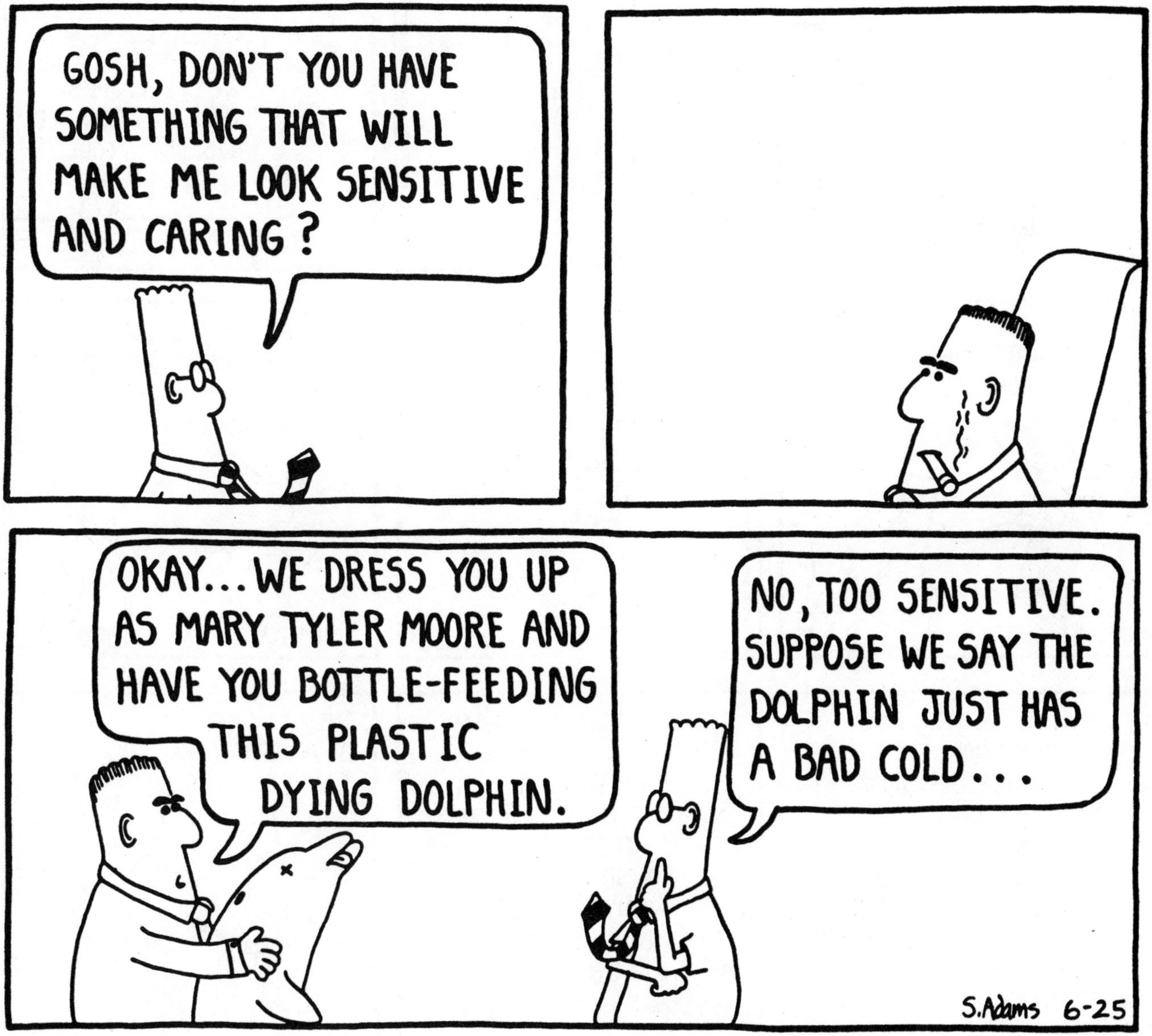
GOSH, DON'T YOU HAVE SOMETHING THAT WILL MAKE ME LOOK SENSITIVE AND CARING?
OKAY... WE DRESS YOU UP AS MARY TYLER MOORE AND HAVE YOU BOTTLE-FEEDING THIS PLASTIC DYING DOLPHIN.
NO, TOO SENSITIVE. SUPPOSE WE SAY THE DOLPHIN JUST HAS A BAD COLD...
S.Adams 6-25

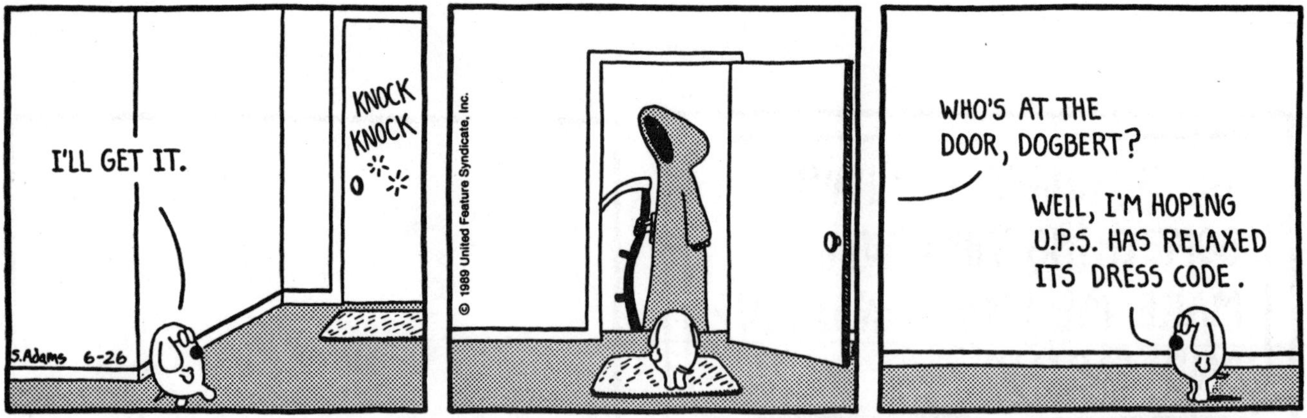
I'LL GET IT.
KNOCK KNOCK
S.Adams 6-26
© 1989 United Feature Syndicate, Inc.
WHO'S AT THE DOOR, DOGBERT?
WELL, I'M HOPING U.P.S. HAS RELAXED ITS DRESS CODE.

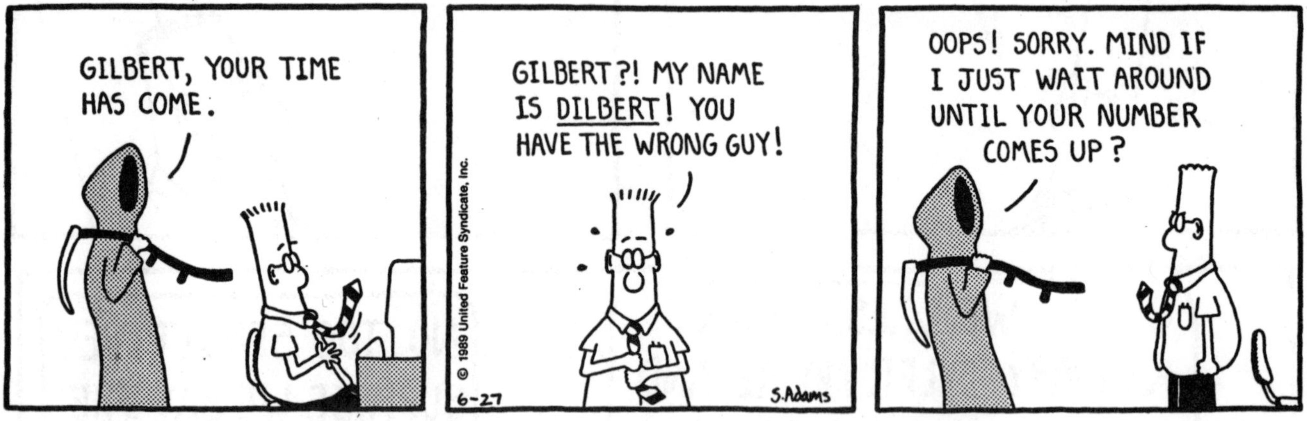
GILBERT, YOUR TIME HAS COME.
GILBERT?! MY NAME IS DILBERT! YOU HAVE THE WRONG GUY!
© 1989 United Feature Syndicate, Inc.
6-27
S.Adams
OOPS! SORRY. MIND IF I JUST WAIT AROUND UNTIL YOUR NUMBER COMES UP?

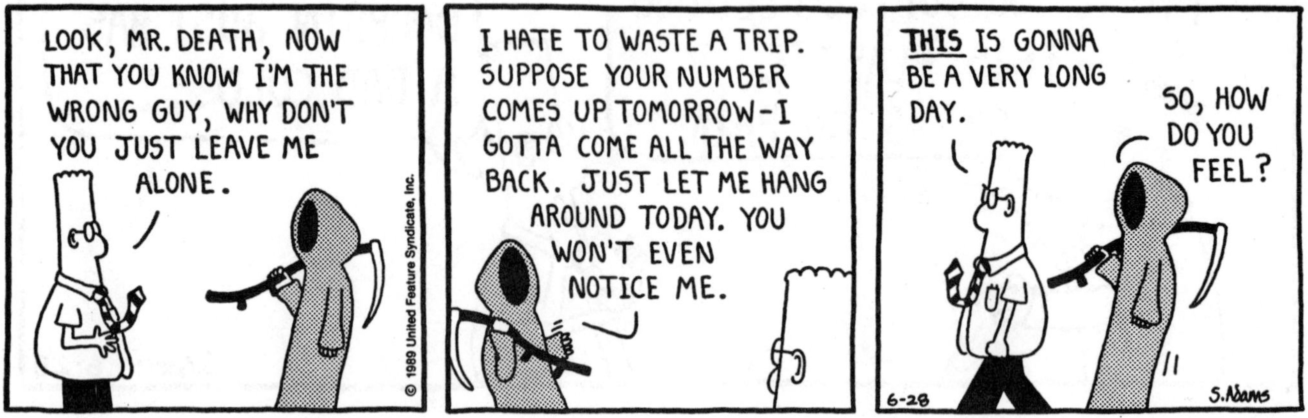
LOOK, MR. DEATH, NOW THAT YOU KNOW I'M THE WRONG GUY, WHY DON'T YOU JUST LEAVE ME ALONE.
© 1989 United Feature Syndicate, Inc.
I HATE TO WASTE A TRIP. SUPPOSE YOUR NUMBER COMES UP TOMORROW - I GOTTA COME ALL THE WAY BACK. JUST LET ME HANG AROUND TODAY. YOU WON'T EVEN NOTICE ME.
THIS IS GONNA BE A VERY LONG DAY.
SO, HOW DO YOU FEEL?
6-28
S.Adams

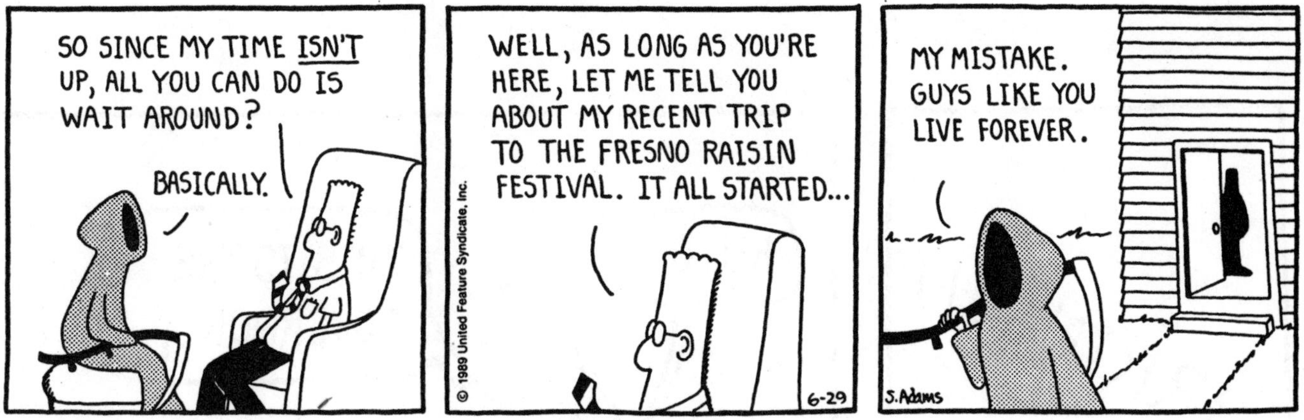
SO SINCE MY TIME ISN'T UP, ALL YOU CAN DO IS WAIT AROUND?
BASICALLY.
WELL, AS LONG AS YOU'RE HERE, LET ME TELL YOU ABOUT MY RECENT TRIP TO THE FRESNO RAISIN FESTIVAL. IT ALL STARTED...
© 1989 United Feature Syndicate, Inc.
6-29
MY MISTAKE. GUYS LIKE YOU LIVE FOREVER.
S. Adams

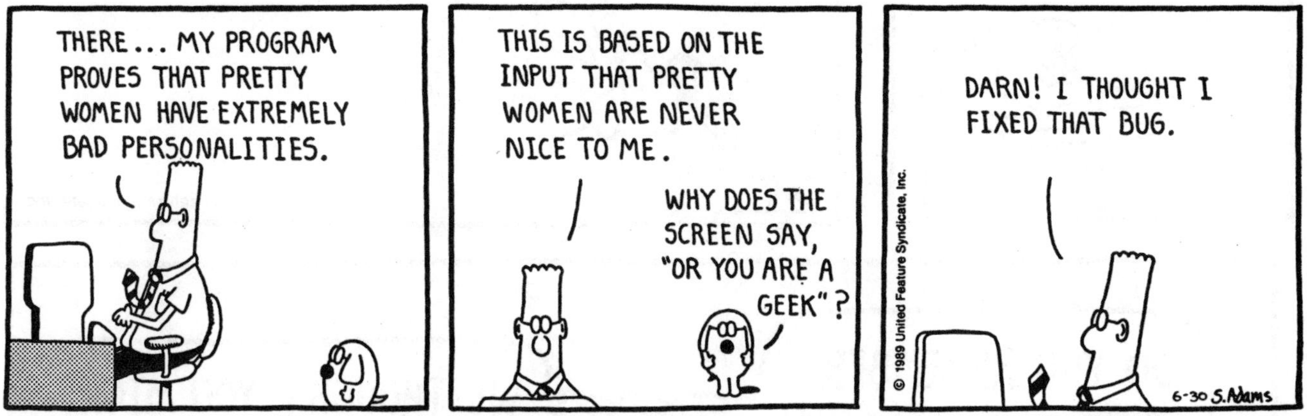
THERE... MY PROGRAM PROVES THAT PRETTY WOMEN HAVE EXTREMELY BAD PERSONALITIES.
THIS IS BASED ON THE INPUT THAT PRETTY WOMEN ARE NEVER NICE TO ME.
WHY DOES THE SCREEN SAY, "OR YOU ARE A GEEK"?
DARN! I THOUGHT I FIXED THAT BUG.
© 1989 United Feature Syndicate, Inc.
6-30 S. Adams

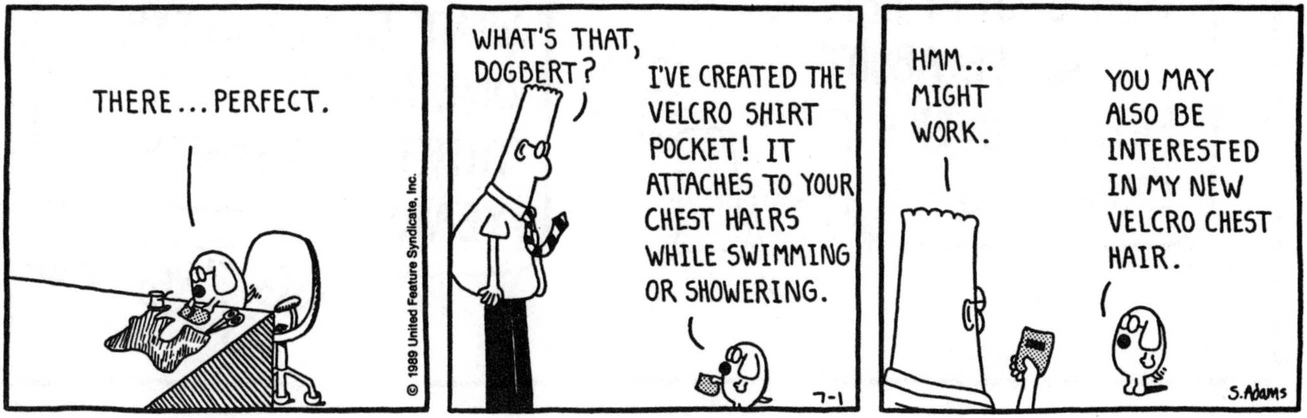
THERE... PERFECT.
© 1989 United Feature Syndicate, Inc.
WHAT'S THAT, DOGBERT?
I'VE CREATED THE VELCRO SHIRT POCKET! IT ATTACHES TO YOUR CHEST HAIRS WHILE SWIMMING OR SHOWERING.
7-1
HMM... MIGHT WORK.
YOU MAY ALSO BE INTERESTED IN MY NEW VELCRO CHEST HAIR.
S. Adams

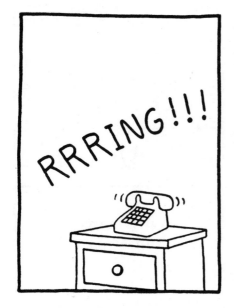

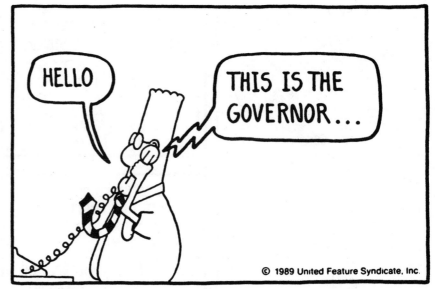

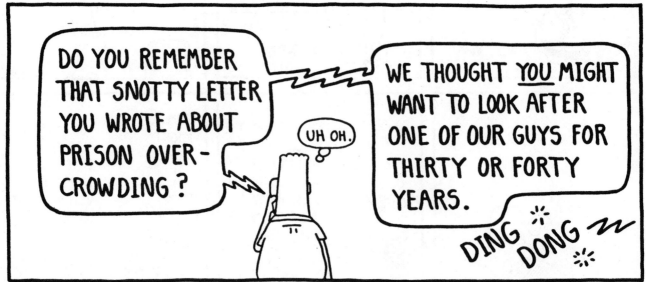

RRRING!!!
HELLO
THIS IS THE GOVERNOR...
© 1989 United Feature Syndicate, Inc.
DO YOU REMEMBER THAT SNOTTY LETTER YOU WROTE ABOUT PRISON OVER-CROWDING?
UH OH.
WE THOUGHT YOU MIGHT WANT TO LOOK AFTER ONE OF OUR GUYS FOR THIRTY OR FORTY YEARS.
DING DONG

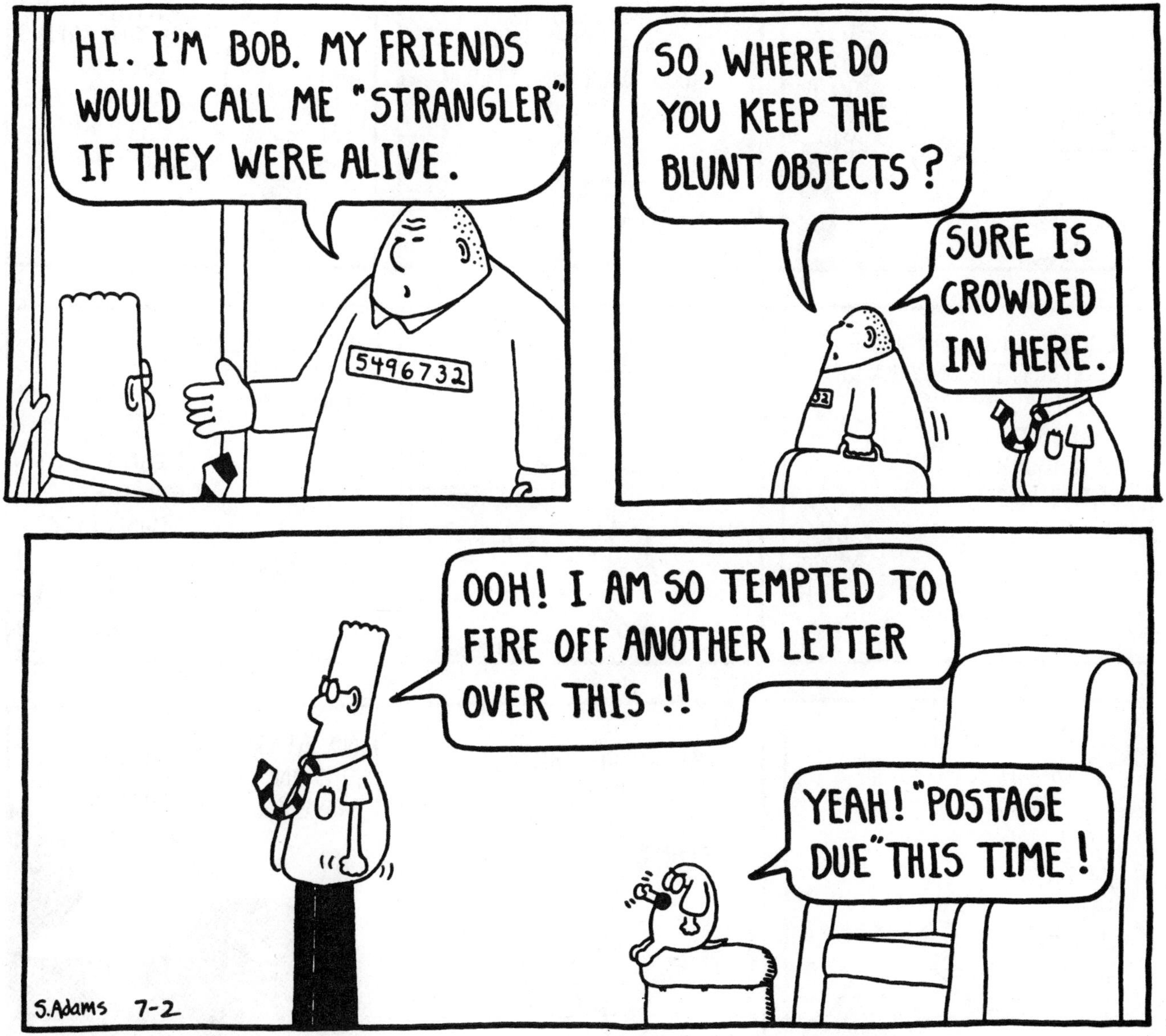
HI. I'M BOB. MY FRIENDS WOULD CALL ME "STRANGLER" IF THEY WERE ALIVE.
5496732
SO, WHERE DO YOU KEEP THE BLUNT OBJECTS?
SURE IS CROWDED IN HERE.
OOH! I AM SO TEMPTED TO FIRE OFF ANOTHER LETTER OVER THIS!!
YEAH! "POSTAGE DUE" THIS TIME!
S.Adams 7-2

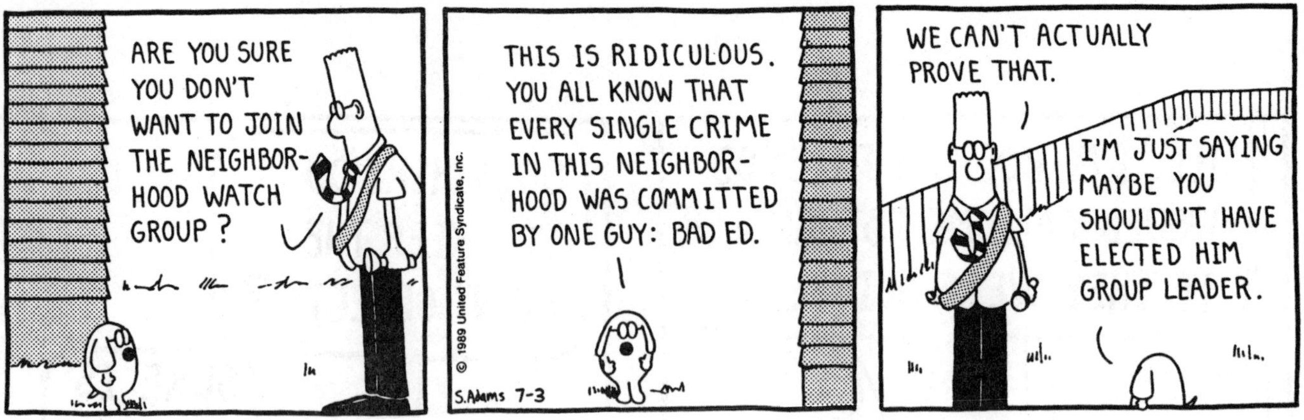
ARE YOU SURE YOU DON'T WANT TO JOIN THE NEIGHBORHOOD WATCH GROUP?
THIS IS RIDICULOUS. YOU ALL KNOW THAT EVERY SINGLE CRIME IN THIS NEIGHBORHOOD WAS COMMITTED BY ONE GUY: BAD ED.
© 1989 United Feature Syndicate, Inc.
S.Adams 7-3
WE CAN'T ACTUALLY PROVE THAT.
I'M JUST SAYING MAYBE YOU SHOULDN'T HAVE ELECTED HIM GROUP LEADER.

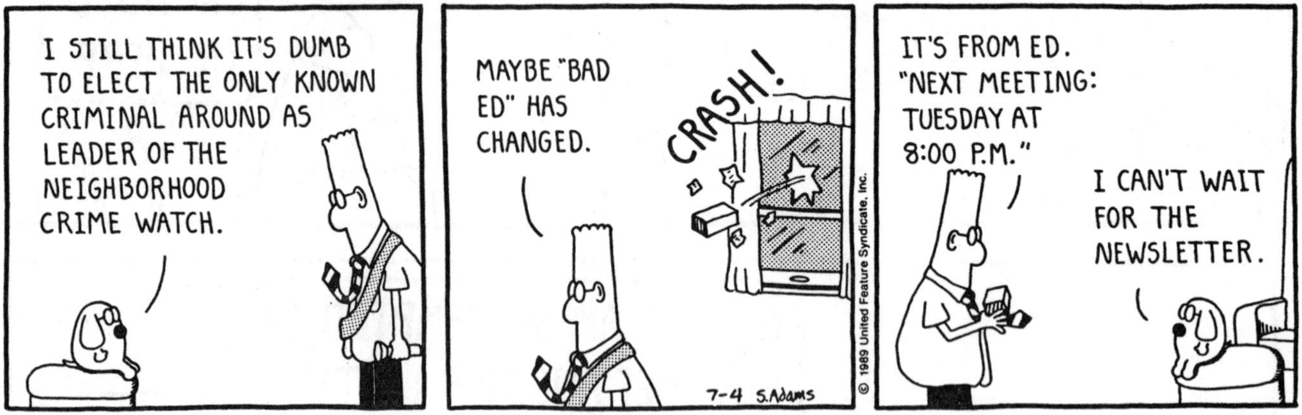
I STILL THINK IT'S DUMB TO ELECT THE ONLY KNOWN CRIMINAL AROUND AS LEADER OF THE NEIGHBORHOOD CRIME WATCH.
MAYBE "BAD ED" HAS CHANGED.
CRASH!
7-4 S.Adams
© 1989 United Feature Syndicate, Inc.
IT'S FROM ED. "NEXT MEETING: TUESDAY AT 8:00 P.M."
I CAN'T WAIT FOR THE NEWSLETTER.

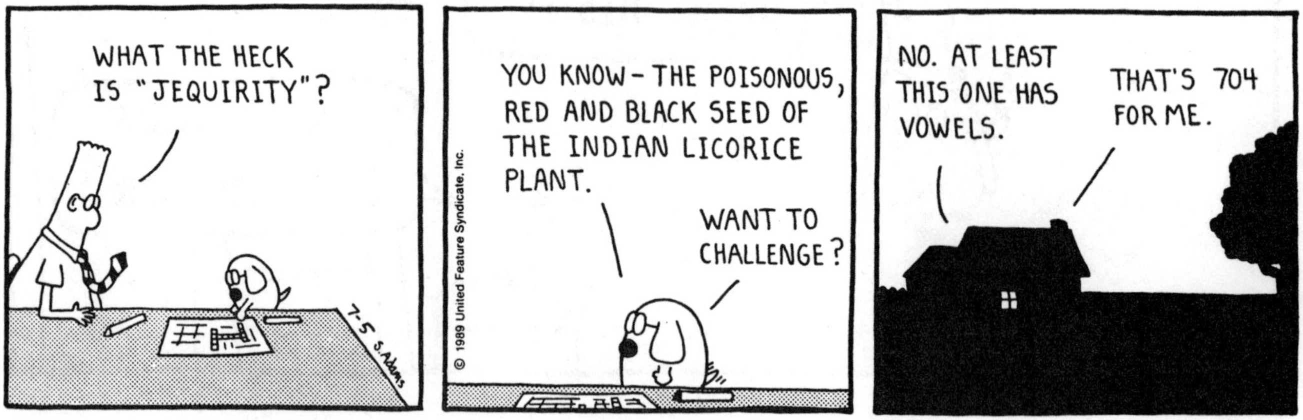
WHAT THE HECK IS "JEQUIRITY"?
7-5 S.Adams
© 1989 United Feature Syndicate, Inc.
YOU KNOW - THE POISONOUS, RED AND BLACK SEED OF THE INDIAN LICORICE PLANT.
WANT TO CHALLENGE?
NO. AT LEAST THIS ONE HAS VOWELS.
THAT'S 704 FOR ME.

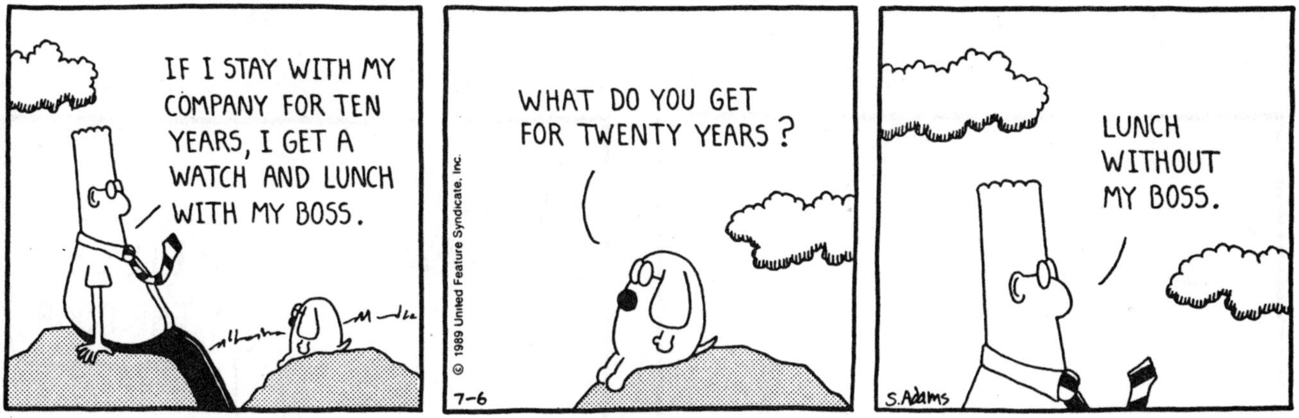
IF I STAY WITH MY COMPANY FOR TEN YEARS, I GET A WATCH AND LUNCH WITH MY BOSS.
WHAT DO YOU GET FOR TWENTY YEARS?
© 1989 United Feature Syndicate, Inc.
7-6
LUNCH WITHOUT MY BOSS.
S. Adams

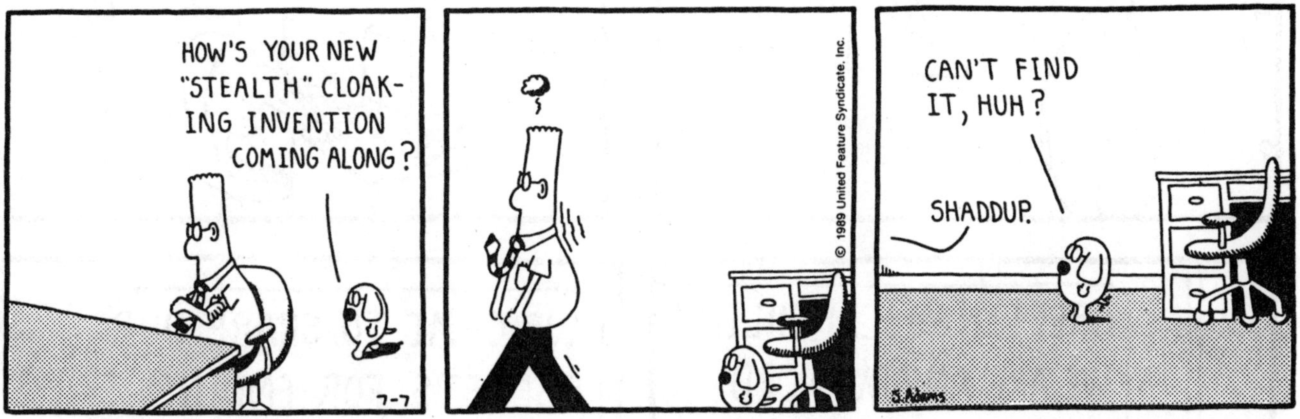
HOW'S YOUR NEW "STEALTH" CLOAKING INVENTION COMING ALONG?
7-7
© 1989 United Feature Syndicate, Inc.
CAN'T FIND IT, HUH?
SHADDUP.
S. Adams

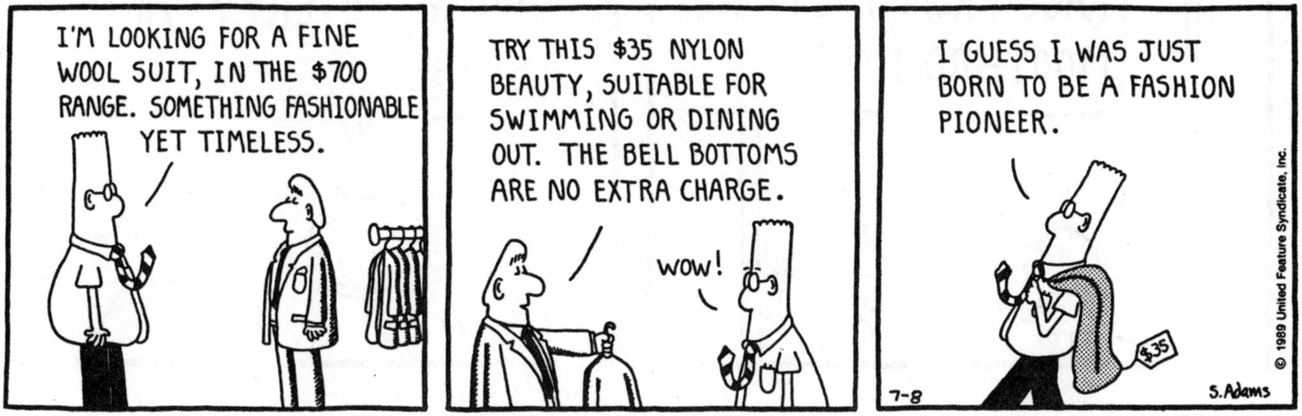
I'M LOOKING FOR A FINE WOOL SUIT, IN THE $700 RANGE. SOMETHING FASHIONABLE YET TIMELESS.
TRY THIS $35 NYLON BEAUTY, SUITABLE FOR SWIMMING OR DINING OUT. THE BELL BOTTOMS ARE NO EXTRA CHARGE.
WOW!
I GUESS I WAS JUST BORN TO BE A FASHION PIONEER.
$35
© 1989 United Feature Syndicate, Inc.
7-8
S. Adams

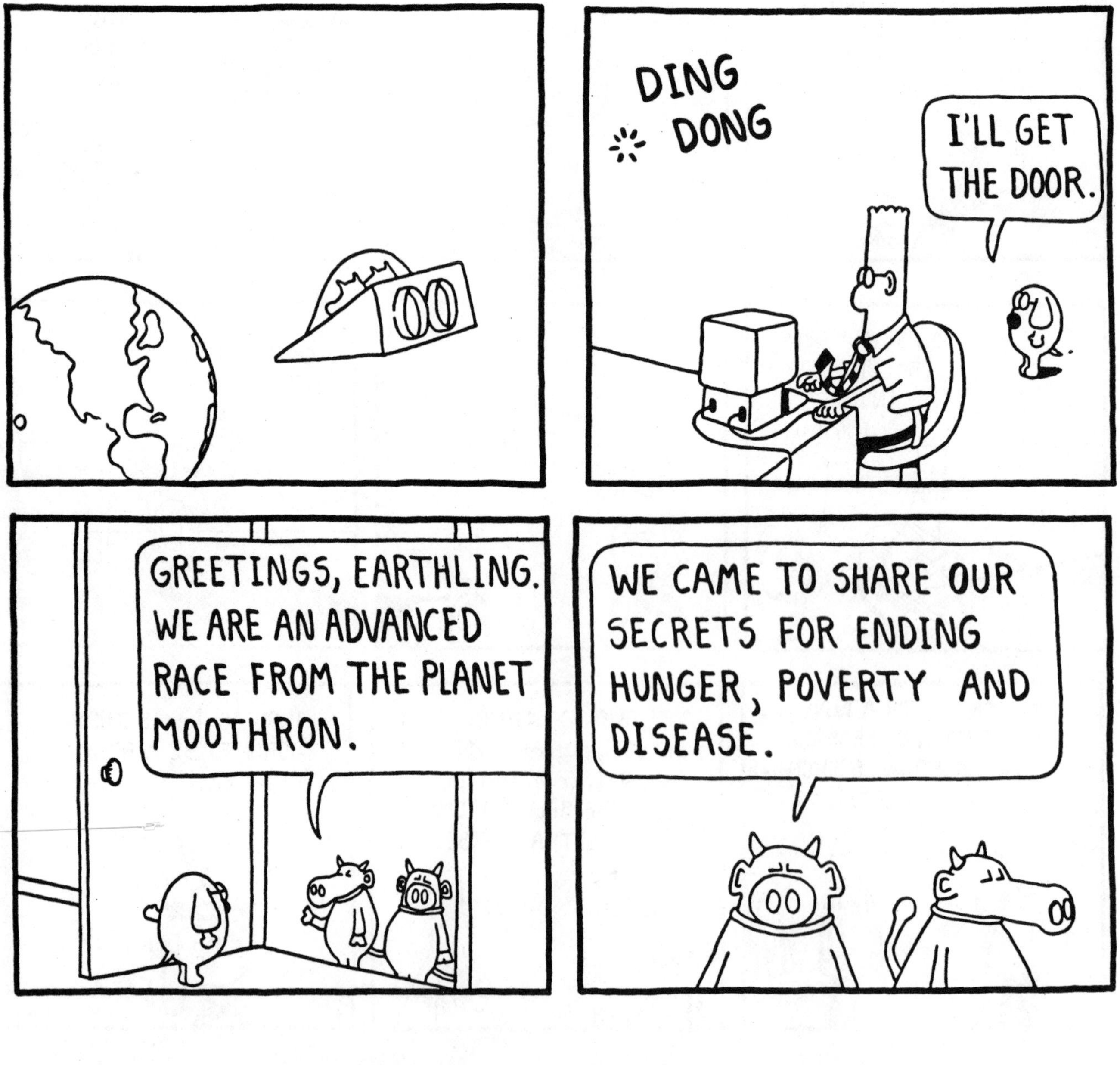
DING
DONG
I'LL GET THE DOOR.
GREETINGS, EARTHLING. WE ARE AN ADVANCED RACE FROM THE PLANET MOOTHRON.
WE CAME TO SHARE OUR SECRETS FOR ENDING HUNGER, POVERTY AND DISEASE.

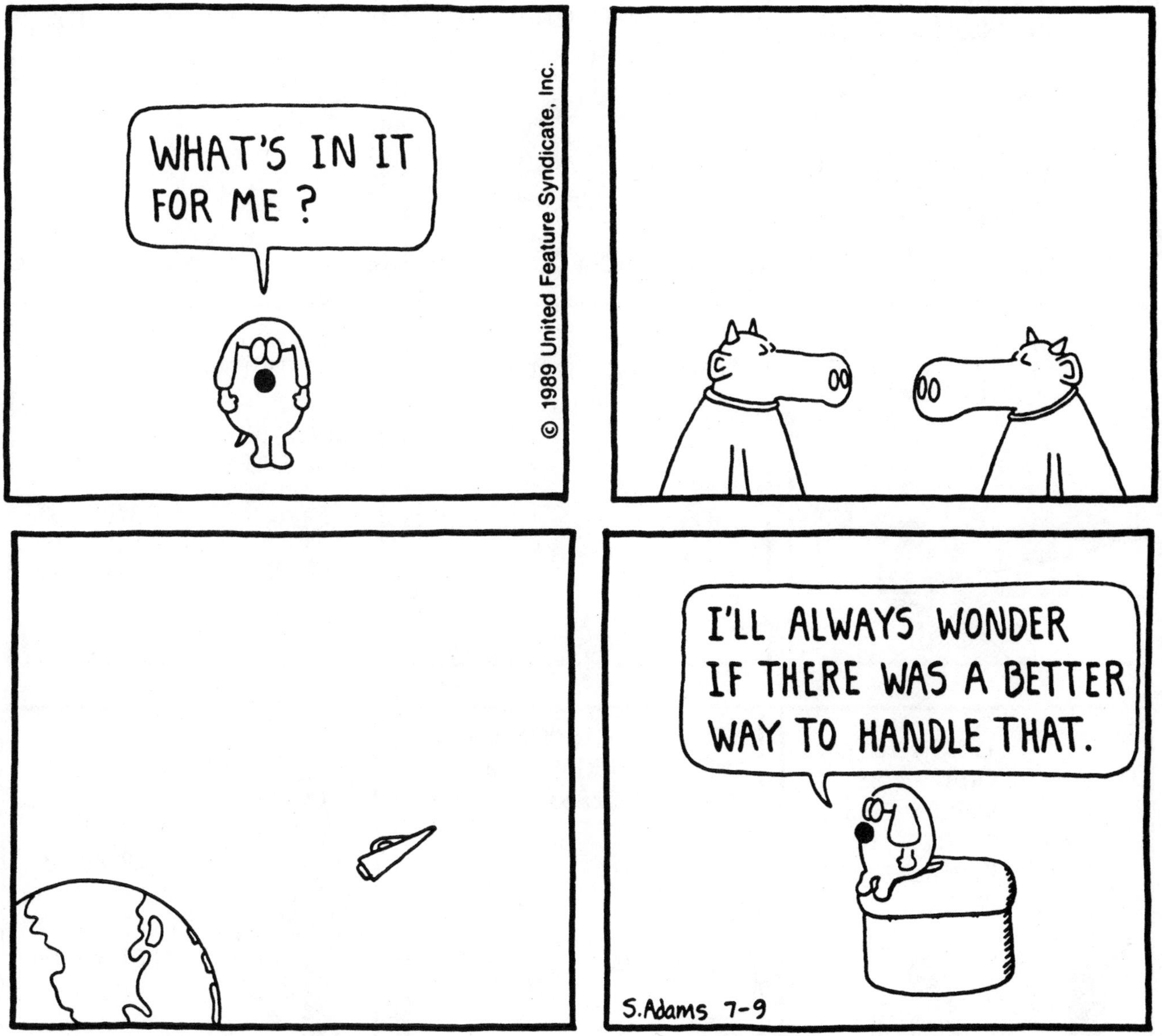
WHAT'S IN IT FOR ME ?
© 1989 United Feature Syndicate, Inc.
I'LL ALWAYS WONDER IF THERE WAS A BETTER WAY TO HANDLE THAT.
S.Adams 7-9

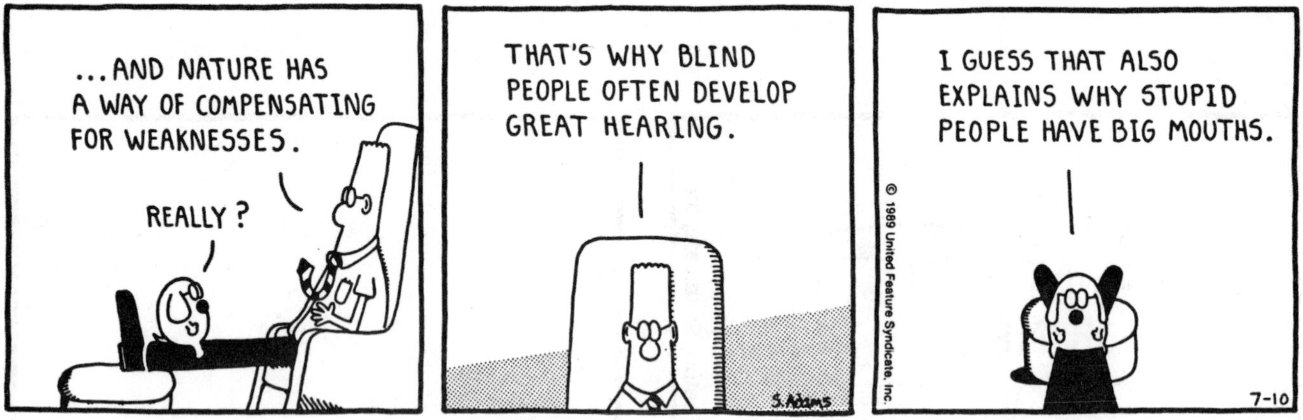

...AND NATURE HAS A WAY OF COMPENSATING FOR WEAKNESSES.
REALLY?
THAT'S WHY BLIND PEOPLE OFTEN DEVELOP GREAT HEARING.
S. Adams
I GUESS THAT ALSO EXPLAINS WHY STUPID PEOPLE HAVE BIG MOUTHS.
© 1989 United Feature Syndicate, Inc.
7-10

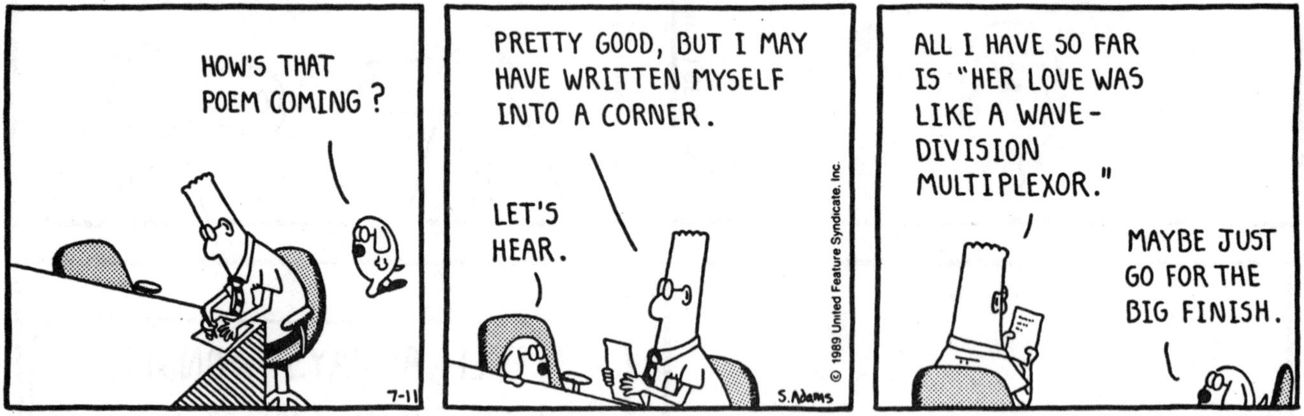

HOW'S THAT POEM COMING?
7-11
PRETTY GOOD, BUT I MAY HAVE WRITTEN MYSELF INTO A CORNER.
LET'S HEAR.
S. Adams
© 1989 United Feature Syndicate, Inc.
ALL I HAVE SO FAR IS "HER LOVE WAS LIKE A WAVE-DIVISION MULTIPLEXOR."
MAYBE JUST GO FOR THE BIG FINISH.

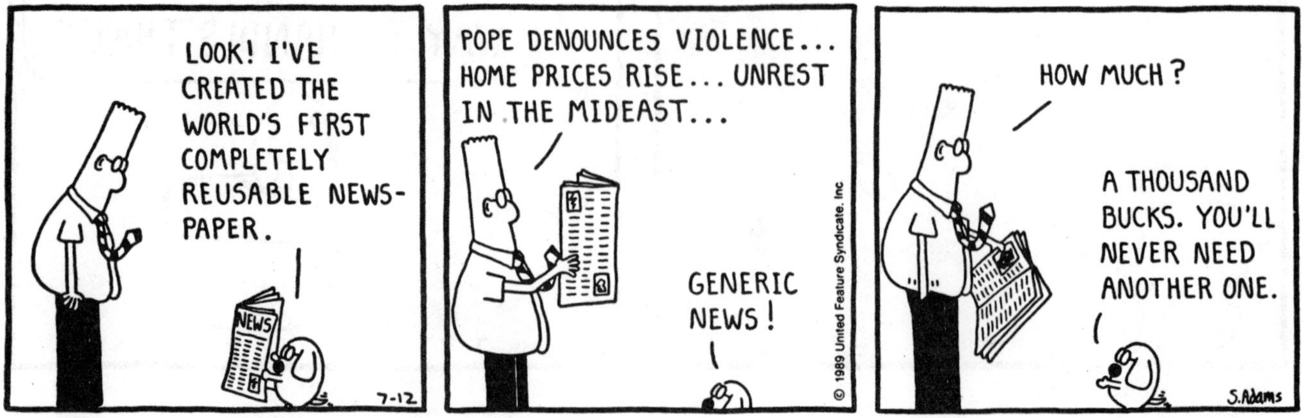

LOOK! I'VE CREATED THE WORLD'S FIRST COMPLETELY REUSABLE NEWS-PAPER.
NEWS
7-12
POPE DENOUNCES VIOLENCE... HOME PRICES RISE... UNREST IN THE MIDEAST...
GENERIC NEWS!
© 1989 United Feature Syndicate, Inc.
HOW MUCH?
A THOUSAND BUCKS. YOU'LL NEVER NEED ANOTHER ONE.
S. Adams

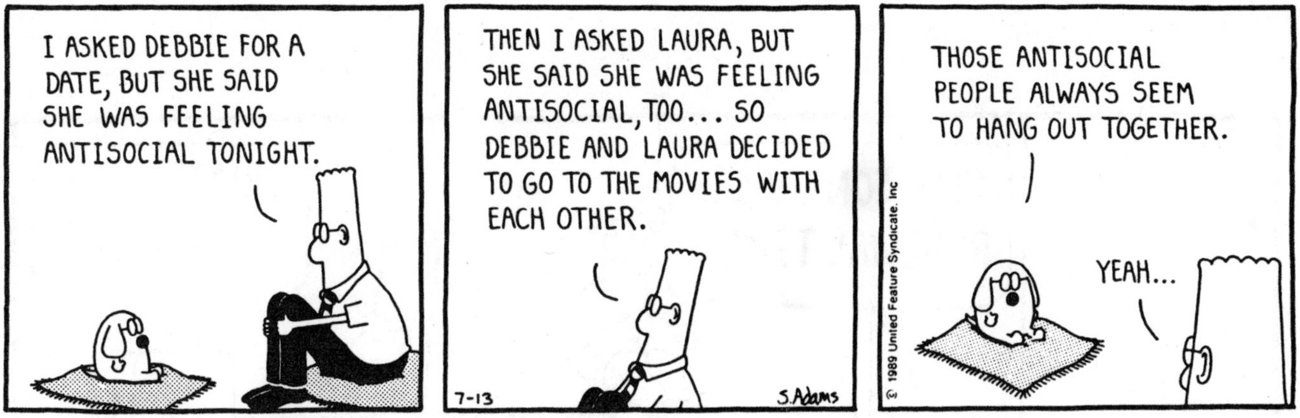
I ASKED DEBBIE FOR A DATE, BUT SHE SAID SHE WAS FEELING ANTISOCIAL TONIGHT.
THEN I ASKED LAURA, BUT SHE SAID SHE WAS FEELING ANTISOCIAL, TOO... SO DEBBIE AND LAURA DECIDED TO GO TO THE MOVIES WITH EACH OTHER.
7-13
S.Adams
THOSE ANTISOCIAL PEOPLE ALWAYS SEEM TO HANG OUT TOGETHER.
YEAH...
© 1989 United Feature Syndicate, Inc

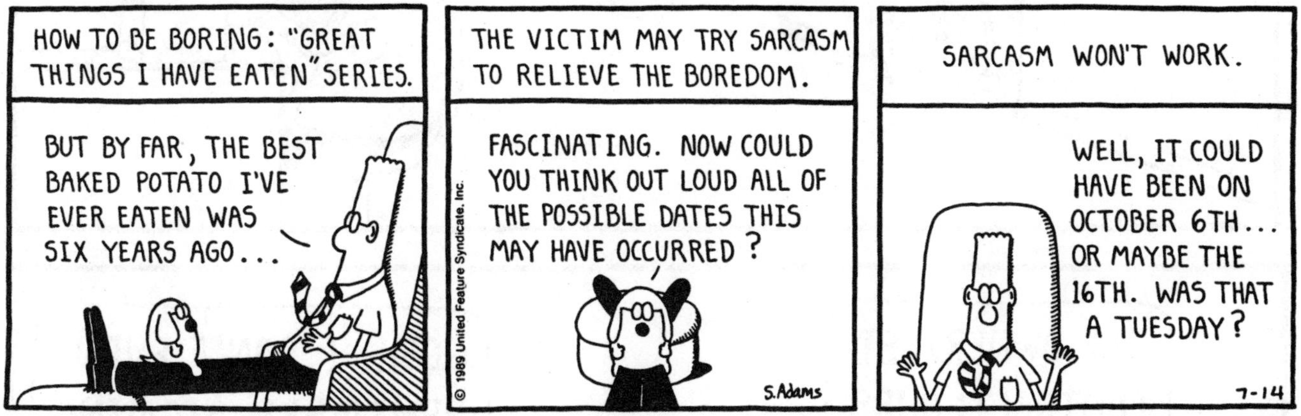
HOW TO BE BORING: "GREAT THINGS I HAVE EATEN" SERIES.
BUT BY FAR, THE BEST BAKED POTATO I'VE EVER EATEN WAS SIX YEARS AGO...
THE VICTIM MAY TRY SARCASM TO RELIEVE THE BOREDOM.
FASCINATING. NOW COULD YOU THINK OUT LOUD ALL OF THE POSSIBLE DATES THIS MAY HAVE OCCURRED?
© 1989 United Feature Syndicate, Inc.
S.Adams
SARCASM WON'T WORK.
WELL, IT COULD HAVE BEEN ON OCTOBER 6TH... OR MAYBE THE 16TH. WAS THAT A TUESDAY?
7-14

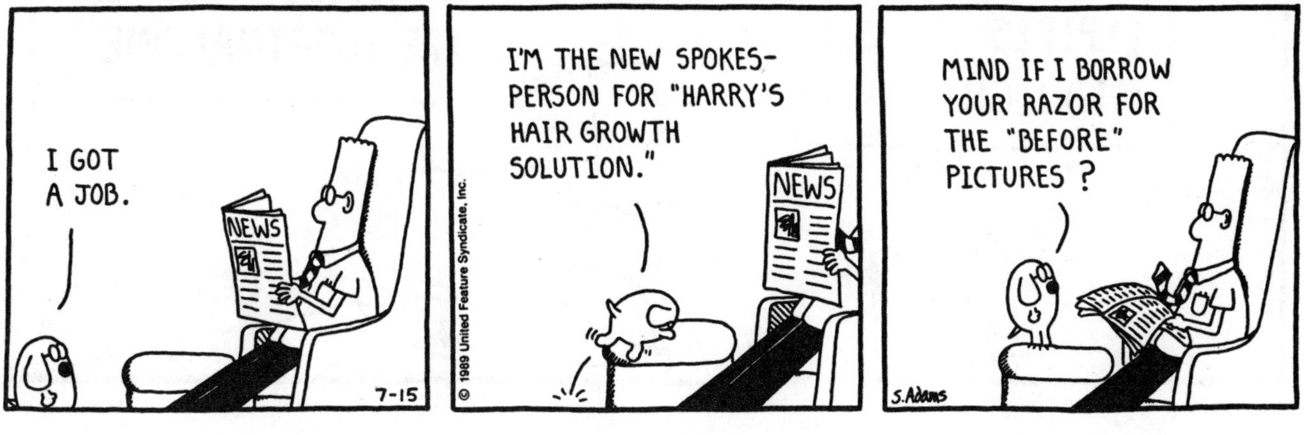
I GOT A JOB.
NEWS
7-15
I'M THE NEW SPOKES-PERSON FOR "HARRY'S HAIR GROWTH SOLUTION."
NEWS
© 1989 United Feature Syndicate, Inc.
MIND IF I BORROW YOUR RAZOR FOR THE "BEFORE" PICTURES?
S.Adams

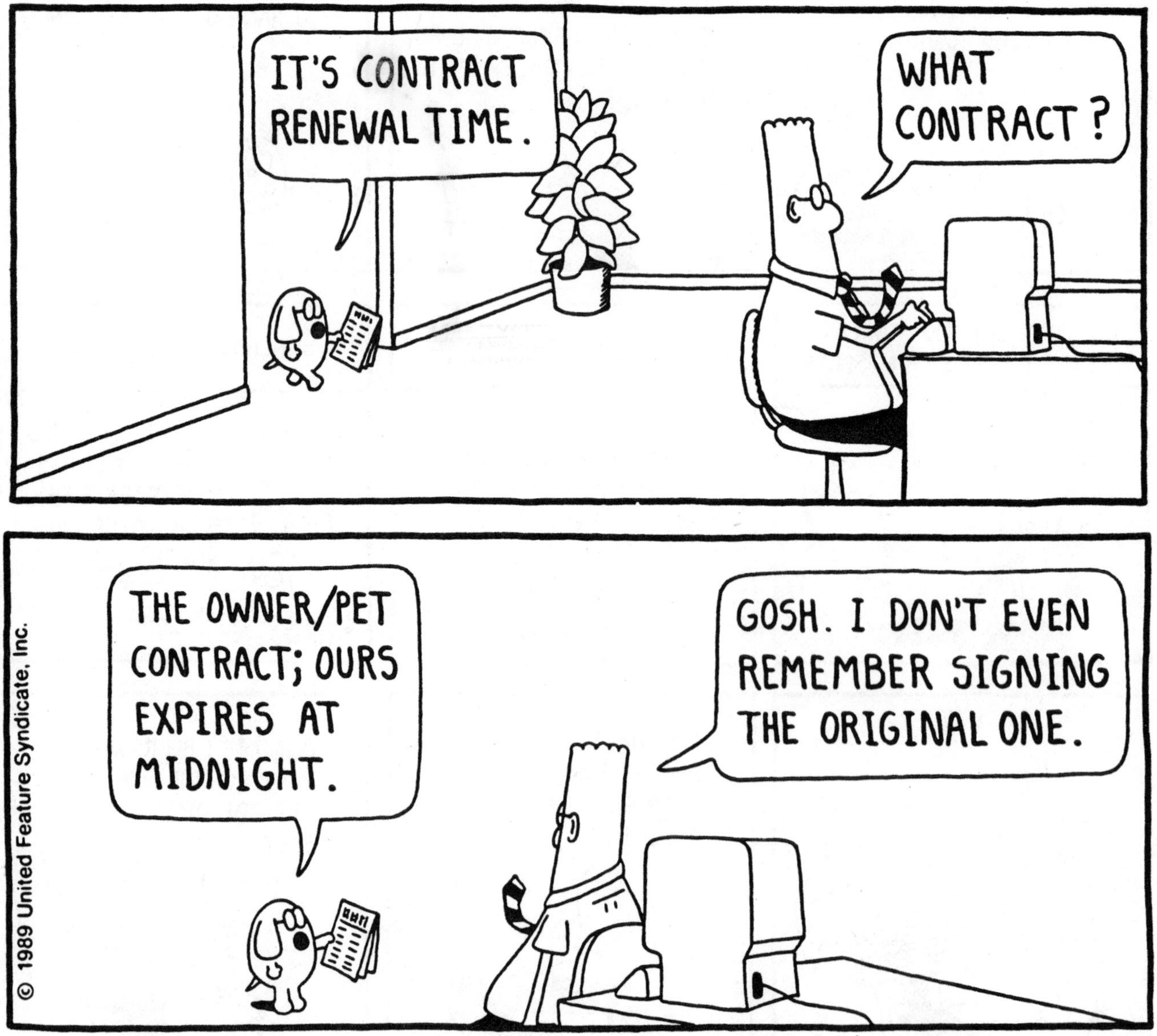
IT'S CONTRACT RENEWAL TIME.
WHAT CONTRACT?
THE OWNER/PET CONTRACT; OURS EXPIRES AT MIDNIGHT.
GOSH. I DON'T EVEN REMEMBER SIGNING THE ORIGINAL ONE.

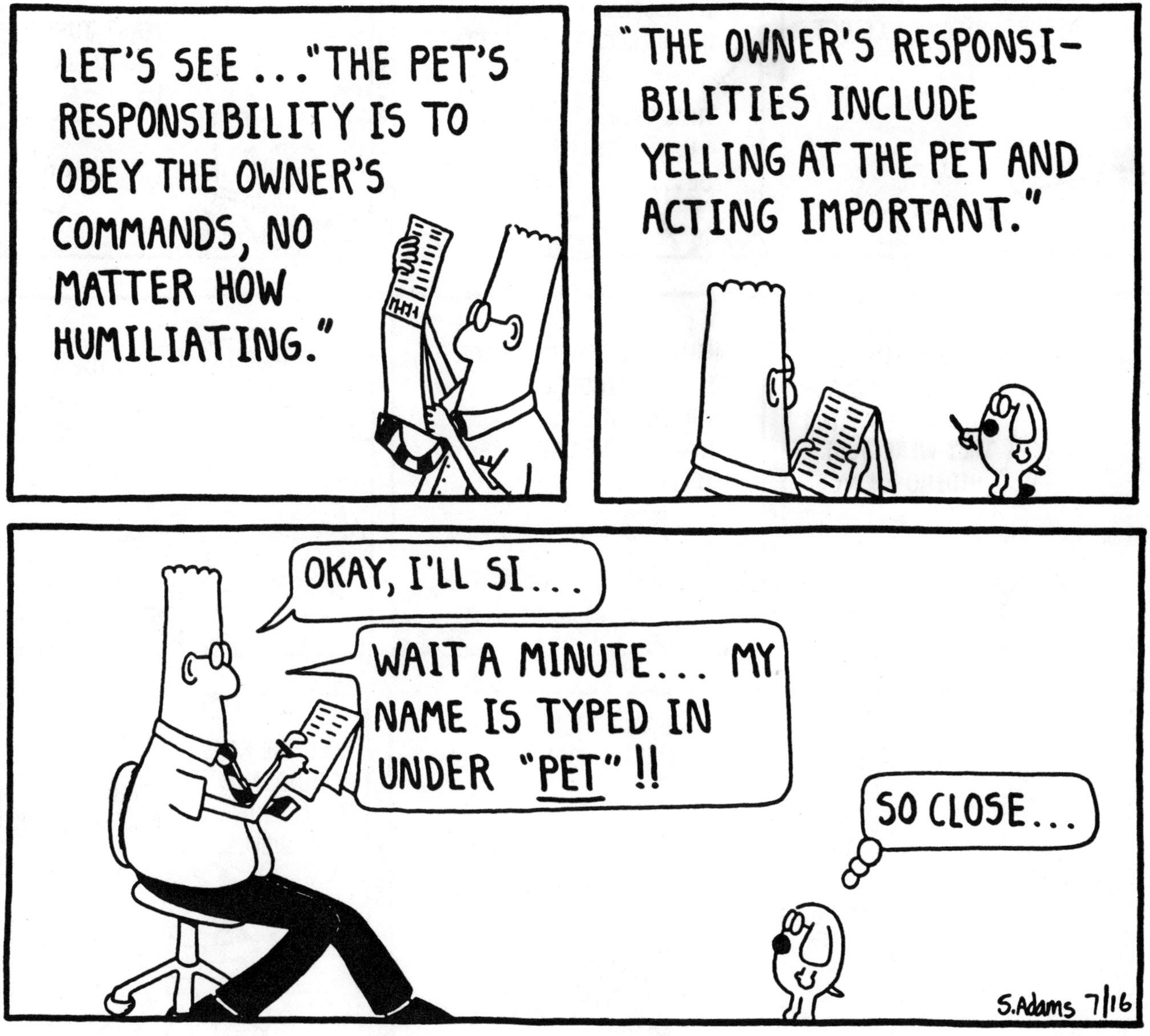
LET'S SEE ..."THE PET'S RESPONSIBILITY IS TO OBEY THE OWNER'S COMMANDS, NO MATTER HOW HUMILIATING."
"THE OWNER'S RESPONSI-BILITIES INCLUDE YELLING AT THE PET AND ACTING IMPORTANT."
OKAY, I'LL SI...
WAIT A MINUTE... MY NAME IS TYPED IN UNDER "PET" !!
SO CLOSE...
S.Adams 7/16

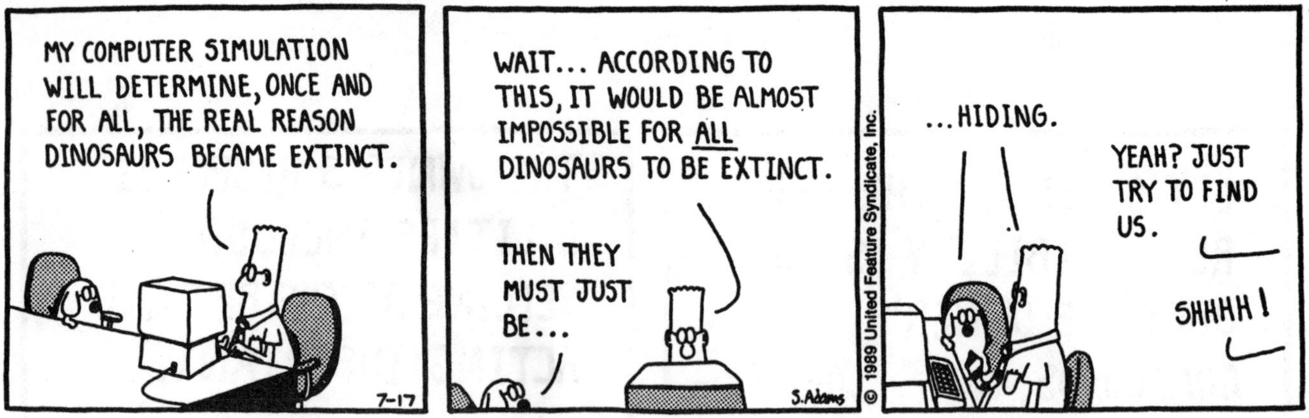
MY COMPUTER SIMULATION WILL DETERMINE, ONCE AND FOR ALL, THE REAL REASON DINOSAURS BECAME EXTINCT.
7-17
WAIT... ACCORDING TO THIS, IT WOULD BE ALMOST IMPOSSIBLE FOR ALL DINOSAURS TO BE EXTINCT.
THEN THEY MUST JUST BE...
S.Adams
© 1989 United Feature Syndicate, Inc.
...HIDING.
YEAH? JUST TRY TO FIND US.
SHHHH!

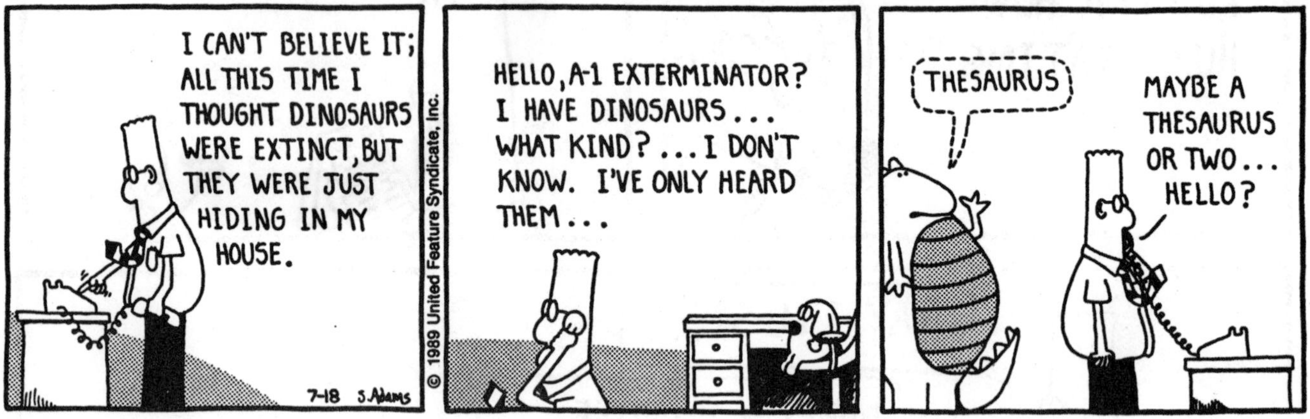
I CAN'T BELIEVE IT; ALL THIS TIME I THOUGHT DINOSAURS WERE EXTINCT, BUT THEY WERE JUST HIDING IN MY HOUSE.
7-18 S.Adams
© 1989 United Feature Syndicate, Inc.
HELLO, A-1 EXTERMINATOR? I HAVE DINOSAURS... WHAT KIND? ... I DON'T KNOW. I'VE ONLY HEARD THEM...
THESAURUS
MAYBE A THESAURUS OR TWO... HELLO?

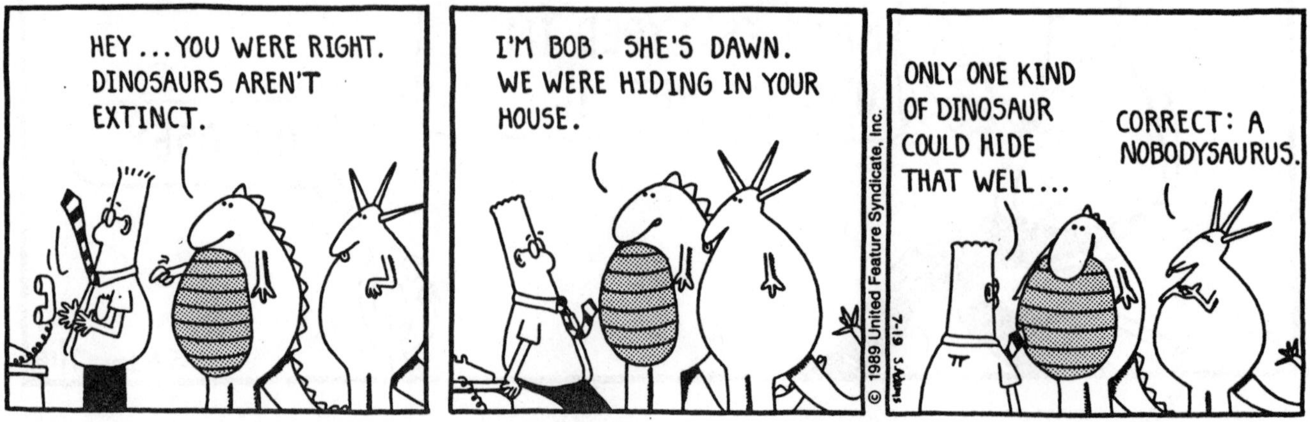
HEY... YOU WERE RIGHT. DINOSAURS AREN'T EXTINCT.
I'M BOB. SHE'S DAWN. WE WERE HIDING IN YOUR HOUSE.
© 1989 United Feature Syndicate, Inc.
7-19 S.Adams
ONLY ONE KIND OF DINOSAUR COULD HIDE THAT WELL...
CORRECT: A NOBODYSAURUS.

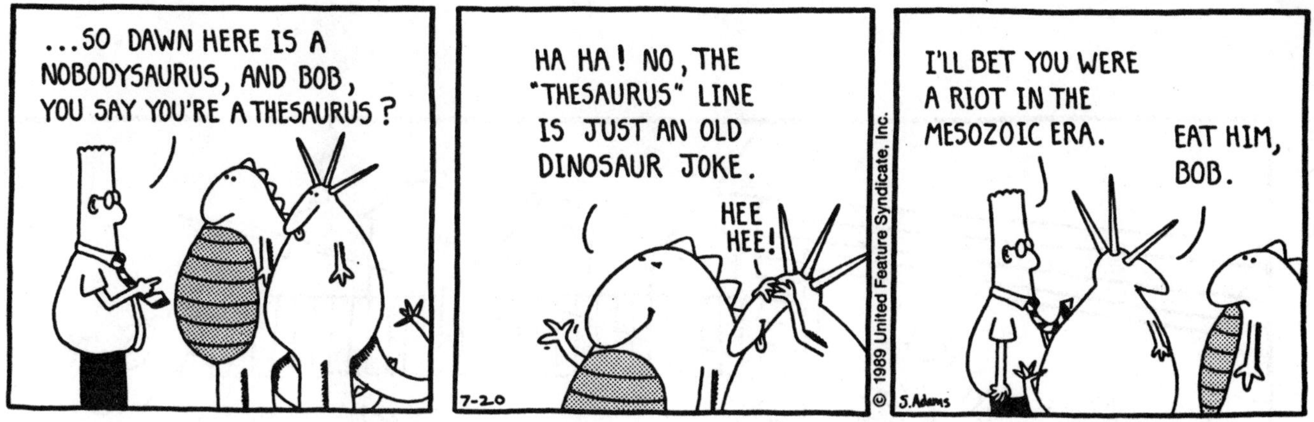
...SO DAWN HERE IS A NOBODYSAURUS, AND BOB, YOU SAY YOU'RE A THESAURUS?
HA HA! NO, THE "THESAURUS" LINE IS JUST AN OLD DINOSAUR JOKE.
HEE HEE!
7-20
I'LL BET YOU WERE A RIOT IN THE MESOZOIC ERA.
EAT HIM, BOB.
S. Adams
© 1989 United Feature Syndicate, Inc.

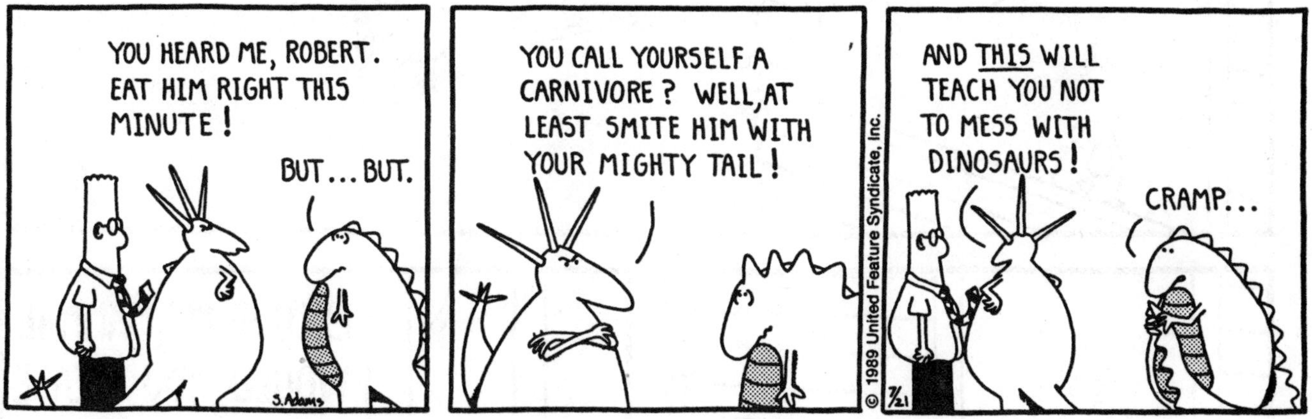
YOU HEARD ME, ROBERT. EAT HIM RIGHT THIS MINUTE!
BUT... BUT.
S. Adams
YOU CALL YOURSELF A CARNIVORE? WELL, AT LEAST SMITE HIM WITH YOUR MIGHTY TAIL!
AND THIS WILL TEACH YOU NOT TO MESS WITH DINOSAURS!
CRAMP...
7/21
© 1989 United Feature Syndicate, Inc.

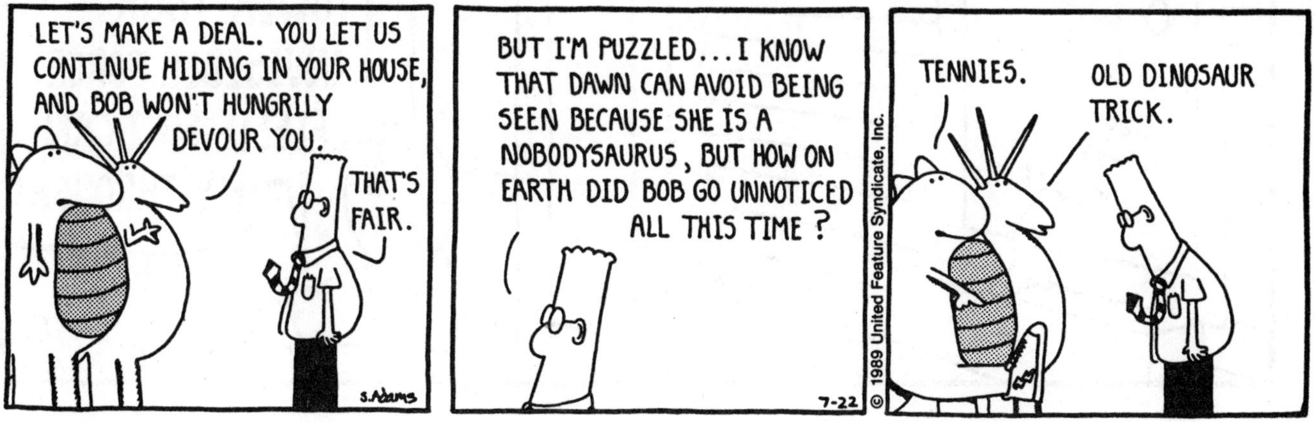
LET'S MAKE A DEAL. YOU LET US CONTINUE HIDING IN YOUR HOUSE, AND BOB WON'T HUNGRILY DEVOUR YOU.
THAT'S FAIR.
S. Adams
BUT I'M PUZZLED... I KNOW THAT DAWN CAN AVOID BEING SEEN BECAUSE SHE IS A NOBODYSAURUS, BUT HOW ON EARTH DID BOB GO UNNOTICED ALL THIS TIME?
7-22
TENNIES.
OLD DINOSAUR TRICK.
© 1989 United Feature Syndicate, Inc.

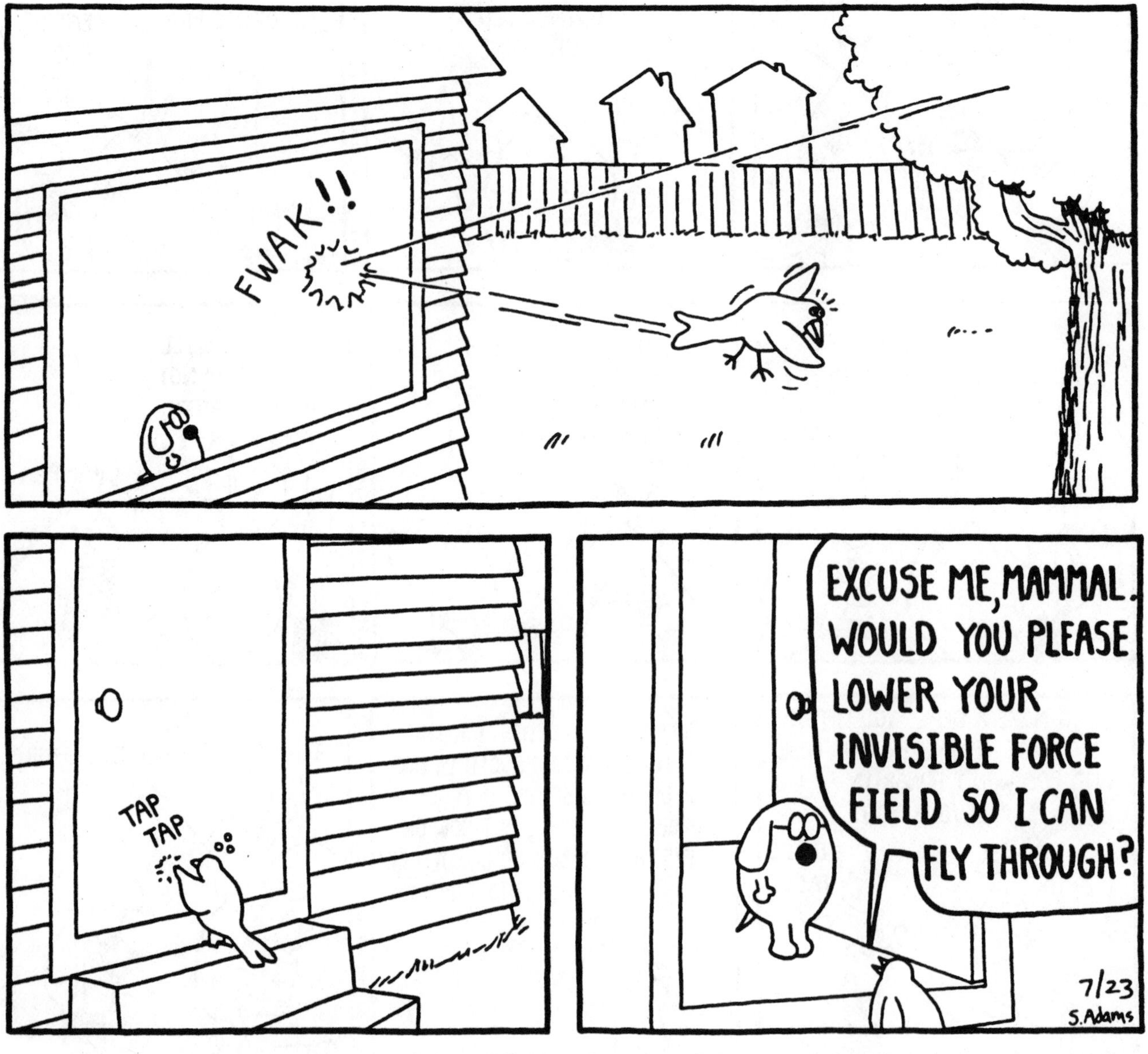
FWAK!!
TAP TAP
EXCUSE ME, MAMMAL. WOULD YOU PLEASE LOWER YOUR INVISIBLE FORCE FIELD SO I CAN FLY THROUGH?
7/23
S. Adams

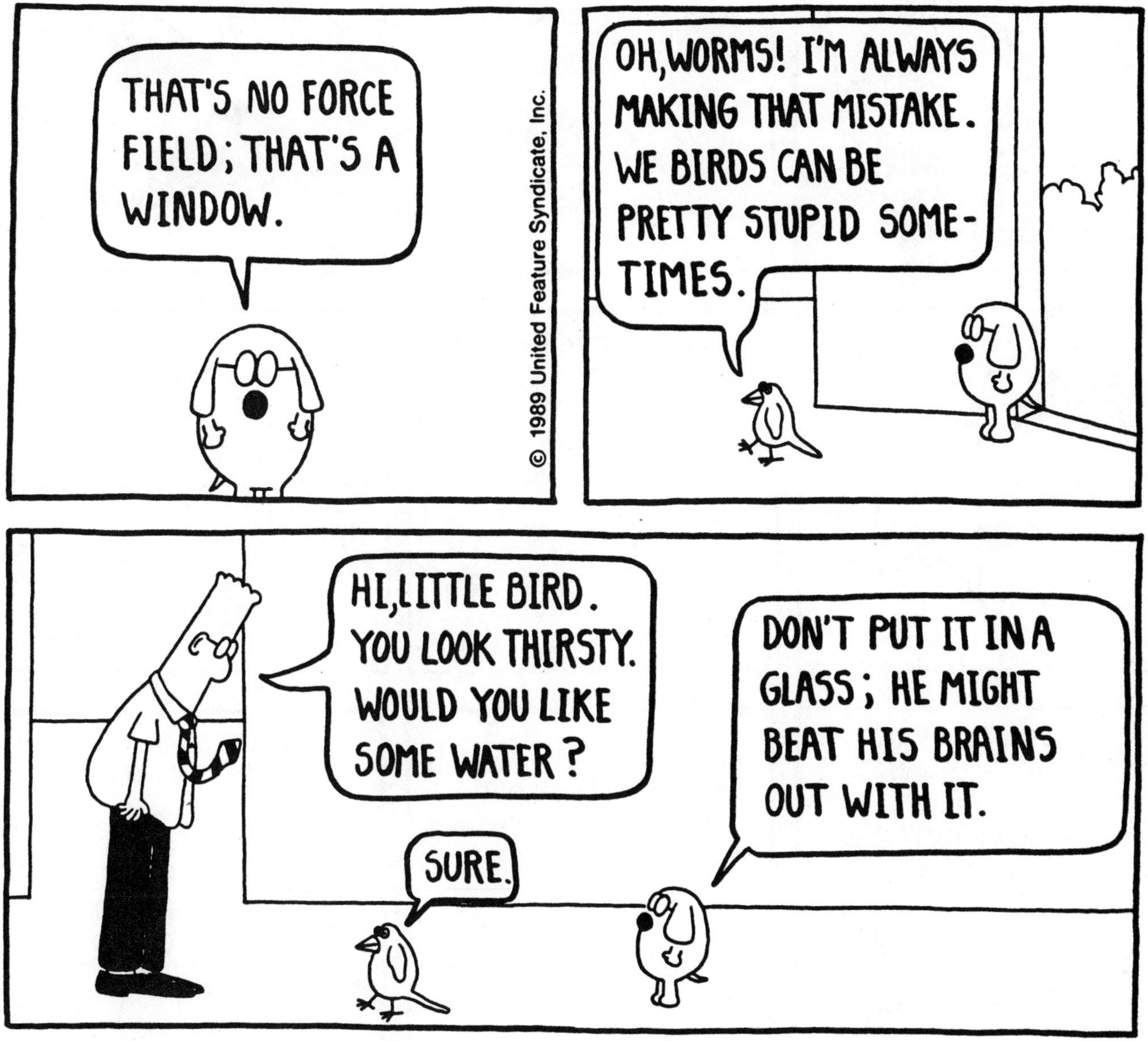
THAT'S NO FORCE FIELD; THAT'S A WINDOW.
© 1989 United Feature Syndicate, Inc.
OH, WORMS! I'M ALWAYS MAKING THAT MISTAKE. WE BIRDS CAN BE PRETTY STUPID SOMETIMES.
HI, LITTLE BIRD. YOU LOOK THIRSTY. WOULD YOU LIKE SOME WATER?
SURE.
DON'T PUT IT IN A GLASS; HE MIGHT BEAT HIS BRAINS OUT WITH IT.

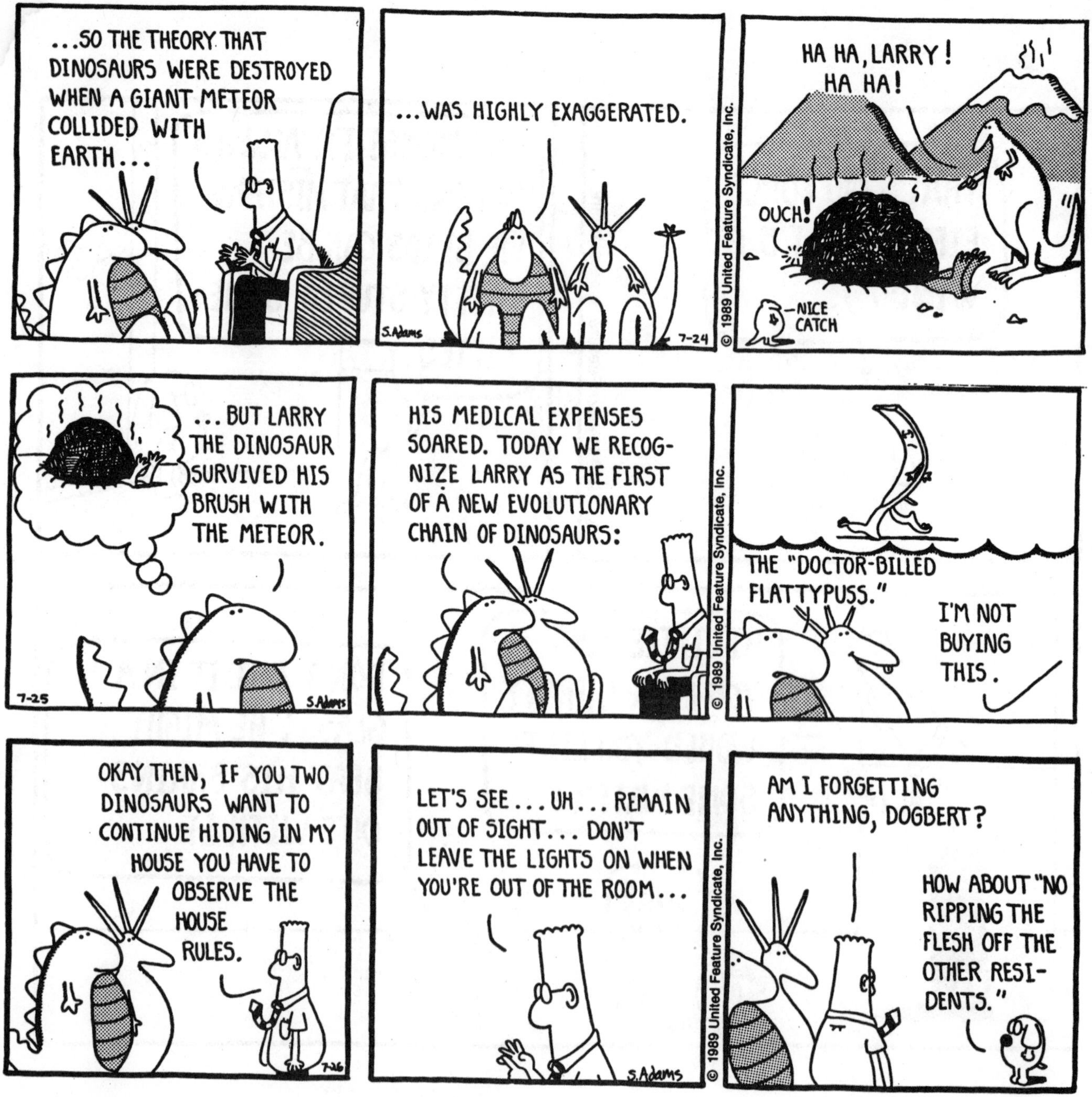

...SO THE THEORY THAT DINOSAURS WERE DESTROYED WHEN A GIANT METEOR COLLIDED WITH EARTH...
...WAS HIGHLY EXAGGERATED.
S.Adams
7-24
HA HA, LARRY! HA HA!
OUCH!
—NICE CATCH
© 1989 United Feature Syndicate, Inc.
...BUT LARRY THE DINOSAUR SURVIVED HIS BRUSH WITH THE METEOR.
7-25
S.Adams
HIS MEDICAL EXPENSES SOARED. TODAY WE RECOGNIZE LARRY AS THE FIRST OF A NEW EVOLUTIONARY CHAIN OF DINOSAURS:
© 1989 United Feature Syndicate, Inc.
THE "DOCTOR-BILLED FLATTYPUSS."
I'M NOT BUYING THIS.
OKAY THEN, IF YOU TWO DINOSAURS WANT TO CONTINUE HIDING IN MY HOUSE YOU HAVE TO OBSERVE THE HOUSE RULES.
7-26
LET'S SEE...UH...REMAIN OUT OF SIGHT...DON'T LEAVE THE LIGHTS ON WHEN YOU'RE OUT OF THE ROOM...
S.Adams
© 1989 United Feature Syndicate, Inc.
AM I FORGETTING ANYTHING, DOGBERT?
HOW ABOUT "NO RIPPING THE FLESH OFF THE OTHER RESIDENTS."

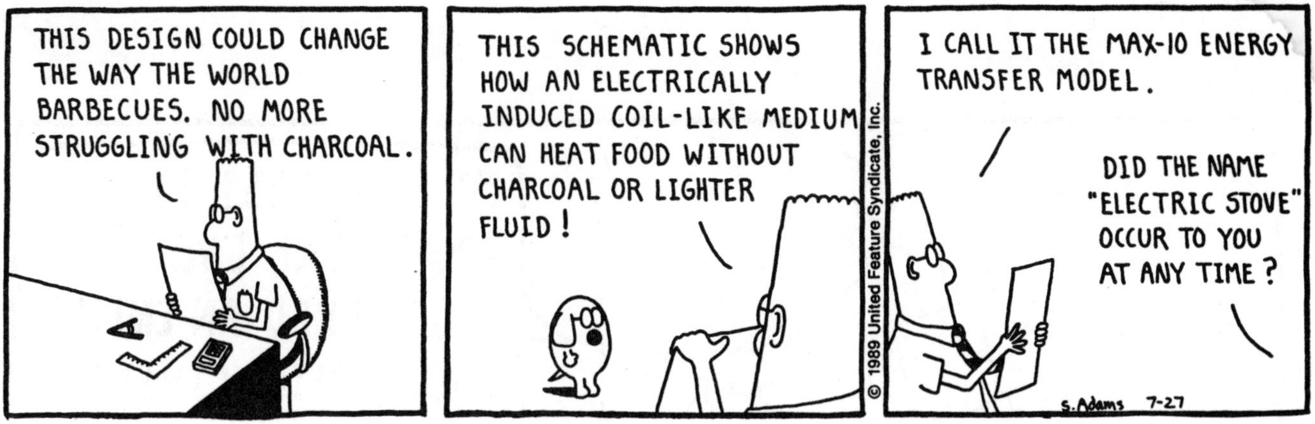
THIS DESIGN COULD CHANGE THE WAY THE WORLD BARBECUES. NO MORE STRUGGLING WITH CHARCOAL.
THIS SCHEMATIC SHOWS HOW AN ELECTRICALLY INDUCED COIL-LIKE MEDIUM CAN HEAT FOOD WITHOUT CHARCOAL OR LIGHTER FLUID!
© 1989 United Feature Syndicate, Inc.
I CALL IT THE MAX-10 ENERGY TRANSFER MODEL.
DID THE NAME "ELECTRIC STOVE" OCCUR TO YOU AT ANY TIME?
S. Adams 7-27

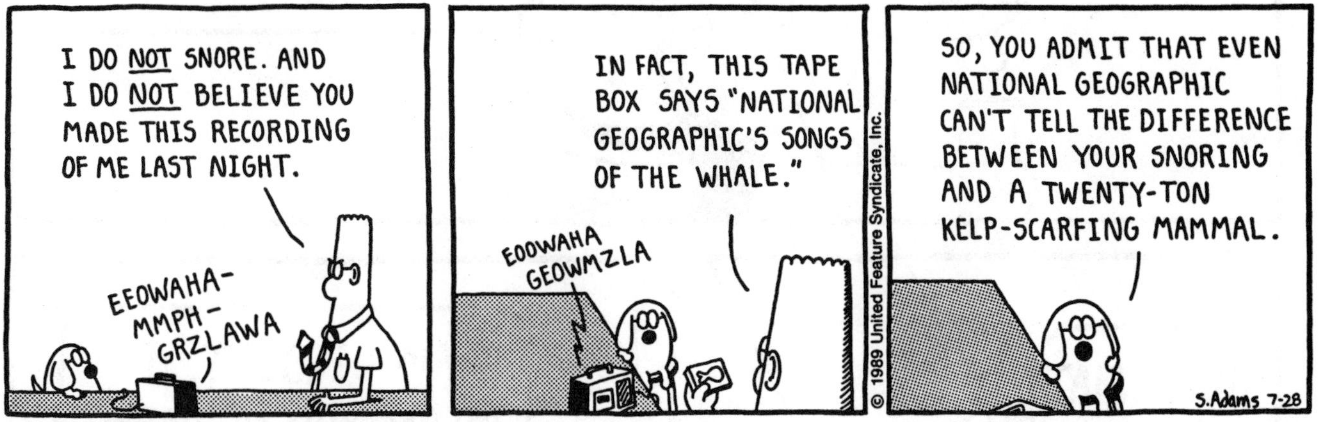
I DO NOT SNORE. AND I DO NOT BELIEVE YOU MADE THIS RECORDING OF ME LAST NIGHT.
EEOWAHA-MMPH-GRZLAWA
IN FACT, THIS TAPE BOX SAYS "NATIONAL GEOGRAPHIC'S SONGS OF THE WHALE."
EOOWAHA GEOWMZLA
© 1989 United Feature Syndicate, Inc.
SO, YOU ADMIT THAT EVEN NATIONAL GEOGRAPHIC CAN'T TELL THE DIFFERENCE BETWEEN YOUR SNORING AND A TWENTY-TON KELP-SCARFING MAMMAL.
S. Adams 7-28

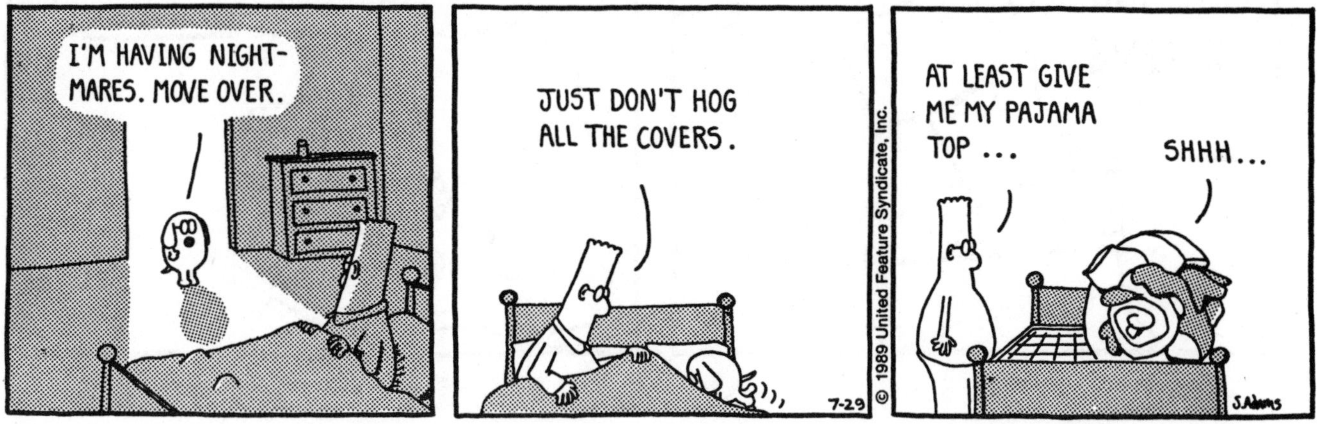
I'M HAVING NIGHT-MARES. MOVE OVER.
JUST DON'T HOG ALL THE COVERS.
7-29
© 1989 United Feature Syndicate, Inc.
AT LEAST GIVE ME MY PAJAMA TOP ...
SHHH...
S. Adams

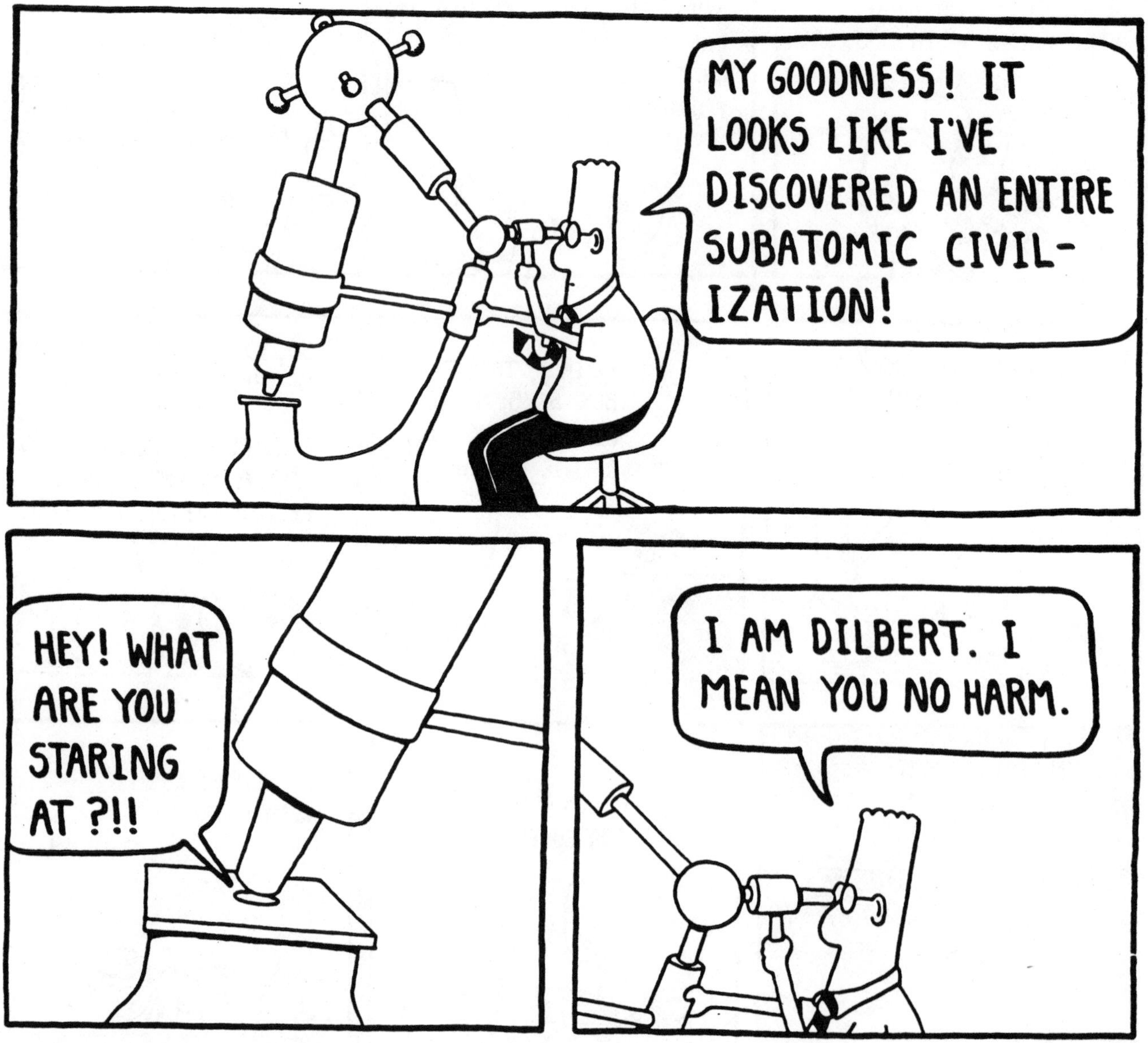
MY GOODNESS! IT LOOKS LIKE I'VE DISCOVERED AN ENTIRE SUBATOMIC CIVIL-IZATION!
HEY! WHAT ARE YOU STARING AT ?!!
I AM DILBERT. I MEAN YOU NO HARM.

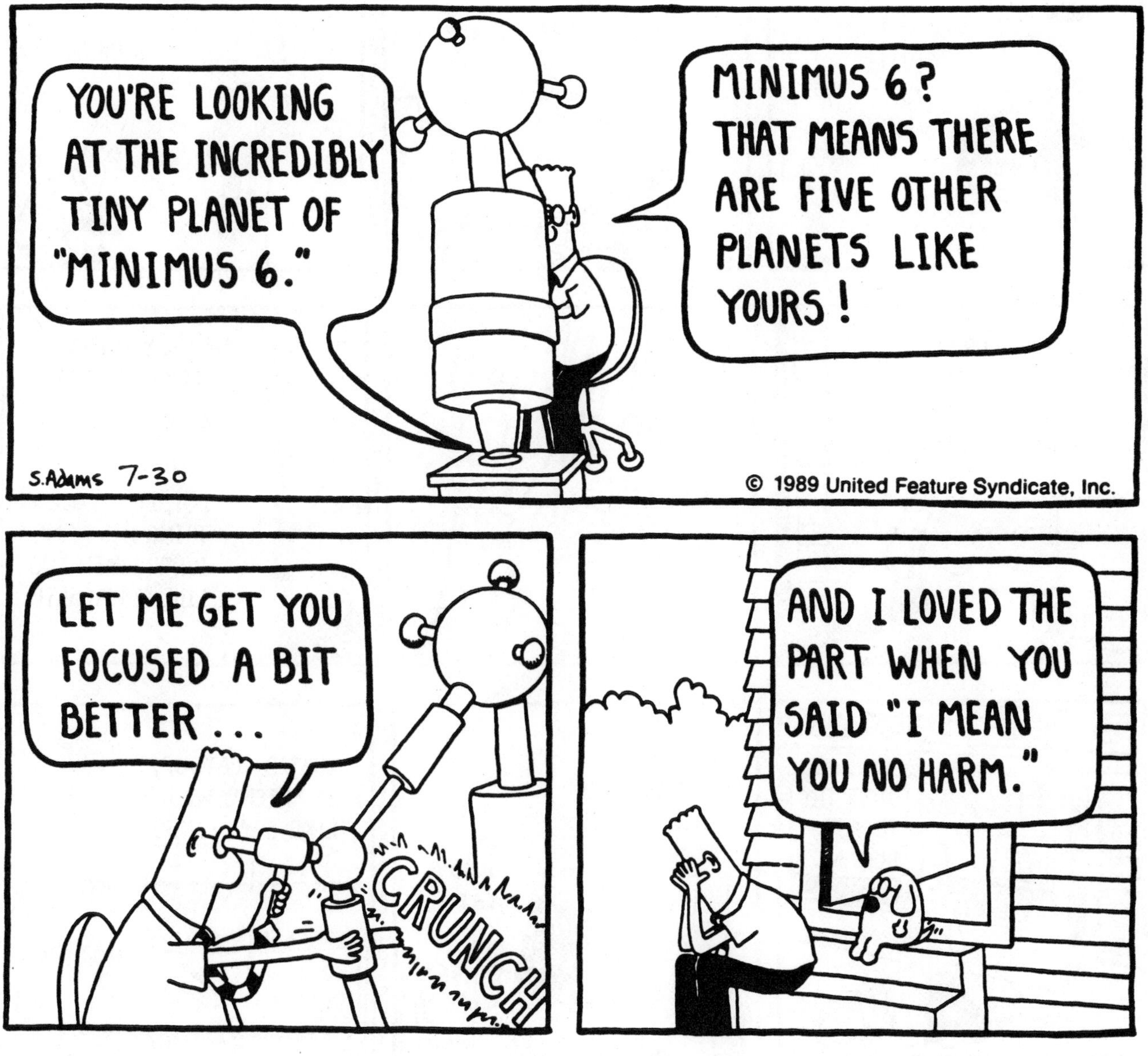
YOU'RE LOOKING AT THE INCREDIBLY TINY PLANET OF "MINIMUS 6."
MINIMUS 6? THAT MEANS THERE ARE FIVE OTHER PLANETS LIKE YOURS!
S.Adams 7-30
© 1989 United Feature Syndicate, Inc.
LET ME GET YOU FOCUSED A BIT BETTER ...
CRUNCH
AND I LOVED THE PART WHEN YOU SAID "I MEAN YOU NO HARM."

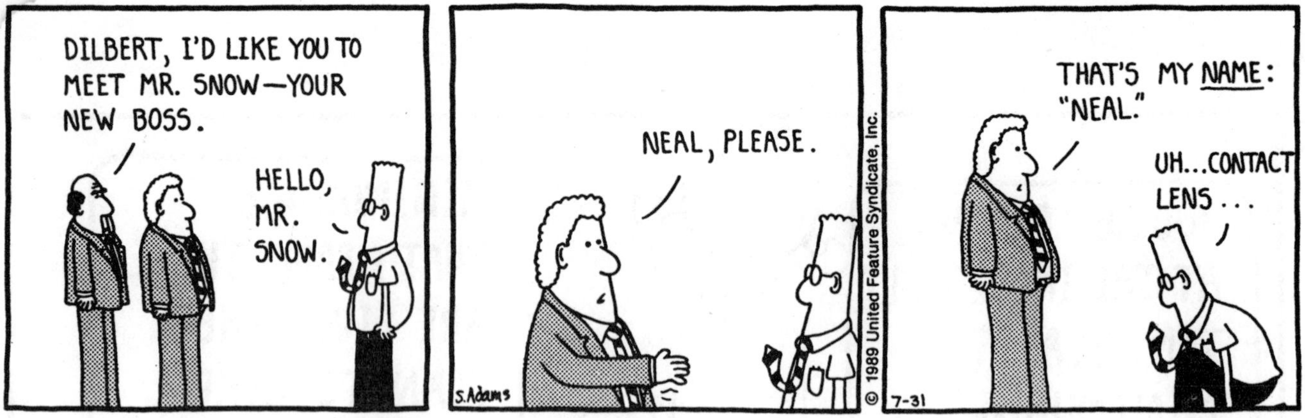
DILBERT, I'D LIKE YOU TO MEET MR. SNOW—YOUR NEW BOSS.
HELLO, MR. SNOW.
NEAL, PLEASE.
S.Adams
© 1989 United Feature Syndicate, Inc.
THAT'S MY NAME: "NEAL."
UH...CONTACT LENS . . .
7-31

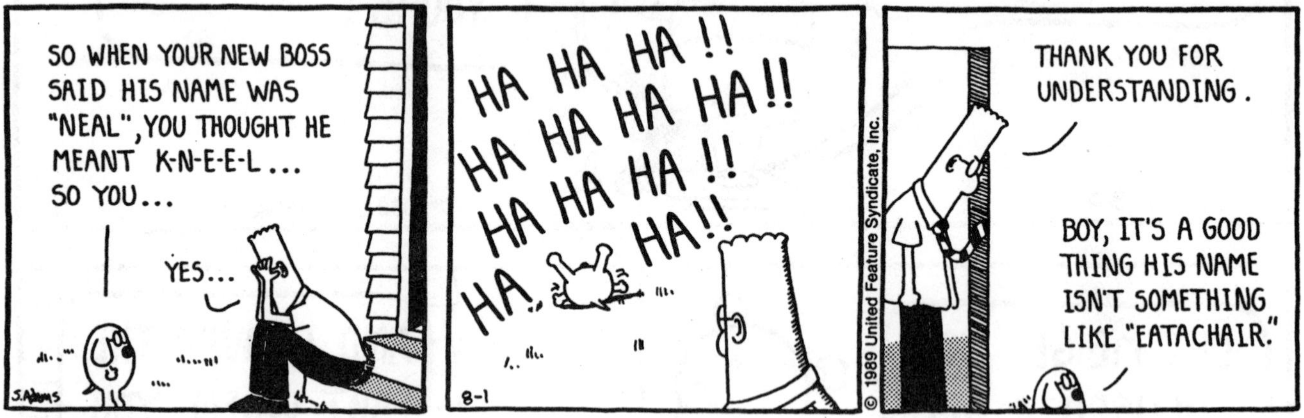
SO WHEN YOUR NEW BOSS SAID HIS NAME WAS "NEAL", YOU THOUGHT HE MEANT K-N-E-E-L . . . SO YOU . . .
YES . . .
S.Adams
HA HA HA !! HA HA HA HA !! HA HA HA !! HA HA !!
8-1
© 1989 United Feature Syndicate, Inc.
THANK YOU FOR UNDERSTANDING.
BOY, IT'S A GOOD THING HIS NAME ISN'T SOMETHING LIKE "EATACHAIR."

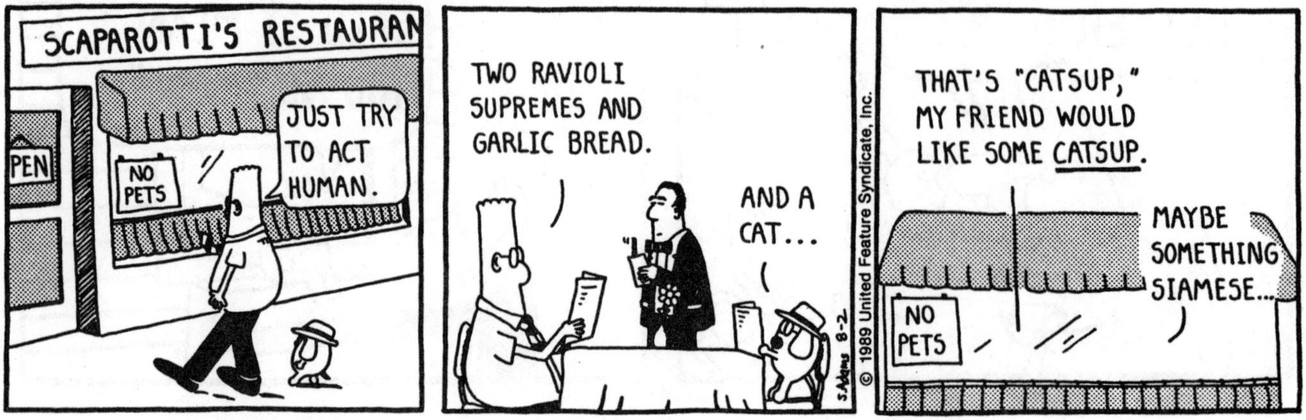
SCAPAROTTI'S RESTAURAN
PEN
NO PETS
JUST TRY TO ACT HUMAN.
TWO RAVIOLI SUPREMES AND GARLIC BREAD.
AND A CAT . . .
S.Adams 8-2
© 1989 United Feature Syndicate, Inc.
THAT'S "CATSUP," MY FRIEND WOULD LIKE SOME CATSUP.
MAYBE SOMETHING SIAMESE...
NO PETS

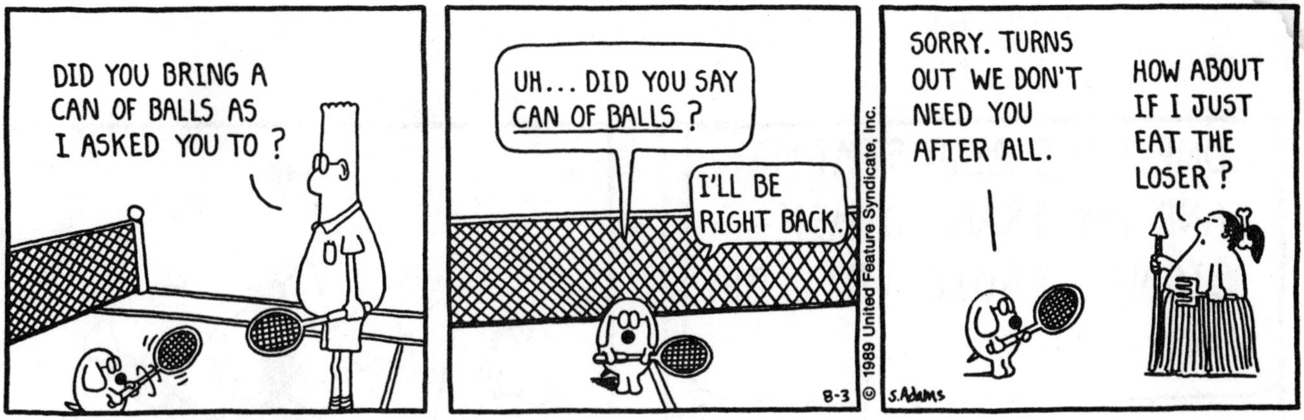
DID YOU BRING A CAN OF BALLS AS I ASKED YOU TO ?
UH... DID YOU SAY CAN OF BALLS ?
I'LL BE RIGHT BACK.
8-3
© 1989 United Feature Syndicate, Inc.
SORRY. TURNS OUT WE DON'T NEED YOU AFTER ALL.
HOW ABOUT IF I JUST EAT THE LOSER ?
S.Adams

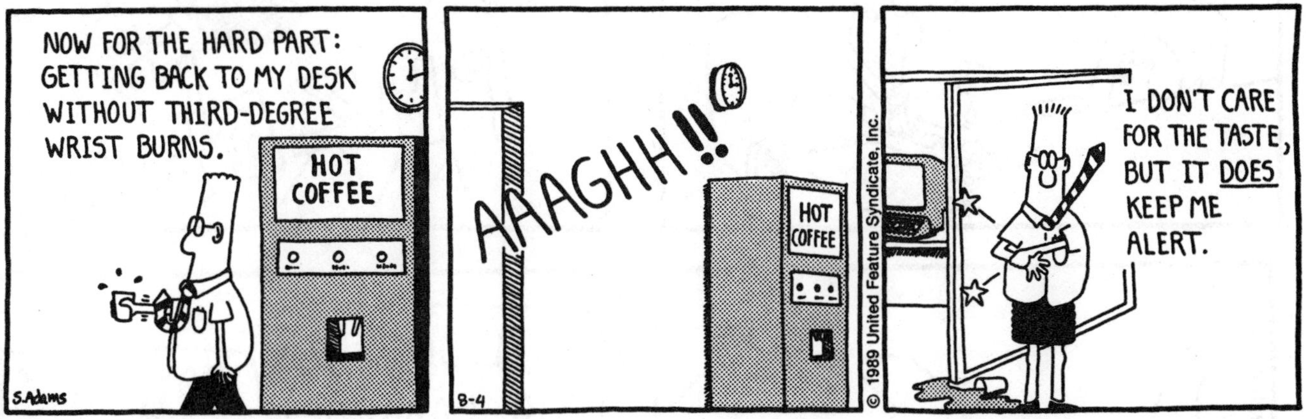
NOW FOR THE HARD PART: GETTING BACK TO MY DESK WITHOUT THIRD-DEGREE WRIST BURNS.
HOT COFFEE
S.Adams
AAAGHH!!
HOT COFFEE
8-4
© 1989 United Feature Syndicate, Inc.
I DON'T CARE FOR THE TASTE, BUT IT DOES KEEP ME ALERT.

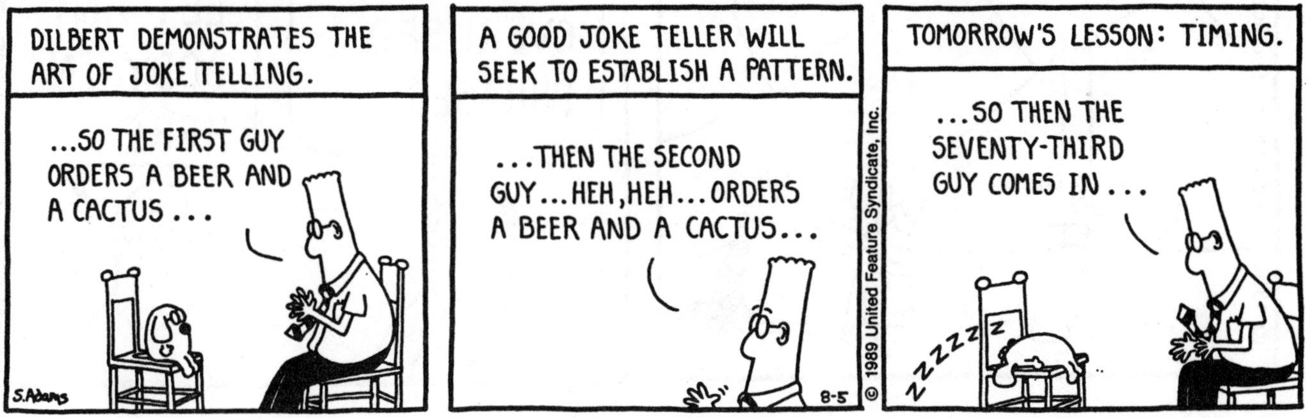
DILBERT DEMONSTRATES THE ART OF JOKE TELLING.
...SO THE FIRST GUY ORDERS A BEER AND A CACTUS ...
S.Adams
A GOOD JOKE TELLER WILL SEEK TO ESTABLISH A PATTERN.
...THEN THE SECOND GUY...HEH,HEH...ORDERS A BEER AND A CACTUS...
8-5
© 1989 United Feature Syndicate, Inc.
TOMORROW'S LESSON: TIMING.
...SO THEN THE SEVENTY-THIRD GUY COMES IN ...
ZZZZZZ

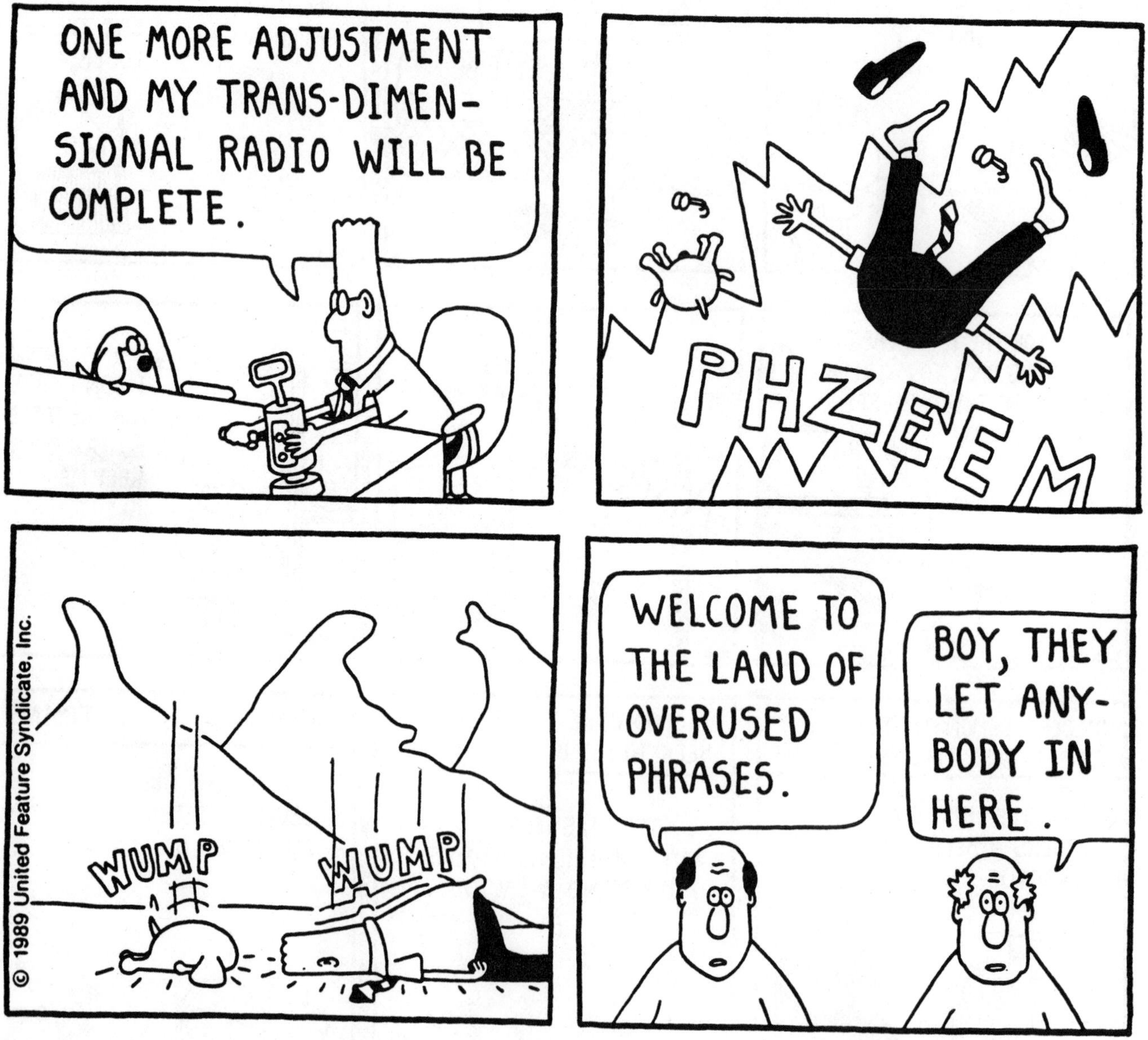
ONE MORE ADJUSTMENT AND MY TRANS-DIMEN-SIONAL RADIO WILL BE COMPLETE.
PHZEEM
© 1989 United Feature Syndicate, Inc.
WUMP
WUMP
WELCOME TO THE LAND OF OVERUSED PHRASES.
BOY, THEY LET ANY-BODY IN HERE.

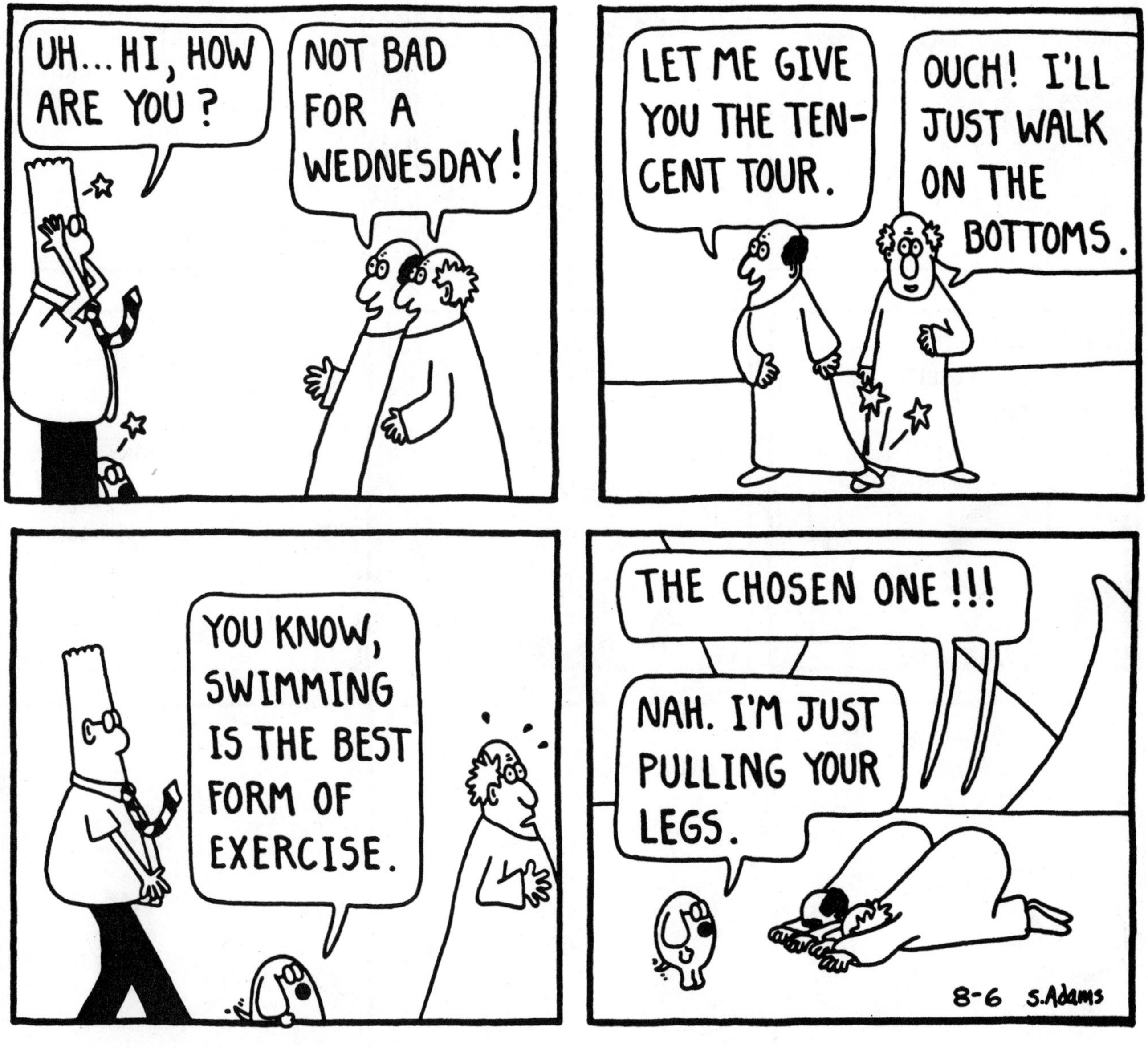
UH... HI, HOW ARE YOU?
NOT BAD FOR A WEDNESDAY!
LET ME GIVE YOU THE TEN-CENT TOUR.
OUCH! I'LL JUST WALK ON THE BOTTOMS.
YOU KNOW, SWIMMING IS THE BEST FORM OF EXERCISE.
THE CHOSEN ONE!!!
NAH. I'M JUST PULLING YOUR LEGS.
8-6 S.Adams

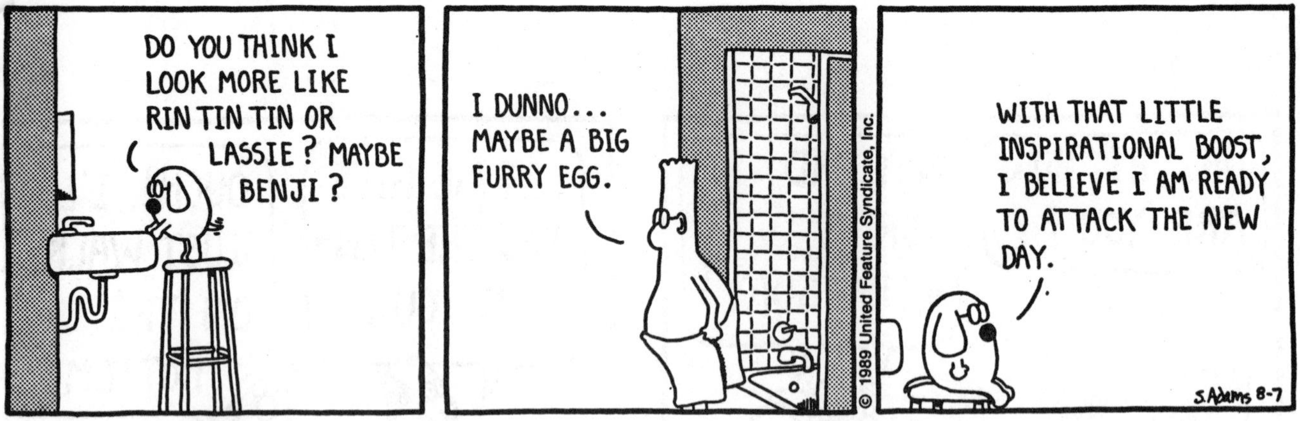
DO YOU THINK I LOOK MORE LIKE RIN TIN TIN OR LASSIE? MAYBE BENJI?
I DUNNO... MAYBE A BIG FURRY EGG.
© 1989 United Feature Syndicate, Inc.
WITH THAT LITTLE INSPIRATIONAL BOOST, I BELIEVE I AM READY TO ATTACK THE NEW DAY.
S.Adams 8-7

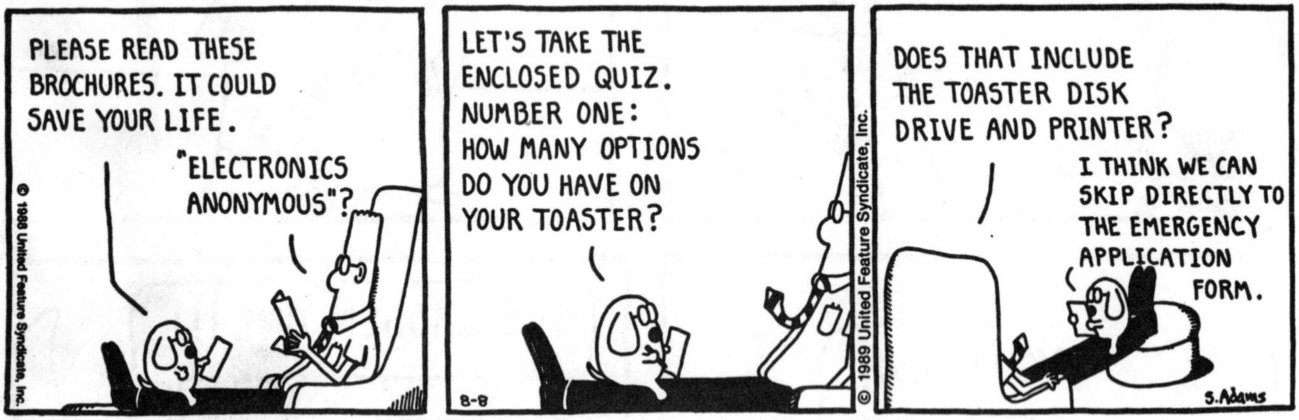
PLEASE READ THESE BROCHURES. IT COULD SAVE YOUR LIFE.
"ELECTRONICS ANONYMOUS"?
© 1988 United Feature Syndicate, Inc.
LET'S TAKE THE ENCLOSED QUIZ. NUMBER ONE: HOW MANY OPTIONS DO YOU HAVE ON YOUR TOASTER?
8-8
© 1989 United Feature Syndicate, Inc.
DOES THAT INCLUDE THE TOASTER DISK DRIVE AND PRINTER?
I THINK WE CAN SKIP DIRECTLY TO THE EMERGENCY APPLICATION FORM.
S.Adams

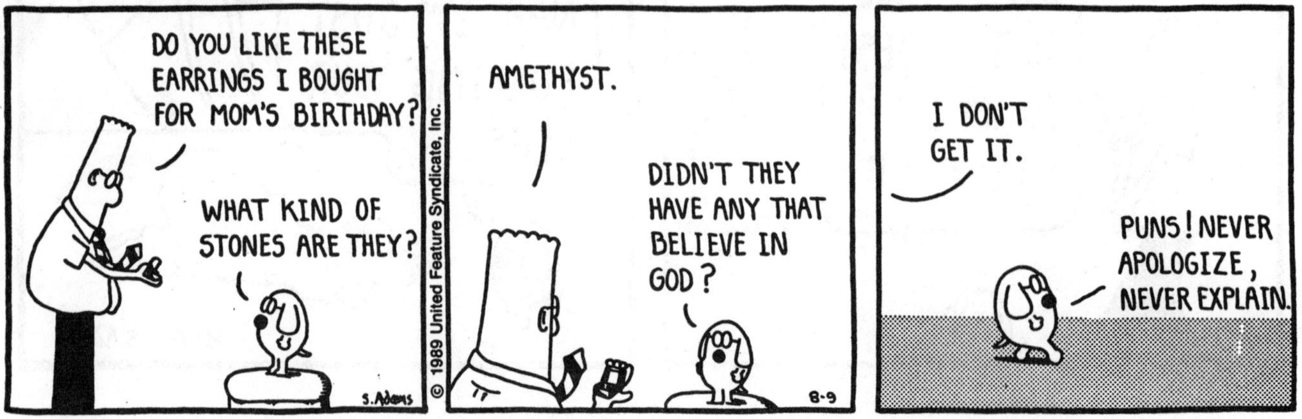
DO YOU LIKE THESE EARRINGS I BOUGHT FOR MOM'S BIRTHDAY?
WHAT KIND OF STONES ARE THEY?
S.Adams
© 1989 United Feature Syndicate, Inc.
AMETHYST.
DIDN'T THEY HAVE ANY THAT BELIEVE IN GOD?
8-9
I DON'T GET IT.
PUNS! NEVER APOLOGIZE, NEVER EXPLAIN.

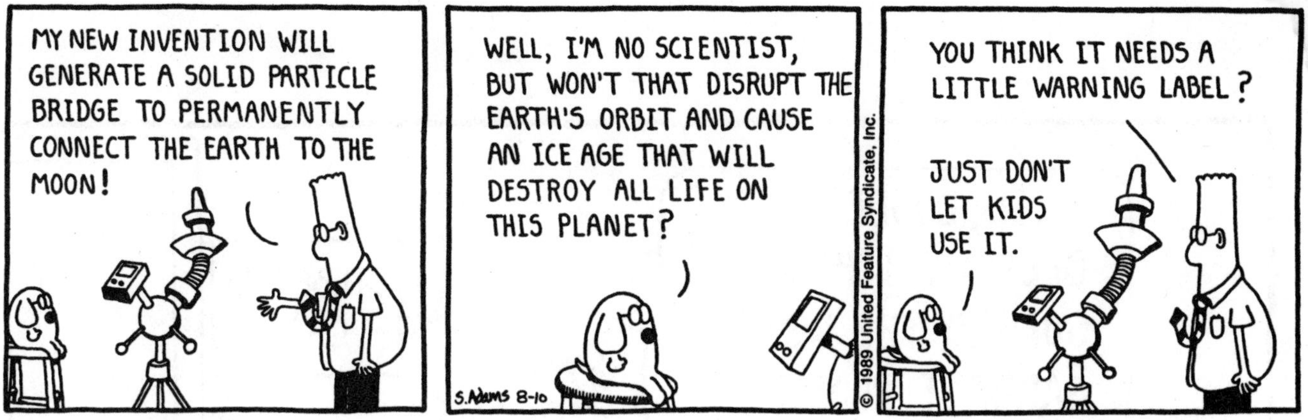
MY NEW INVENTION WILL GENERATE A SOLID PARTICLE BRIDGE TO PERMANENTLY CONNECT THE EARTH TO THE MOON!
WELL, I'M NO SCIENTIST, BUT WON'T THAT DISRUPT THE EARTH'S ORBIT AND CAUSE AN ICE AGE THAT WILL DESTROY ALL LIFE ON THIS PLANET?
S.Adams 8-10
© 1989 United Feature Syndicate, Inc.
YOU THINK IT NEEDS A LITTLE WARNING LABEL?
JUST DON'T LET KIDS USE IT.

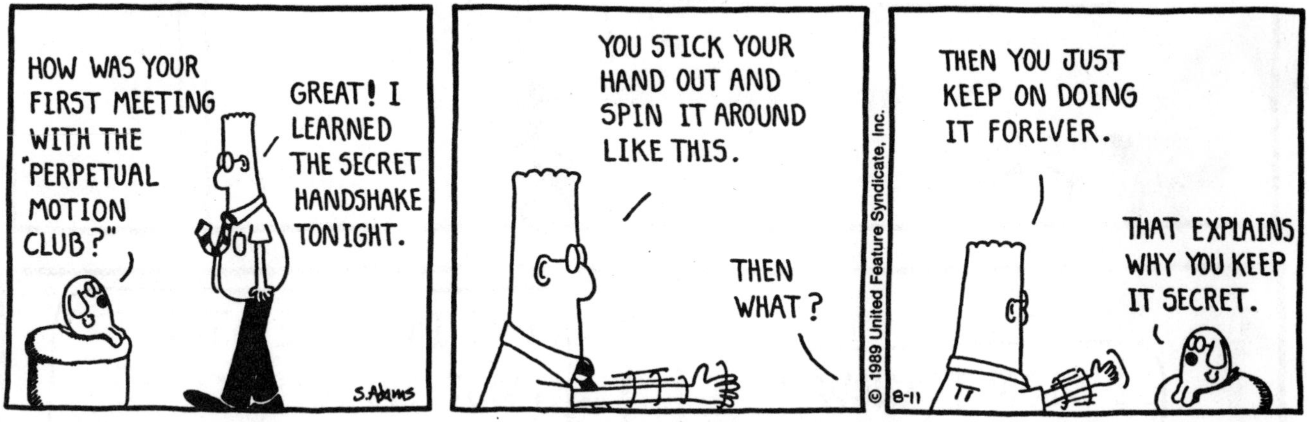
HOW WAS YOUR FIRST MEETING WITH THE "PERPETUAL MOTION CLUB?"
GREAT! I LEARNED THE SECRET HANDSHAKE TONIGHT.
S.Adams
YOU STICK YOUR HAND OUT AND SPIN IT AROUND LIKE THIS.
THEN WHAT?
© 1989 United Feature Syndicate, Inc.
THEN YOU JUST KEEP ON DOING IT FOREVER.
THAT EXPLAINS WHY YOU KEEP IT SECRET.
8-11

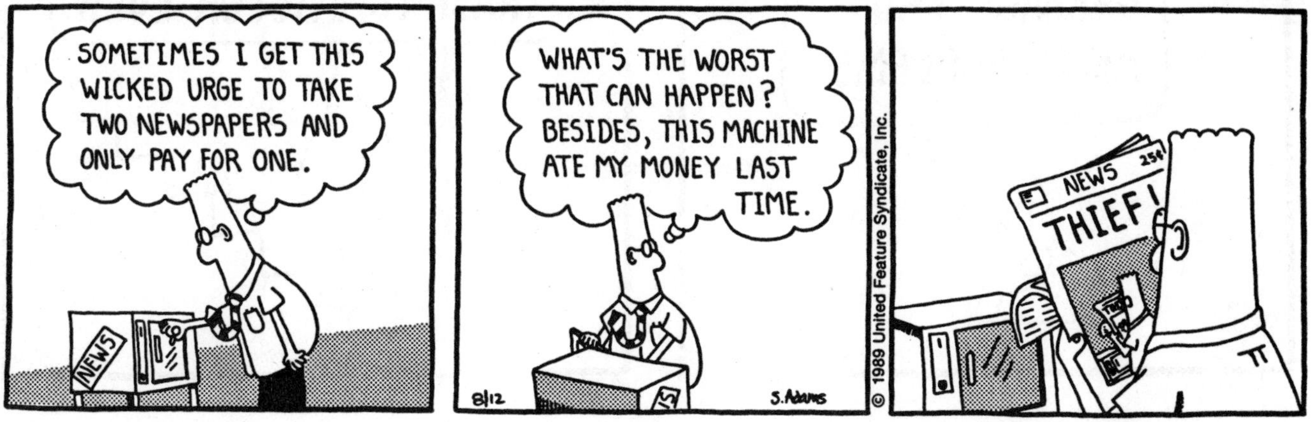
SOMETIMES I GET THIS WICKED URGE TO TAKE TWO NEWSPAPERS AND ONLY PAY FOR ONE.
NEWS
WHAT'S THE WORST THAT CAN HAPPEN? BESIDES, THIS MACHINE ATE MY MONEY LAST TIME.
8/12
S.Adams
© 1989 United Feature Syndicate, Inc.
NEWS
25¢
THIEF!

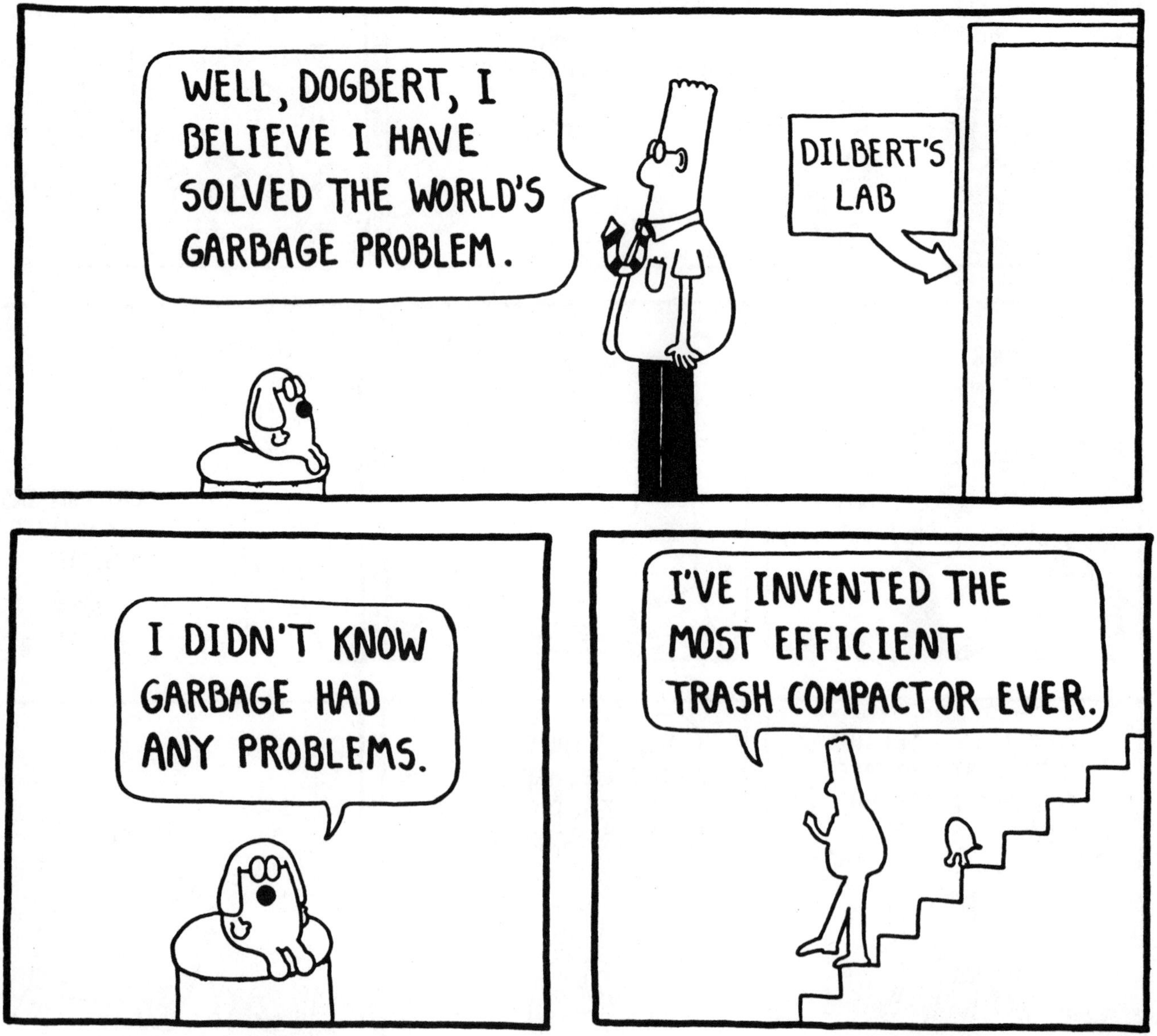
WELL, DOGBERT, I BELIEVE I HAVE SOLVED THE WORLD'S GARBAGE PROBLEM.
DILBERT'S LAB
I DIDN'T KNOW GARBAGE HAD ANY PROBLEMS.
I'VE INVENTED THE MOST EFFICIENT TRASH COMPACTOR EVER.

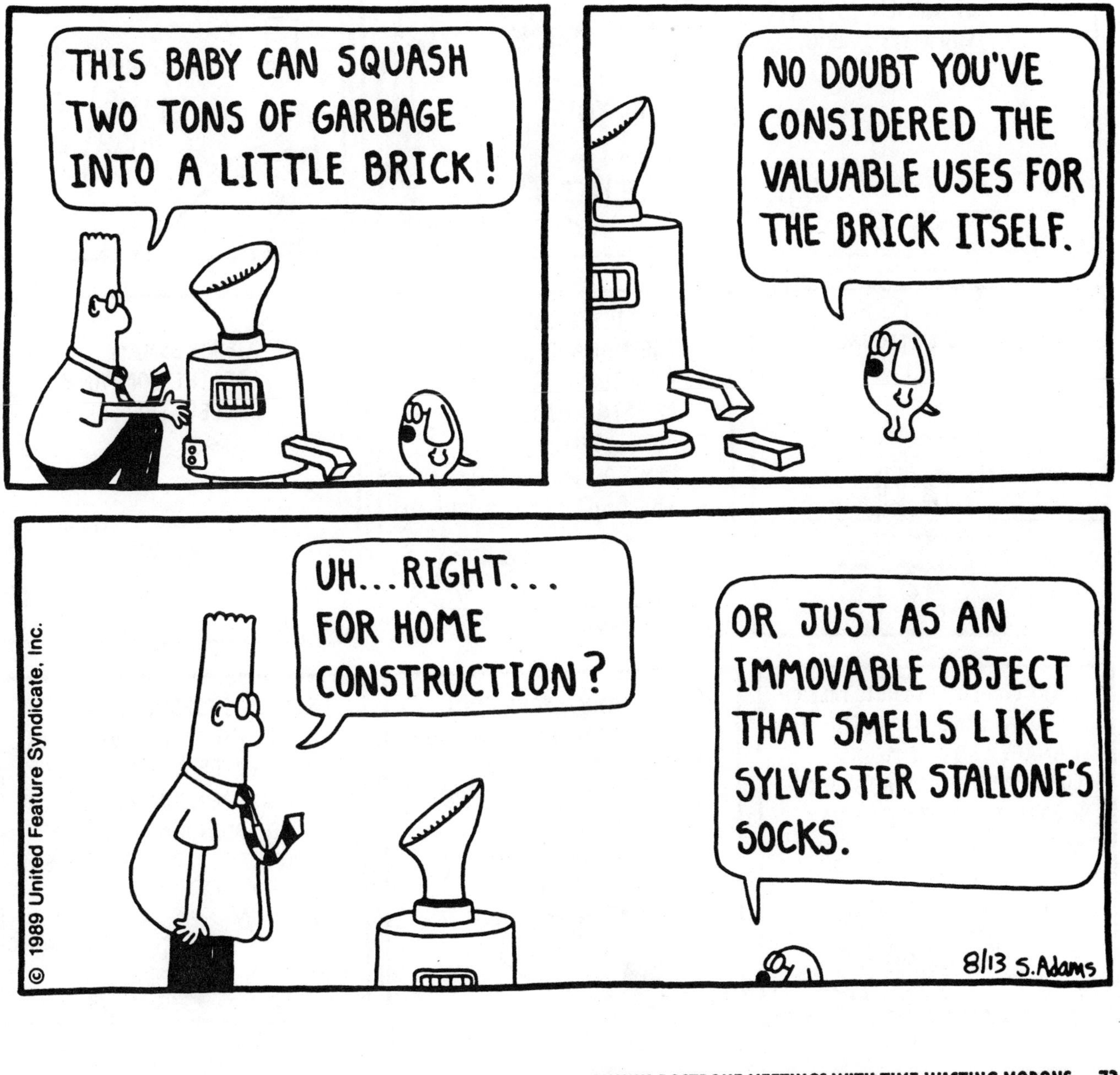
THIS BABY CAN SQUASH TWO TONS OF GARBAGE INTO A LITTLE BRICK!
NO DOUBT YOU'VE CONSIDERED THE VALUABLE USES FOR THE BRICK ITSELF.
UH...RIGHT... FOR HOME CONSTRUCTION?
OR JUST AS AN IMMOVABLE OBJECT THAT SMELLS LIKE SYLVESTER STALLONE'S SOCKS.
8/13 S. Adams

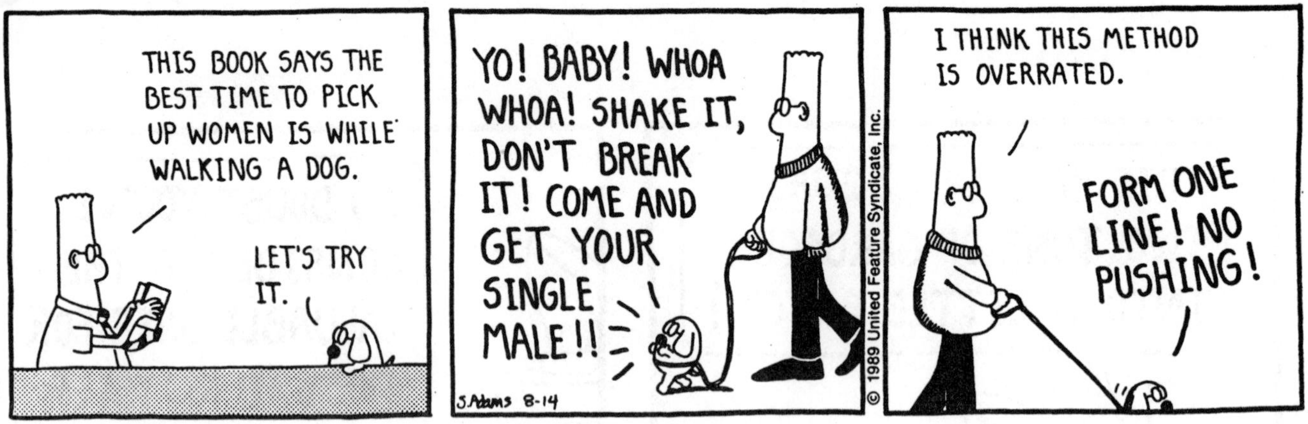
THIS BOOK SAYS THE BEST TIME TO PICK UP WOMEN IS WHILE WALKING A DOG.
LET'S TRY IT.
YO! BABY! WHOA WHOA! SHAKE IT, DON'T BREAK IT! COME AND GET YOUR SINGLE MALE!!
S.Adams 8-14
© 1989 United Feature Syndicate, Inc.
I THINK THIS METHOD IS OVERRATED.
FORM ONE LINE! NO PUSHING!

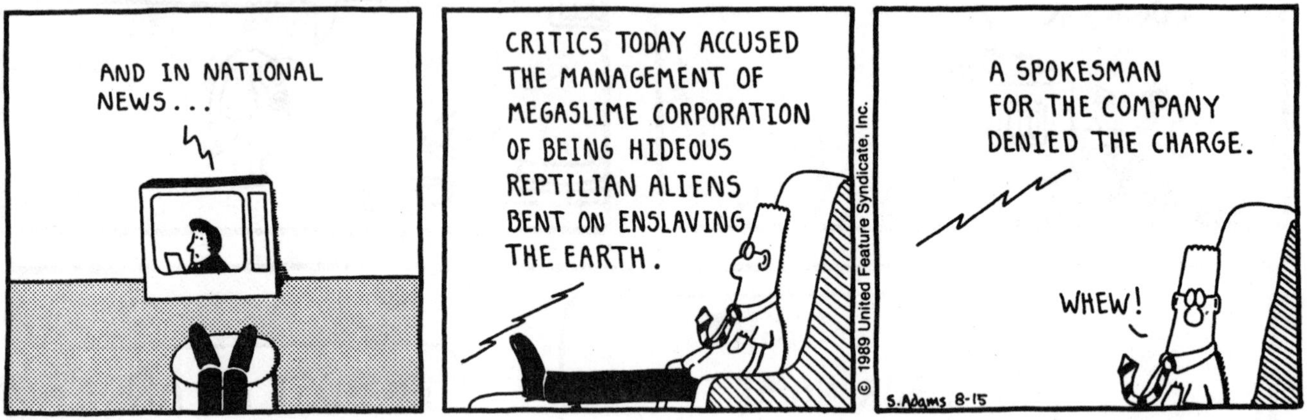
AND IN NATIONAL NEWS...
CRITICS TODAY ACCUSED THE MANAGEMENT OF MEGASLIME CORPORATION OF BEING HIDEOUS REPTILIAN ALIENS BENT ON ENSLAVING THE EARTH.
© 1989 United Feature Syndicate, Inc.
A SPOKESMAN FOR THE COMPANY DENIED THE CHARGE.
WHEW!
S.Adams 8-15

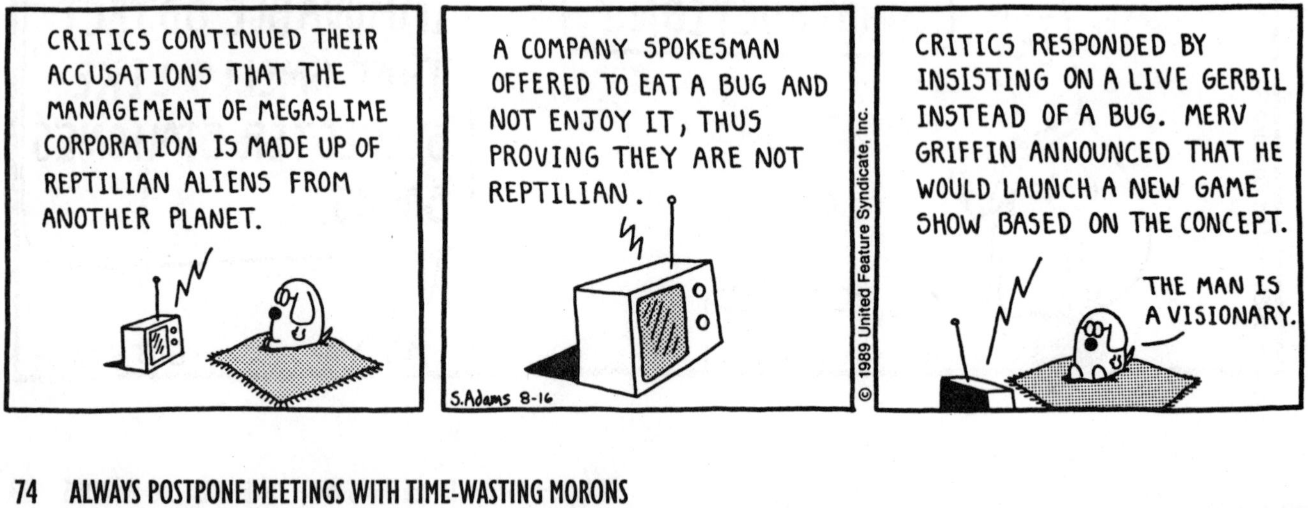
CRITICS CONTINUED THEIR ACCUSATIONS THAT THE MANAGEMENT OF MEGASLIME CORPORATION IS MADE UP OF REPTILIAN ALIENS FROM ANOTHER PLANET.
A COMPANY SPOKESMAN OFFERED TO EAT A BUG AND NOT ENJOY IT, THUS PROVING THEY ARE NOT REPTILIAN.
S.Adams 8-16
© 1989 United Feature Syndicate, Inc.
CRITICS RESPONDED BY INSISTING ON A LIVE GERBIL INSTEAD OF A BUG. MERV GRIFFIN ANNOUNCED THAT HE WOULD LAUNCH A NEW GAME SHOW BASED ON THE CONCEPT.
THE MAN IS A VISIONARY.

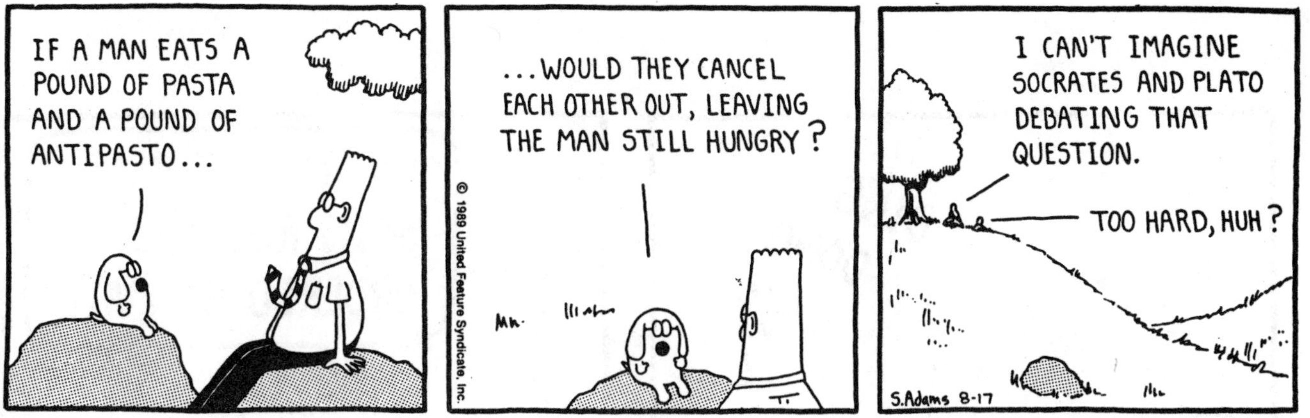
IF A MAN EATS A POUND OF PASTA AND A POUND OF ANTIPASTO...
...WOULD THEY CANCEL EACH OTHER OUT, LEAVING THE MAN STILL HUNGRY?
© 1989 United Feature Syndicate, Inc.
I CAN'T IMAGINE SOCRATES AND PLATO DEBATING THAT QUESTION.
TOO HARD, HUH?
S.Adams 8-17

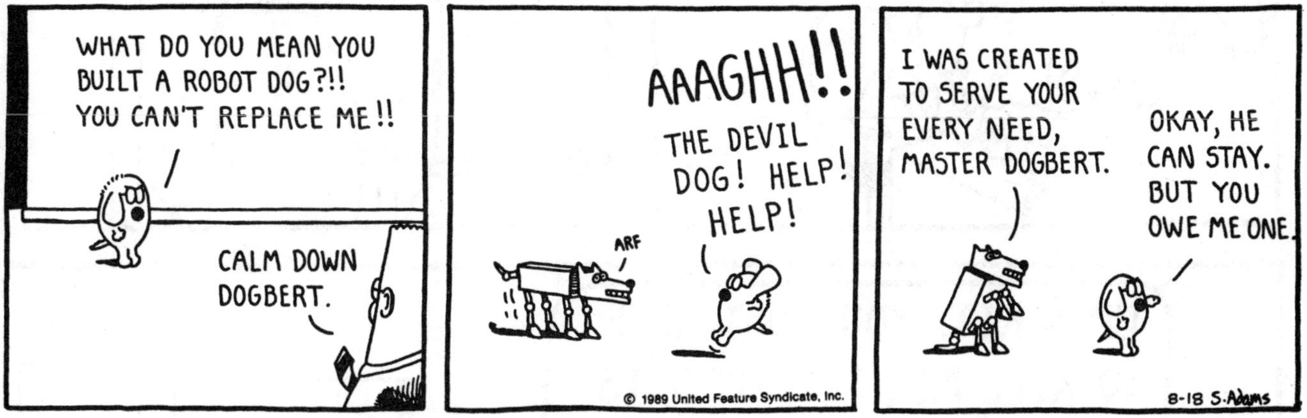
WHAT DO YOU MEAN YOU BUILT A ROBOT DOG?!! YOU CAN'T REPLACE ME!!
CALM DOWN DOGBERT.
AAAGHH!!
THE DEVIL DOG! HELP! HELP!
ARF
© 1989 United Feature Syndicate, Inc.
I WAS CREATED TO SERVE YOUR EVERY NEED, MASTER DOGBERT.
OKAY, HE CAN STAY. BUT YOU OWE ME ONE.
8-18 S.Adams

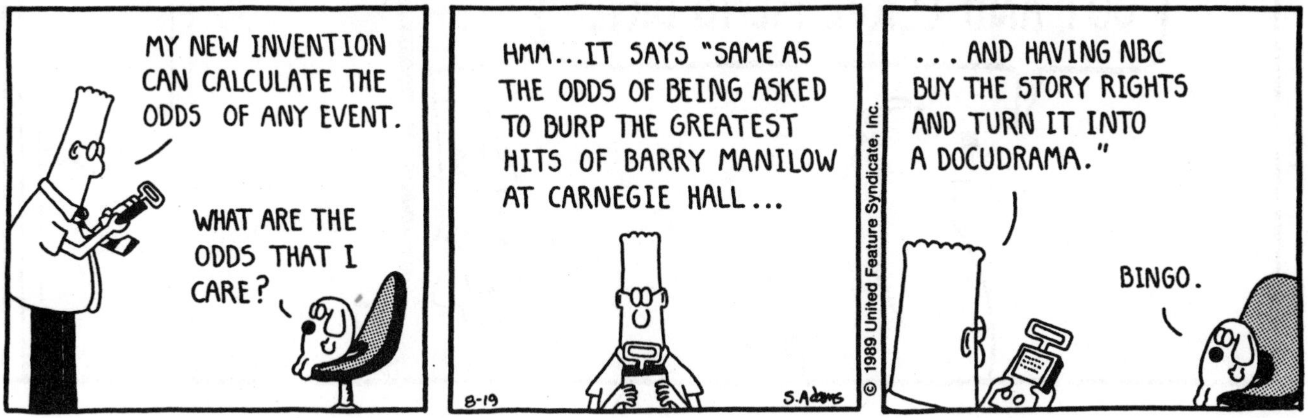
MY NEW INVENTION CAN CALCULATE THE ODDS OF ANY EVENT.
WHAT ARE THE ODDS THAT I CARE?
HMM...IT SAYS "SAME AS THE ODDS OF BEING ASKED TO BURP THE GREATEST HITS OF BARRY MANILOW AT CARNEGIE HALL...
8-19
S.Adams
© 1989 United Feature Syndicate, Inc.
...AND HAVING NBC BUY THE STORY RIGHTS AND TURN IT INTO A DOCUDRAMA."
BINGO.

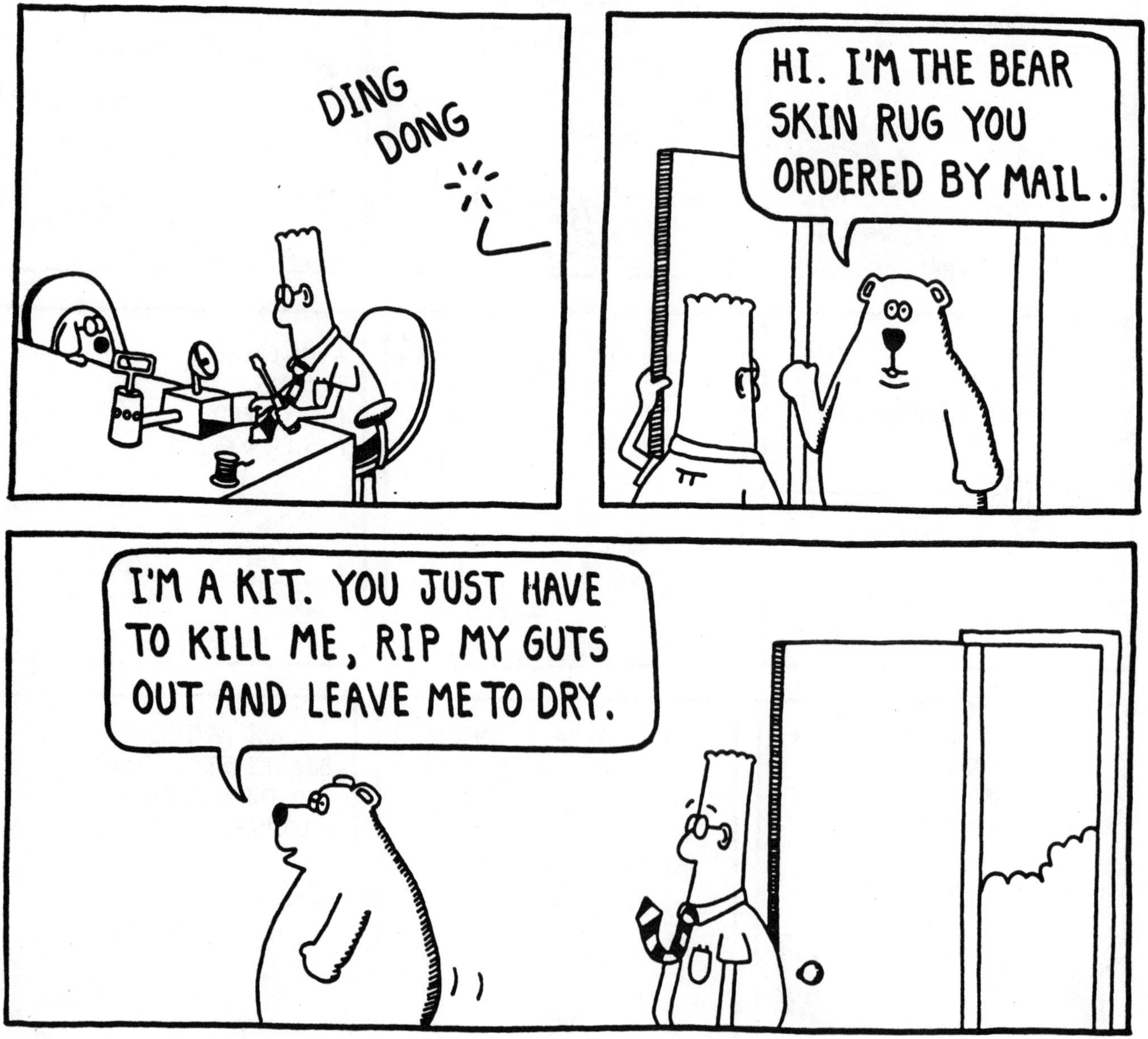
DING DONG
HI. I'M THE BEAR SKIN RUG YOU ORDERED BY MAIL.
I'M A KIT. YOU JUST HAVE TO KILL ME, RIP MY GUTS OUT AND LEAVE ME TO DRY.

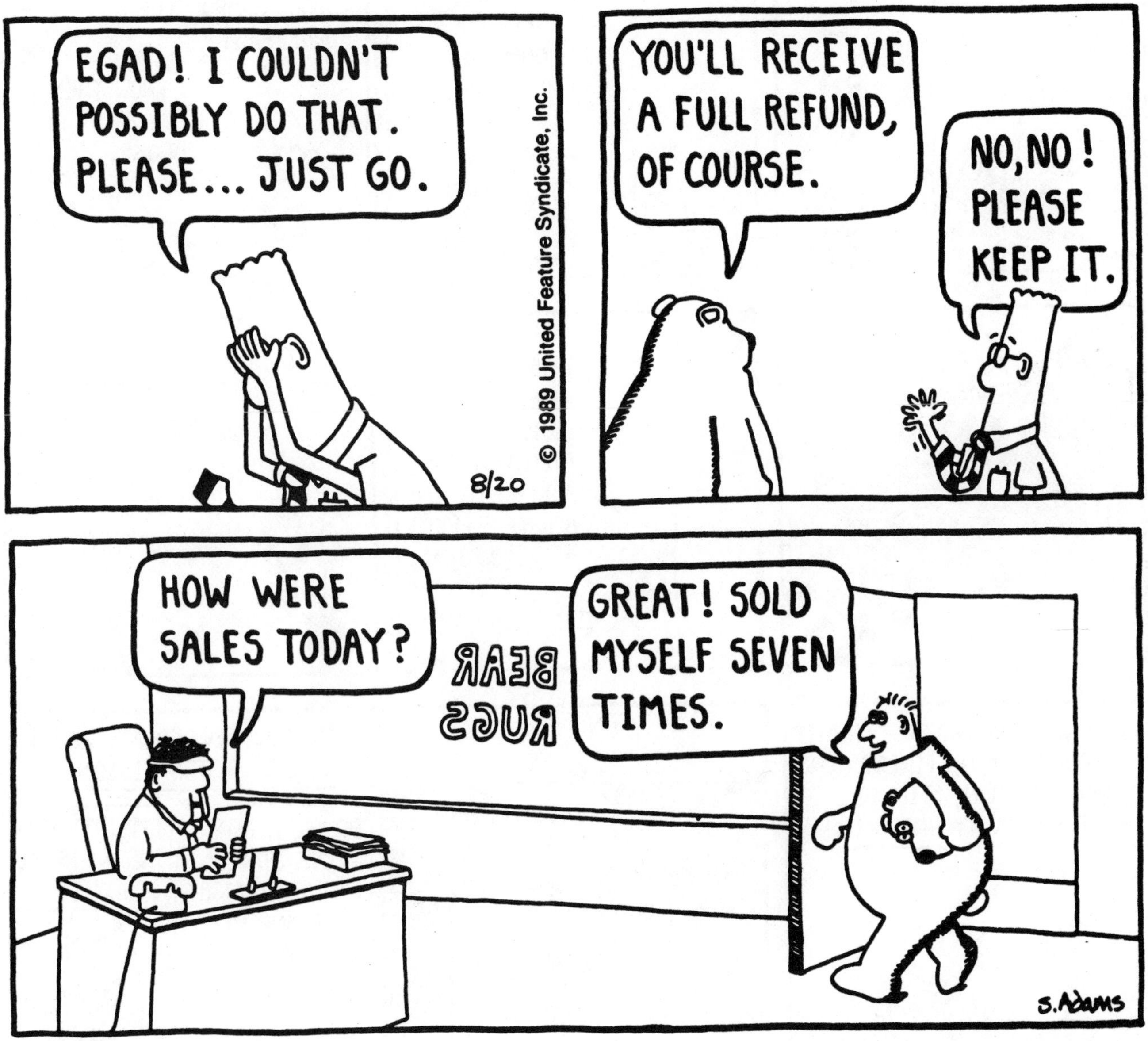
EGAD! I COULDN'T POSSIBLY DO THAT. PLEASE... JUST GO.
© 1989 United Feature Syndicate, Inc.
8/20
YOU'LL RECEIVE A FULL REFUND, OF COURSE.
NO, NO! PLEASE KEEP IT.
HOW WERE SALES TODAY?
BEAR RUGS
GREAT! SOLD MYSELF SEVEN TIMES.
S. Adams

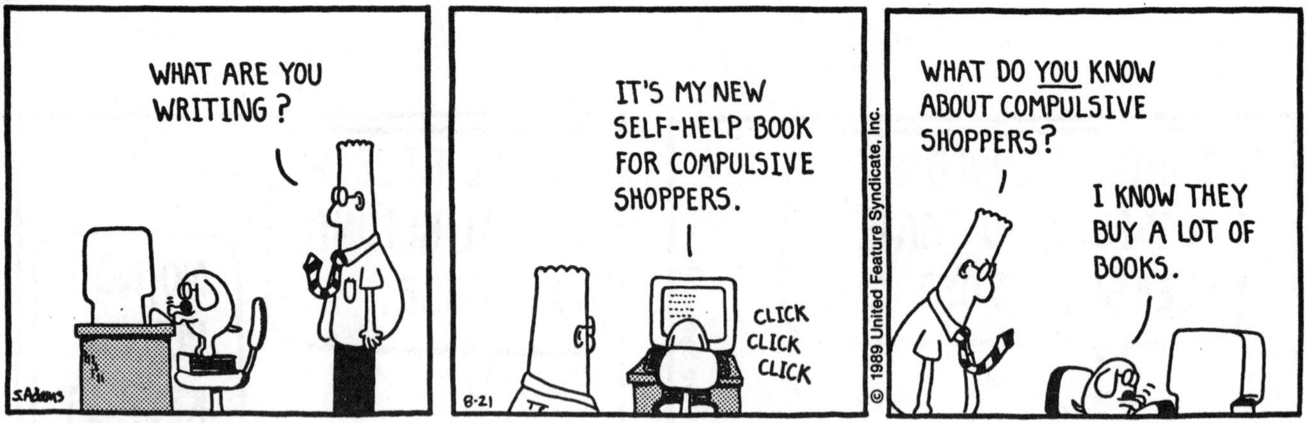
WHAT ARE YOU WRITING?
IT'S MY NEW SELF-HELP BOOK FOR COMPULSIVE SHOPPERS.
CLICK CLICK CLICK
WHAT DO YOU KNOW ABOUT COMPULSIVE SHOPPERS?
I KNOW THEY BUY A LOT OF BOOKS.
S.Adams
8-21
© 1989 United Feature Syndicate, Inc.

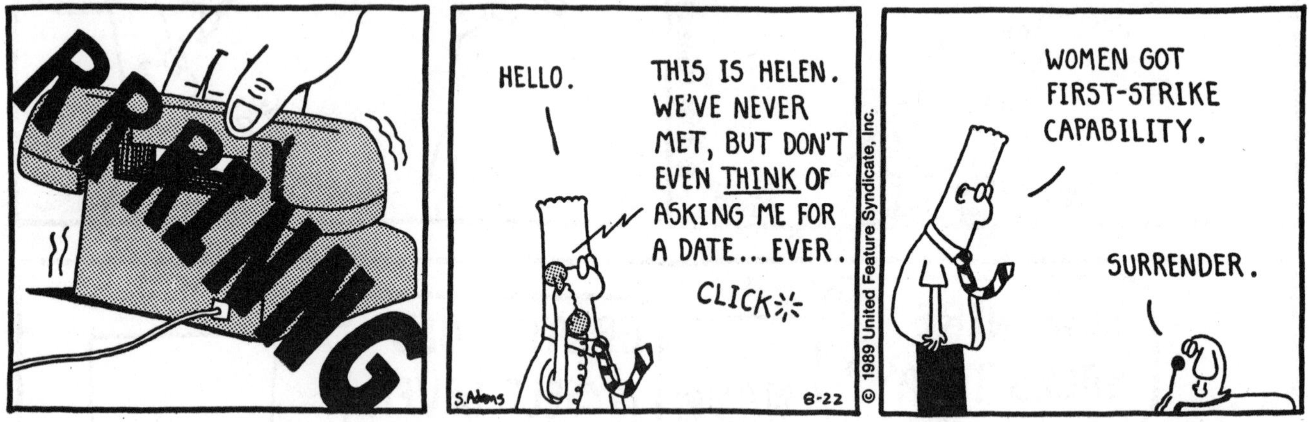
RRRINNG
HELLO.
THIS IS HELEN. WE'VE NEVER MET, BUT DON'T EVEN THINK OF ASKING ME FOR A DATE... EVER.
CLICK
WOMEN GOT FIRST-STRIKE CAPABILITY.
SURRENDER.
S.Adams
8-22
© 1989 United Feature Syndicate, Inc.

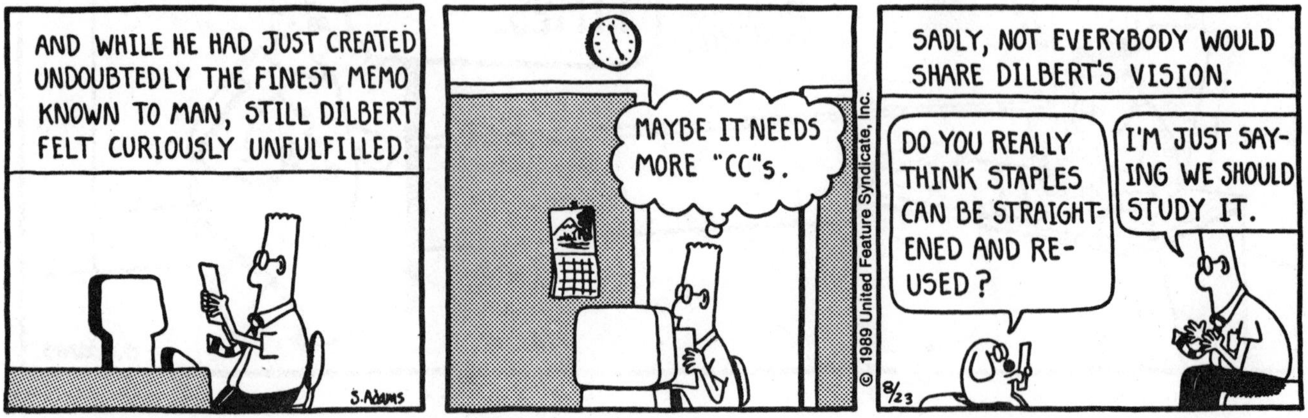
AND WHILE HE HAD JUST CREATED UNDOUBTEDLY THE FINEST MEMO KNOWN TO MAN, STILL DILBERT FELT CURIOUSLY UNFULFILLED.
MAYBE IT NEEDS MORE "CC"s.
SADLY, NOT EVERYBODY WOULD SHARE DILBERT'S VISION.
DO YOU REALLY THINK STAPLES CAN BE STRAIGHT-ENED AND RE-USED?
I'M JUST SAY-ING WE SHOULD STUDY IT.
S.Adams
8/23
© 1989 United Feature Syndicate, Inc.

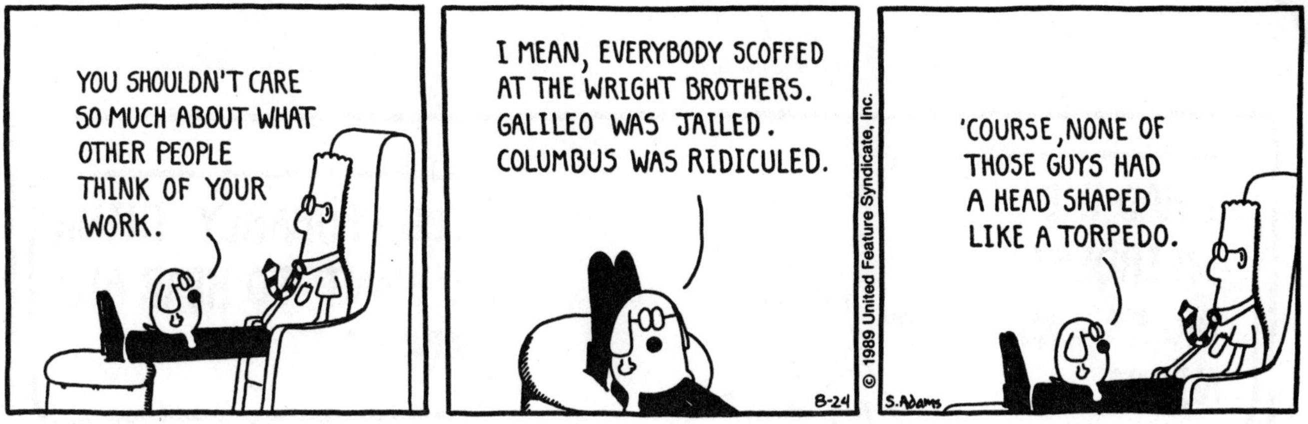
YOU SHOULDN'T CARE SO MUCH ABOUT WHAT OTHER PEOPLE THINK OF YOUR WORK.
I MEAN, EVERYBODY SCOFFED AT THE WRIGHT BROTHERS. GALILEO WAS JAILED. COLUMBUS WAS RIDICULED.
8-24
'COURSE, NONE OF THOSE GUYS HAD A HEAD SHAPED LIKE A TORPEDO.
S. Adams

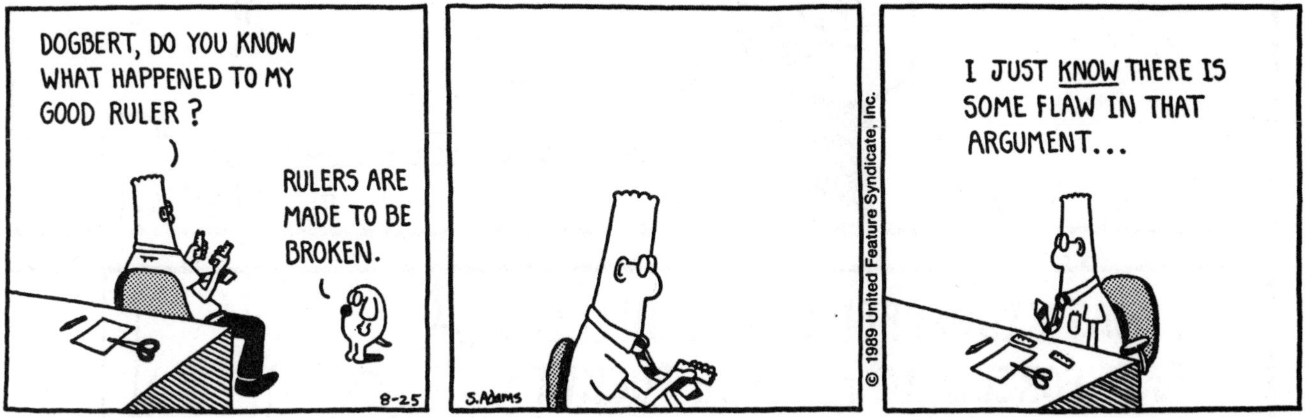
DOGBERT, DO YOU KNOW WHAT HAPPENED TO MY GOOD RULER?
RULERS ARE MADE TO BE BROKEN.
8-25
S. Adams
I JUST KNOW THERE IS SOME FLAW IN THAT ARGUMENT...

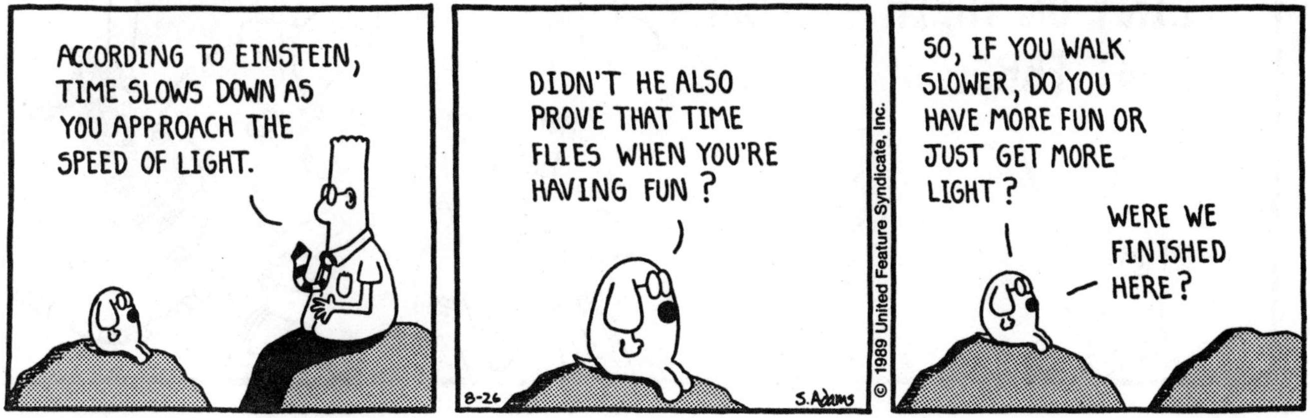
ACCORDING TO EINSTEIN, TIME SLOWS DOWN AS YOU APPROACH THE SPEED OF LIGHT.
DIDN'T HE ALSO PROVE THAT TIME FLIES WHEN YOU'RE HAVING FUN?
8-26
S. Adams
SO, IF YOU WALK SLOWER, DO YOU HAVE MORE FUN OR JUST GET MORE LIGHT?
WERE WE FINISHED HERE?

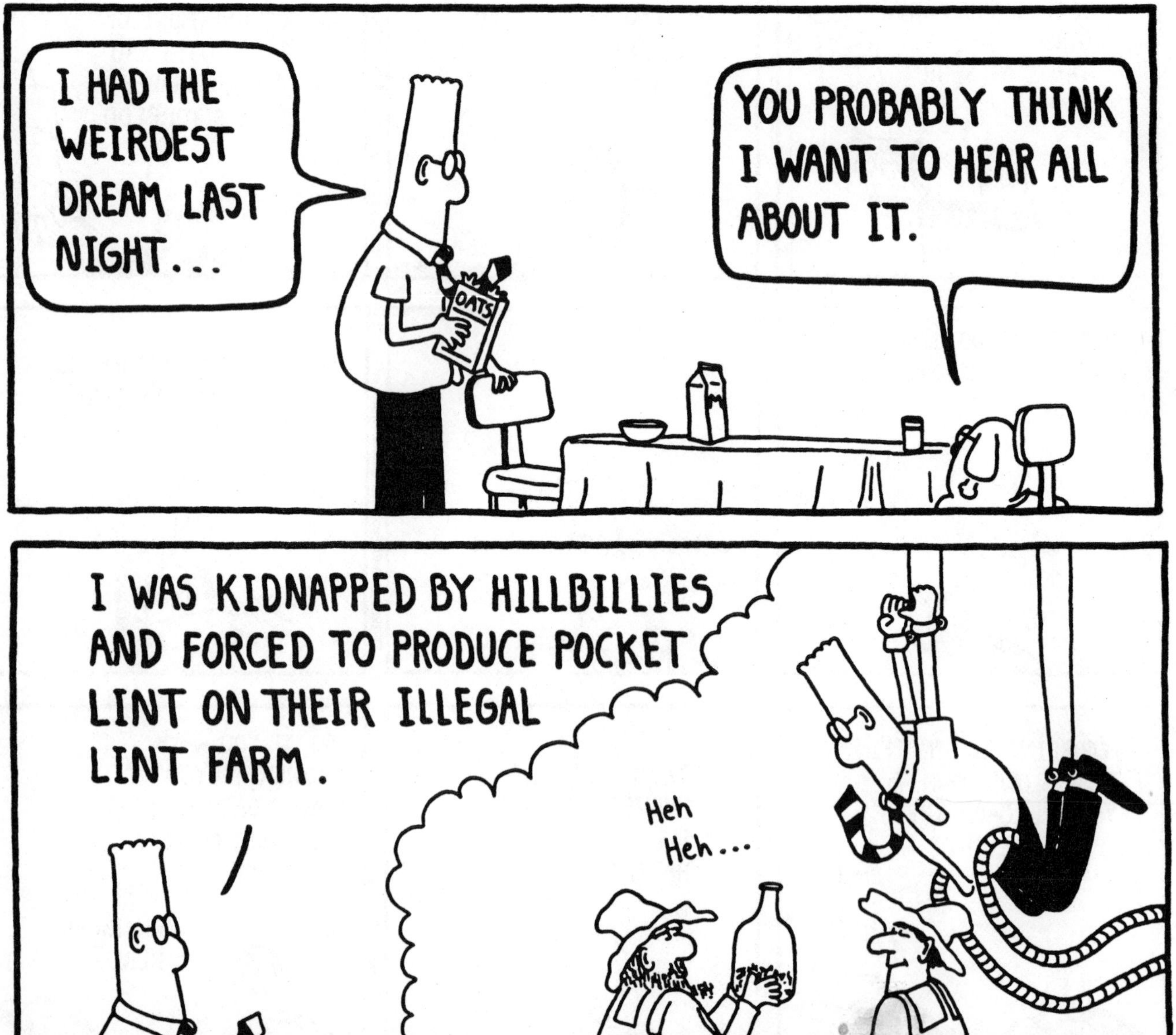
I HAD THE WEIRDEST DREAM LAST NIGHT...
OATS
YOU PROBABLY THINK I WANT TO HEAR ALL ABOUT IT.
I WAS KIDNAPPED BY HILLBILLIES AND FORCED TO PRODUCE POCKET LINT ON THEIR ILLEGAL LINT FARM.
Heh Heh...

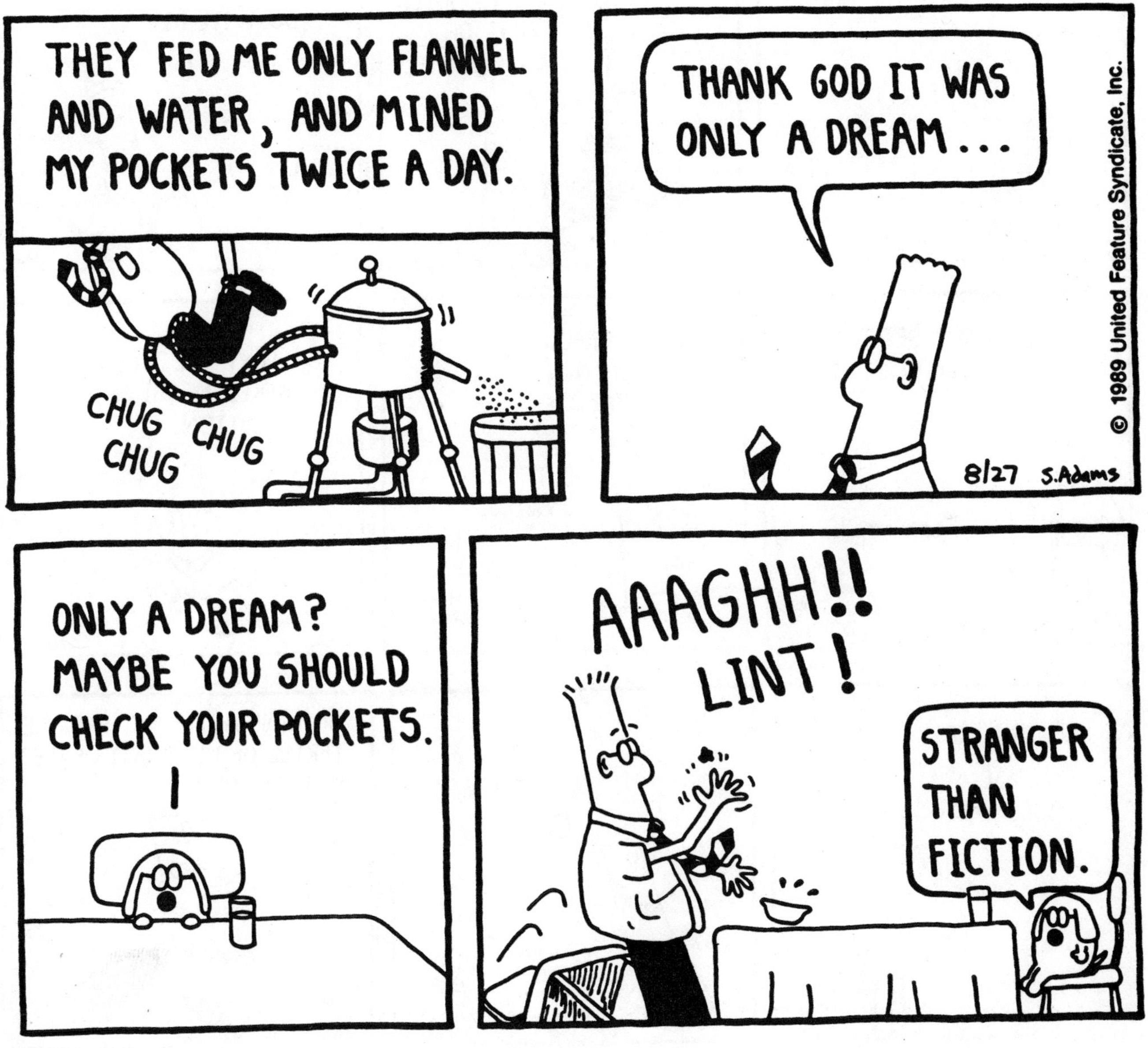
THEY FED ME ONLY FLANNEL AND WATER, AND MINED MY POCKETS TWICE A DAY.
CHUG CHUG CHUG
THANK GOD IT WAS ONLY A DREAM...
© 1989 United Feature Syndicate, Inc.
8/27 S.Adams
ONLY A DREAM? MAYBE YOU SHOULD CHECK YOUR POCKETS.
AAAGHH!! LINT!
STRANGER THAN FICTION.

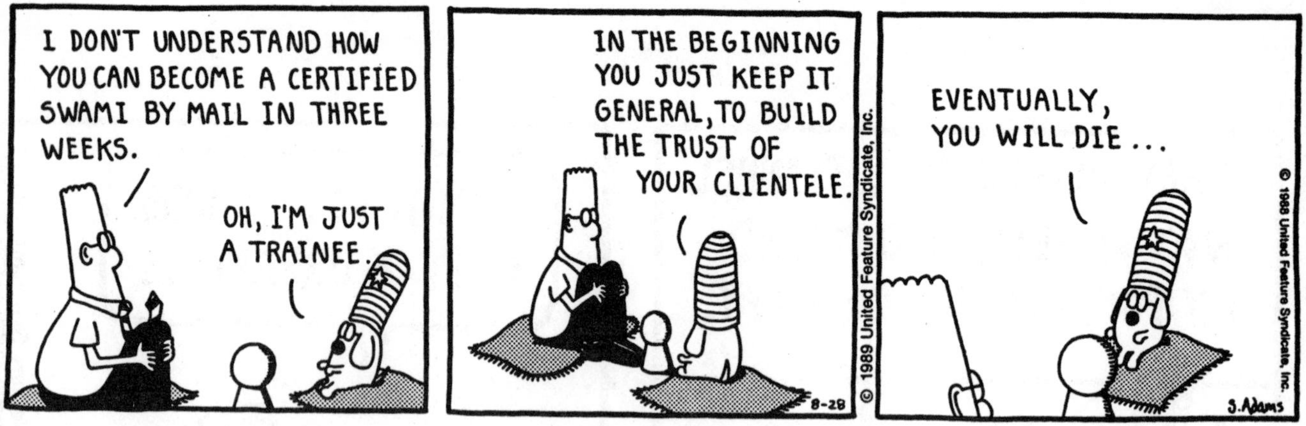
I DON'T UNDERSTAND HOW YOU CAN BECOME A CERTIFIED SWAMI BY MAIL IN THREE WEEKS.
OH, I'M JUST A TRAINEE.
IN THE BEGINNING YOU JUST KEEP IT GENERAL, TO BUILD THE TRUST OF YOUR CLIENTELE.
8-28
© 1989 United Feature Syndicate, Inc.
EVENTUALLY, YOU WILL DIE ...
© 1988 United Feature Syndicate, Inc.
S. Adams

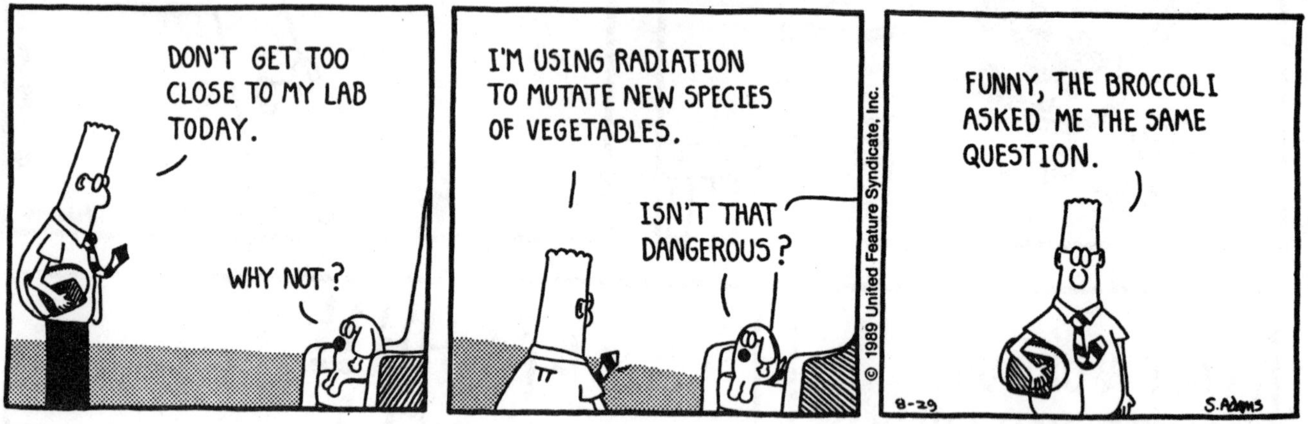
DON'T GET TOO CLOSE TO MY LAB TODAY.
WHY NOT?
I'M USING RADIATION TO MUTATE NEW SPECIES OF VEGETABLES.
ISN'T THAT DANGEROUS?
© 1989 United Feature Syndicate, Inc.
FUNNY, THE BROCCOLI ASKED ME THE SAME QUESTION.
8-29
S. Adams

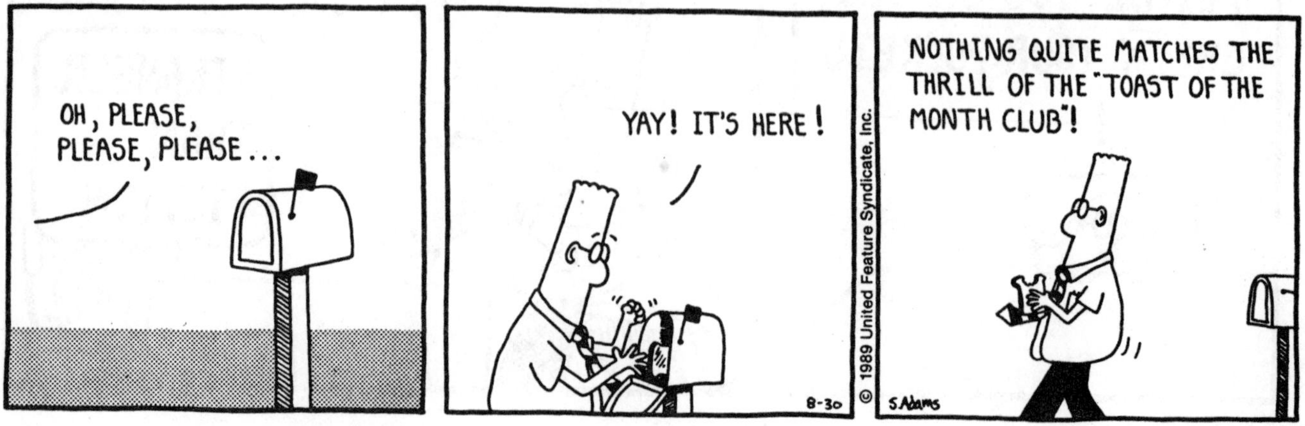
OH, PLEASE, PLEASE, PLEASE ...
YAY! IT'S HERE!
8-30
© 1989 United Feature Syndicate, Inc.
NOTHING QUITE MATCHES THE THRILL OF THE "TOAST OF THE MONTH CLUB"!
S. Adams

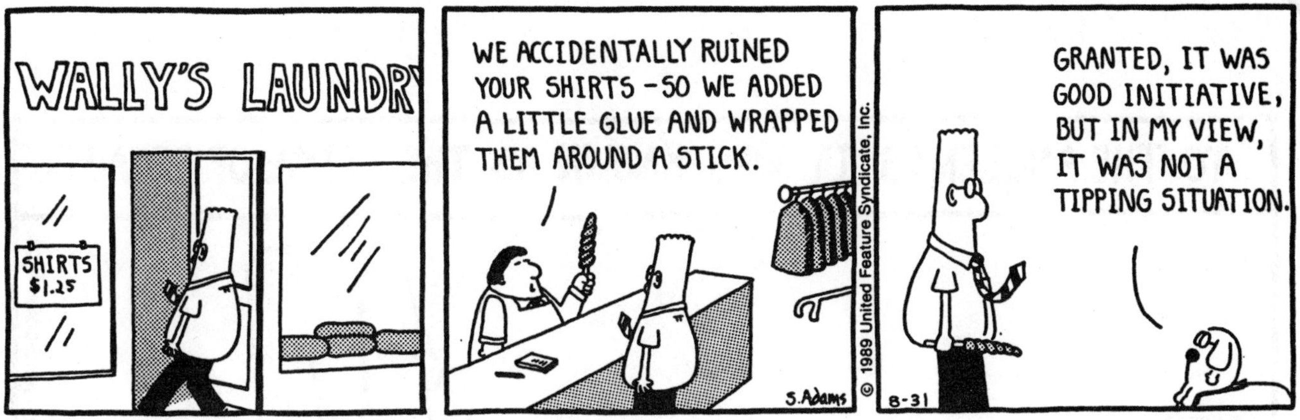
WALLY'S LAUNDRY
SHIRTS $1.25
WE ACCIDENTALLY RUINED YOUR SHIRTS – SO WE ADDED A LITTLE GLUE AND WRAPPED THEM AROUND A STICK.
S.Adams
© 1989 United Feature Syndicate, Inc.
GRANTED, IT WAS GOOD INITIATIVE, BUT IN MY VIEW, IT WAS NOT A TIPPING SITUATION.
8-31

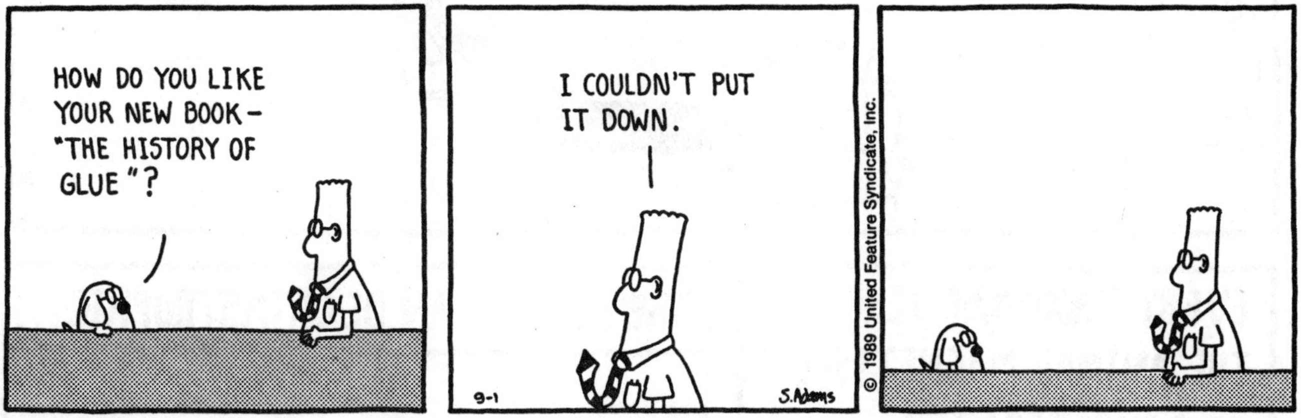
HOW DO YOU LIKE YOUR NEW BOOK – "THE HISTORY OF GLUE"?
I COULDN'T PUT IT DOWN.
9-1
S.Adams
© 1989 United Feature Syndicate, Inc.

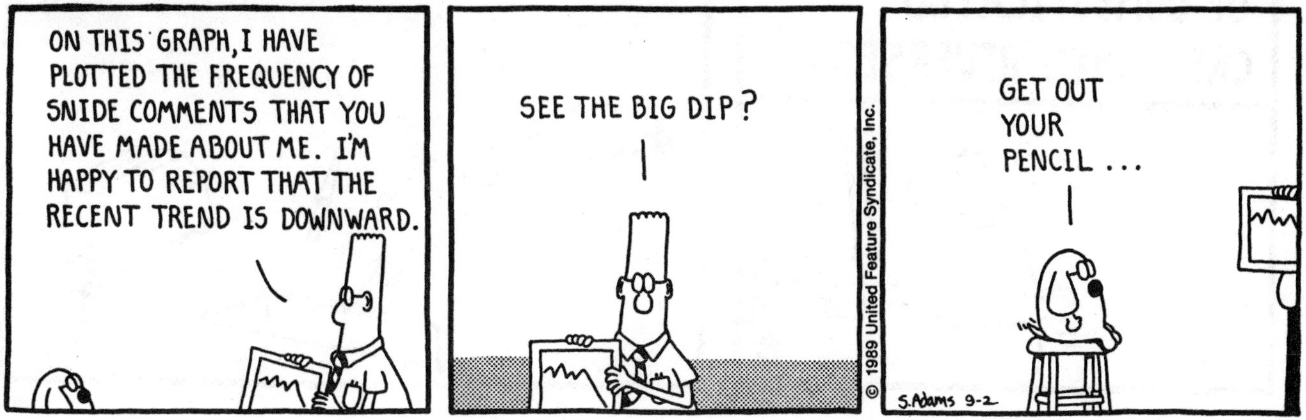
ON THIS GRAPH, I HAVE PLOTTED THE FREQUENCY OF SNIDE COMMENTS THAT YOU HAVE MADE ABOUT ME. I'M HAPPY TO REPORT THAT THE RECENT TREND IS DOWNWARD.
SEE THE BIG DIP?
© 1989 United Feature Syndicate, Inc.
GET OUT YOUR PENCIL ...
S.Adams 9-2

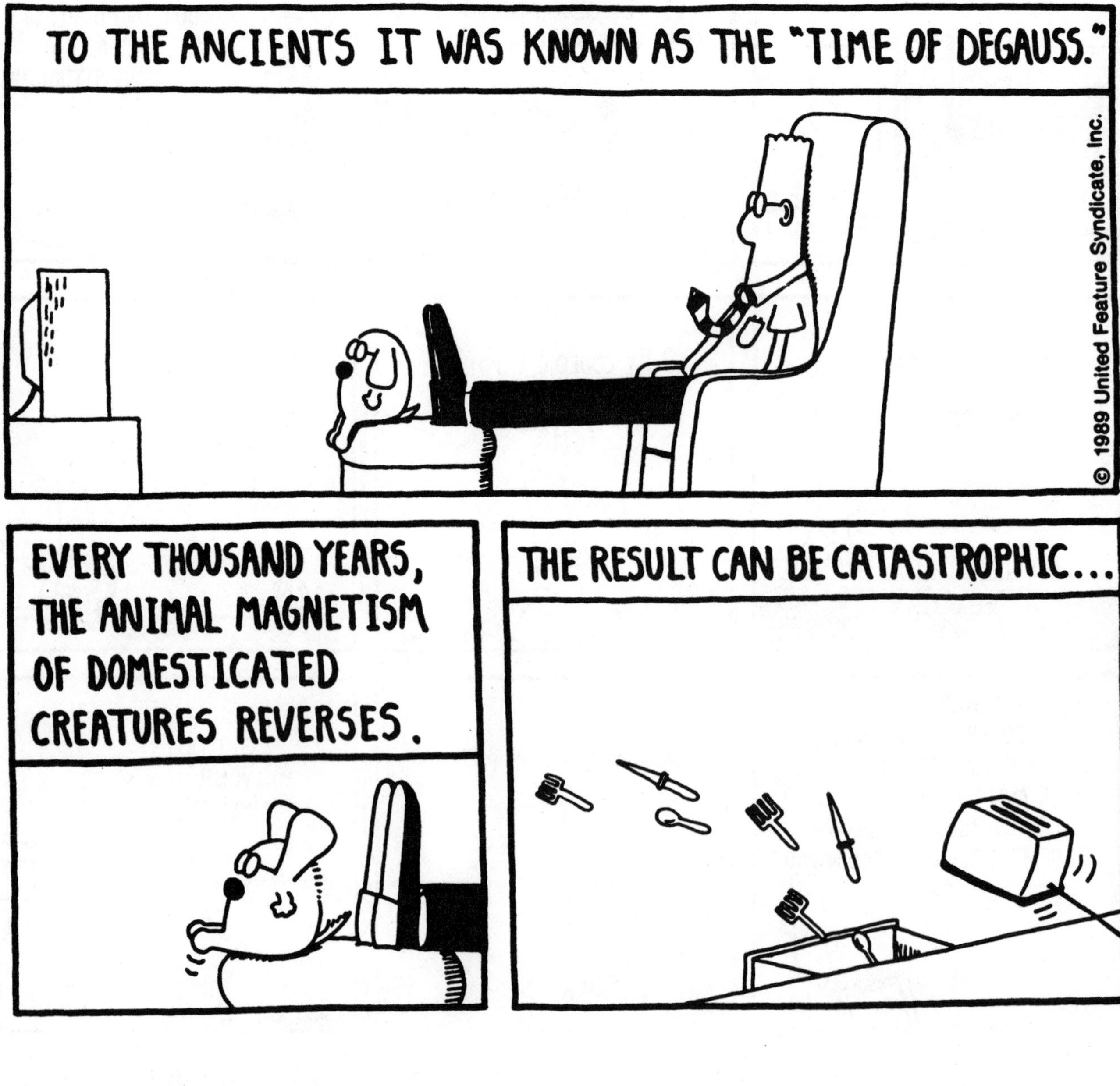
TO THE ANCIENTS IT WAS KNOWN AS THE "TIME OF DEGAUSS."
© 1989 United Feature Syndicate, Inc.
EVERY THOUSAND YEARS, THE ANIMAL MAGNETISM OF DOMESTICATED CREATURES REVERSES.
THE RESULT CAN BE CATASTROPHIC...

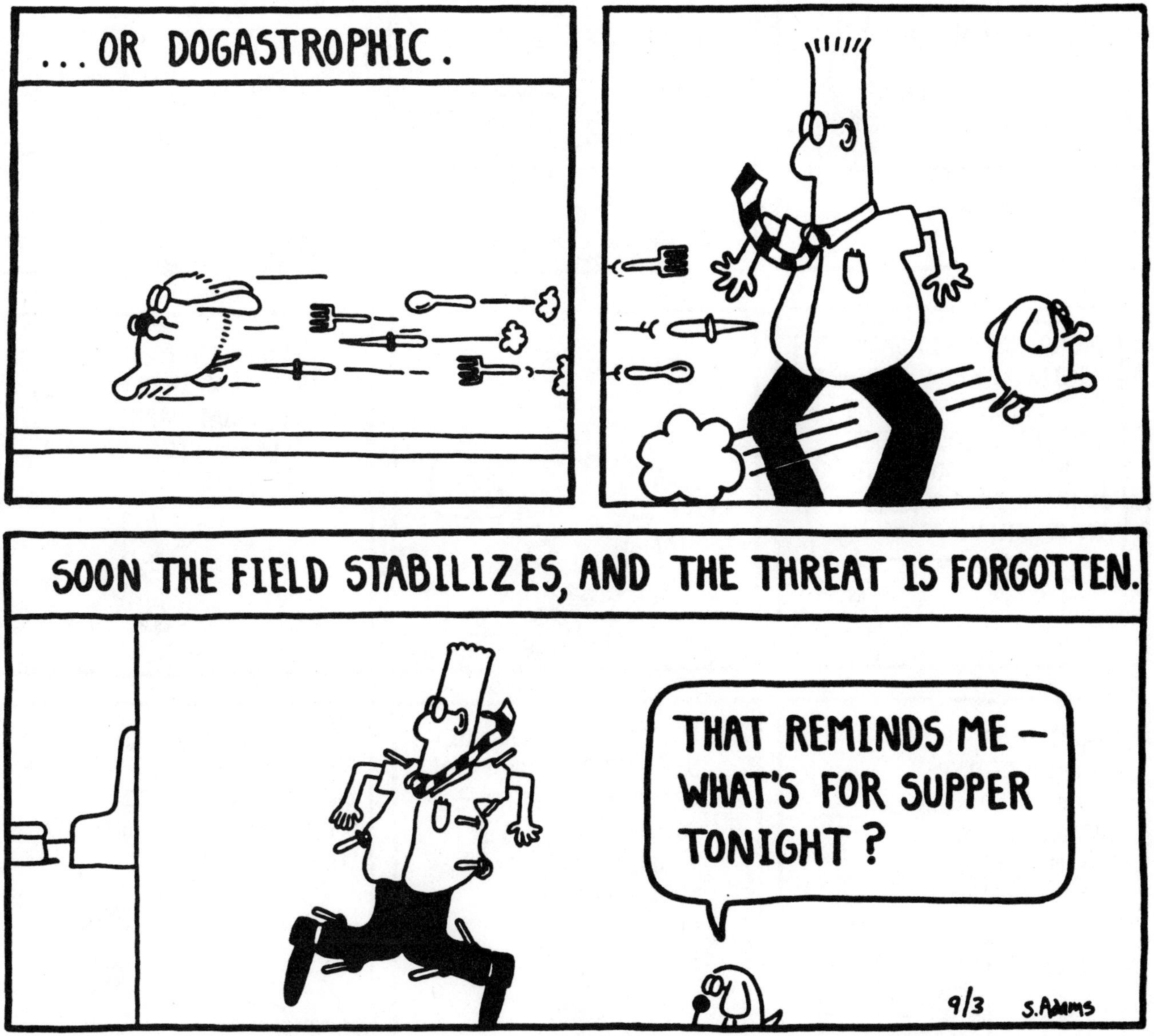
....OR DOGASTROPHIC.
SOON THE FIELD STABILIZES, AND THE THREAT IS FORGOTTEN.
THAT REMINDS ME — WHAT'S FOR SUPPER TONIGHT?
9/3 S.Adams

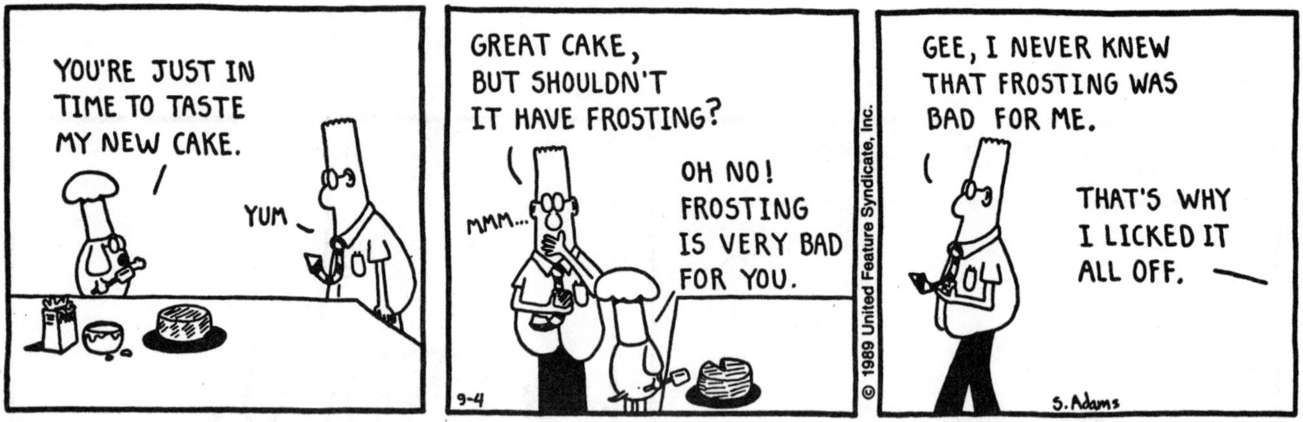
YOU'RE JUST IN TIME TO TASTE MY NEW CAKE.
YUM
GREAT CAKE, BUT SHOULDN'T IT HAVE FROSTING?
MMM...
OH NO! FROSTING IS VERY BAD FOR YOU.
9-4
© 1989 United Feature Syndicate, Inc.
GEE, I NEVER KNEW THAT FROSTING WAS BAD FOR ME.
THAT'S WHY I LICKED IT ALL OFF.
S. Adams

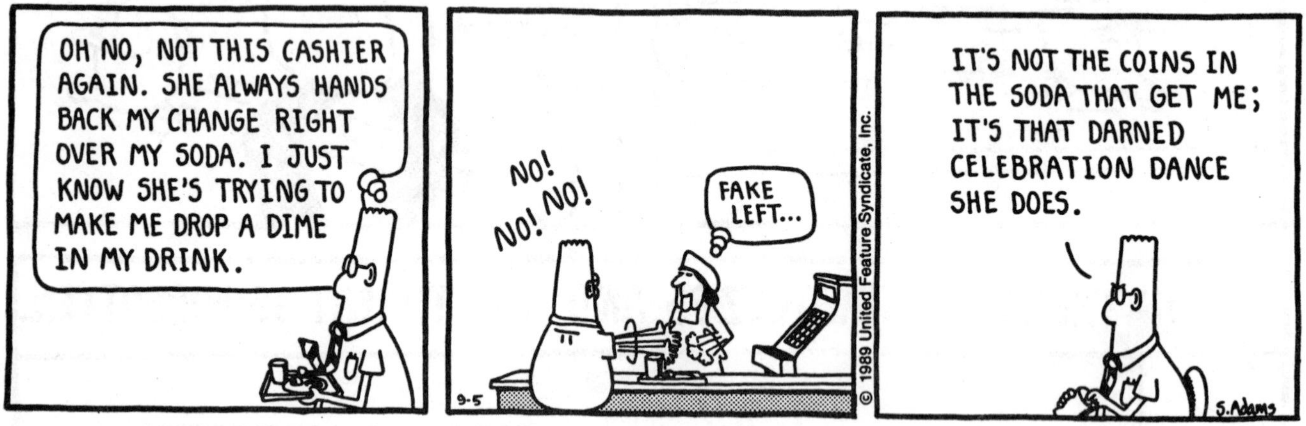
OH NO, NOT THIS CASHIER AGAIN. SHE ALWAYS HANDS BACK MY CHANGE RIGHT OVER MY SODA. I JUST KNOW SHE'S TRYING TO MAKE ME DROP A DIME IN MY DRINK.
NO! NO! NO!
FAKE LEFT...
9-5
© 1989 United Feature Syndicate, Inc.
IT'S NOT THE COINS IN THE SODA THAT GET ME; IT'S THAT DARNED CELEBRATION DANCE SHE DOES.
S. Adams

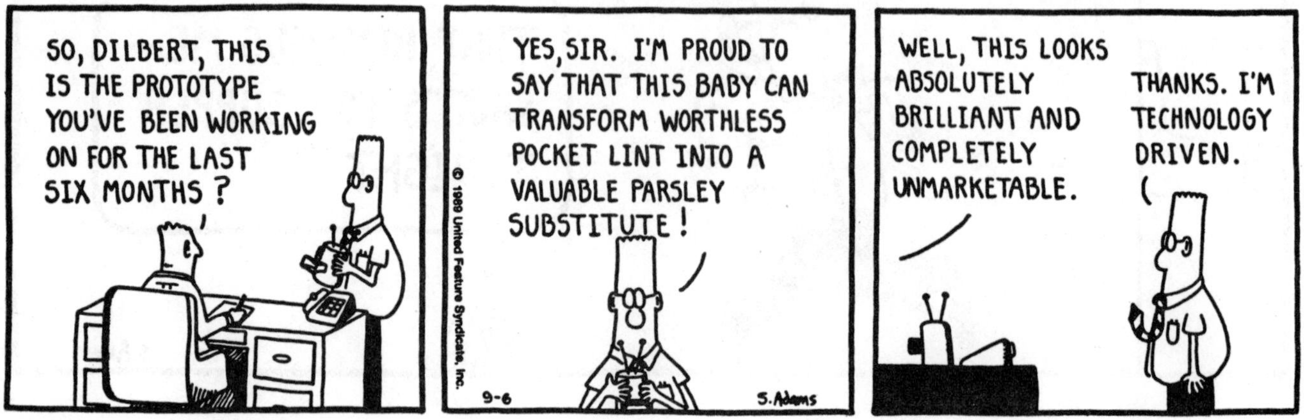
SO, DILBERT, THIS IS THE PROTOTYPE YOU'VE BEEN WORKING ON FOR THE LAST SIX MONTHS?
© 1989 United Feature Syndicate, Inc.
YES, SIR. I'M PROUD TO SAY THAT THIS BABY CAN TRANSFORM WORTHLESS POCKET LINT INTO A VALUABLE PARSLEY SUBSTITUTE!
9-6
S. Adams
WELL, THIS LOOKS ABSOLUTELY BRILLIANT AND COMPLETELY UNMARKETABLE.
THANKS. I'M TECHNOLOGY DRIVEN.

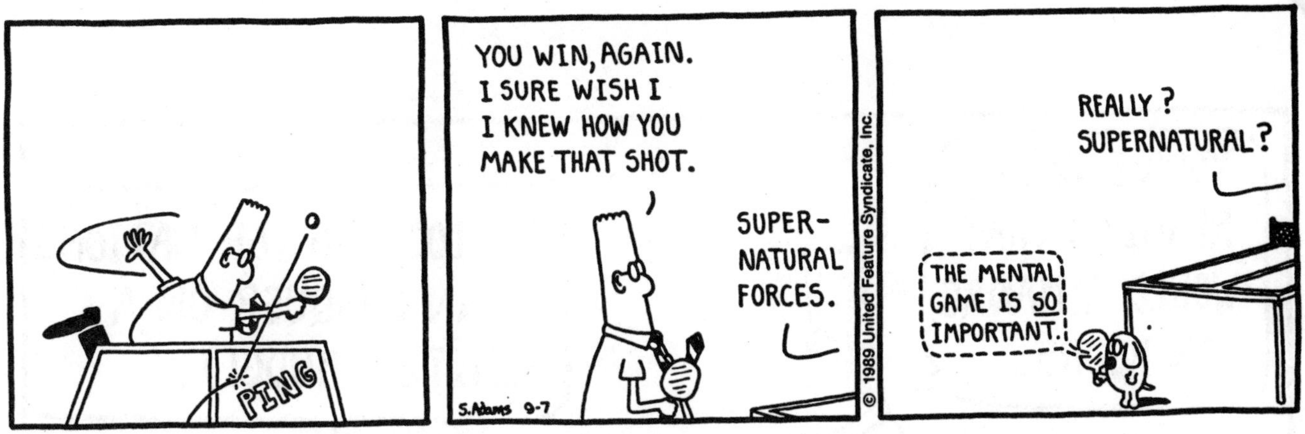
PING
YOU WIN, AGAIN. I SURE WISH I I KNEW HOW YOU MAKE THAT SHOT.
SUPER-NATURAL FORCES.
S.Adams 9-7
© 1989 United Feature Syndicate, Inc.
THE MENTAL GAME IS SO IMPORTANT.
REALLY? SUPERNATURAL?

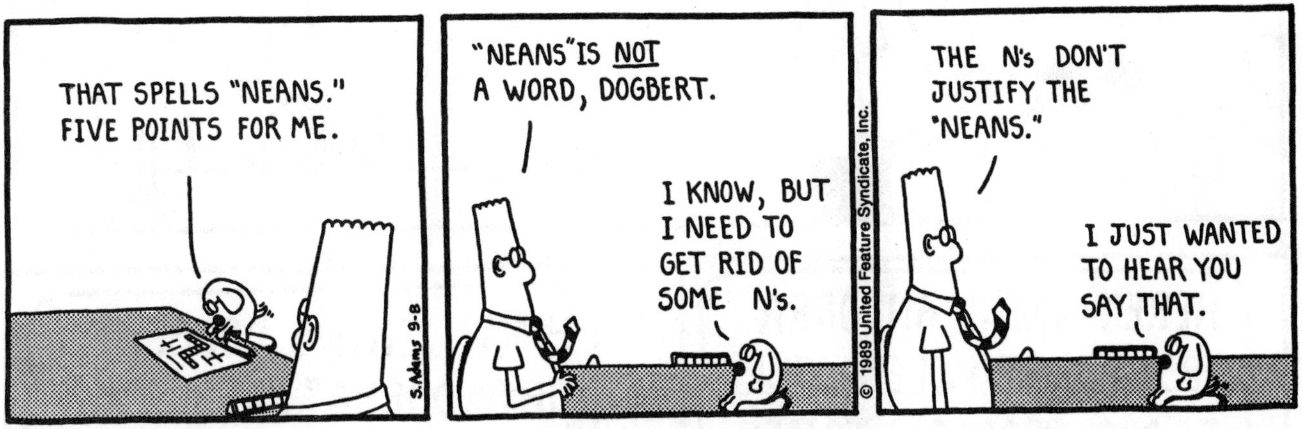
THAT SPELLS "NEANS." FIVE POINTS FOR ME.
S.Adams 9-8
"NEANS" IS NOT A WORD, DOGBERT.
I KNOW, BUT I NEED TO GET RID OF SOME N's.
© 1989 United Feature Syndicate, Inc.
THE N's DON'T JUSTIFY THE "NEANS."
I JUST WANTED TO HEAR YOU SAY THAT.

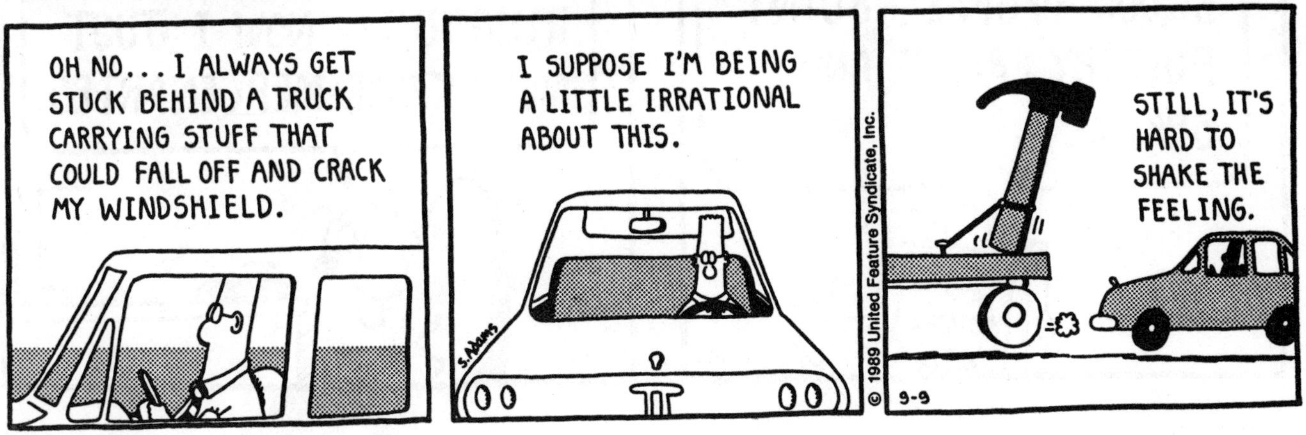
OH NO... I ALWAYS GET STUCK BEHIND A TRUCK CARRYING STUFF THAT COULD FALL OFF AND CRACK MY WINDSHIELD.
I SUPPOSE I'M BEING A LITTLE IRRATIONAL ABOUT THIS.
S.Adams
© 1989 United Feature Syndicate, Inc.
STILL, IT'S HARD TO SHAKE THE FEELING.
9-9

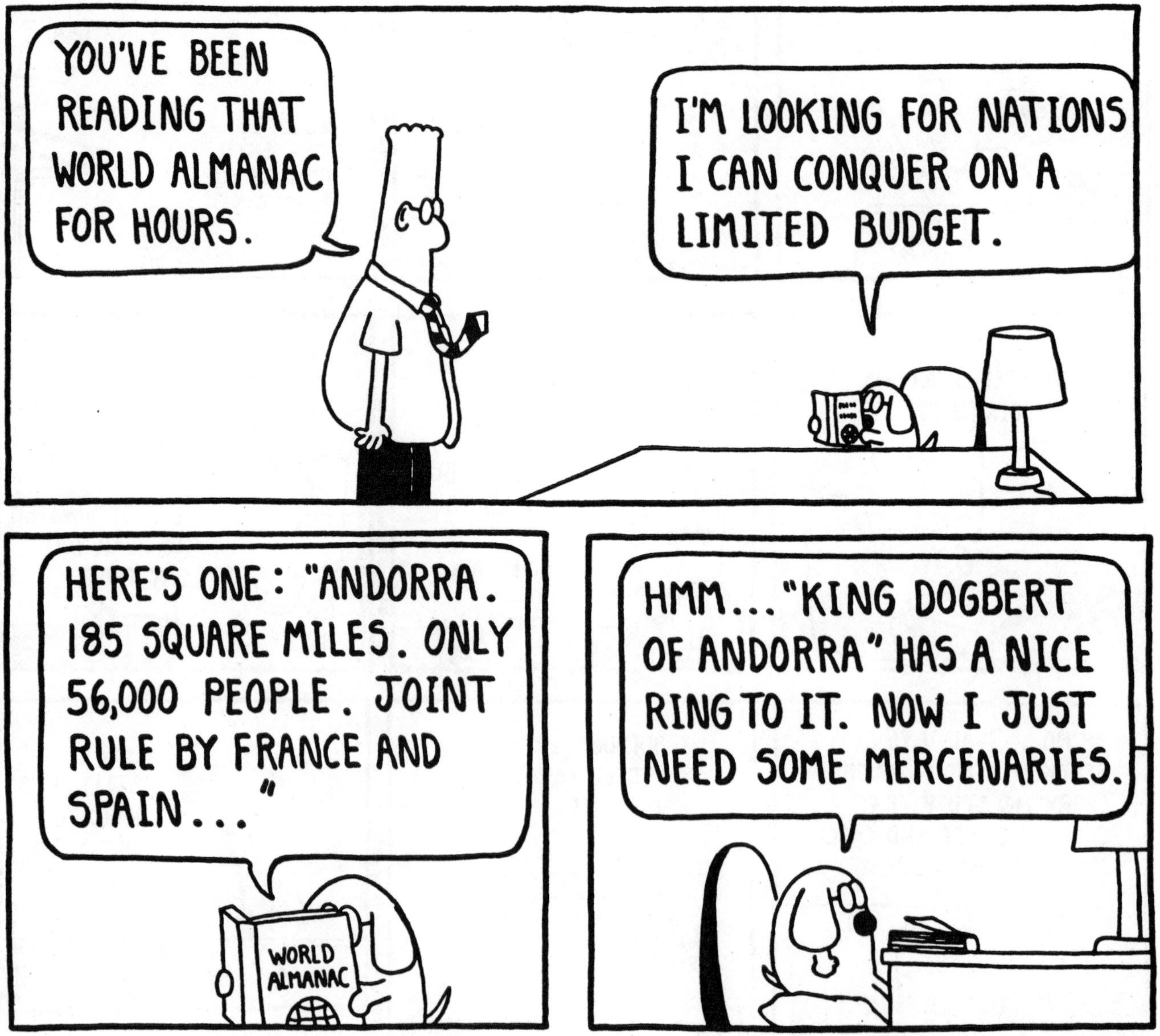
YOU'VE BEEN READING THAT WORLD ALMANAC FOR HOURS.
I'M LOOKING FOR NATIONS I CAN CONQUER ON A LIMITED BUDGET.
HERE'S ONE: "ANDORRA. 185 SQUARE MILES. ONLY 56,000 PEOPLE. JOINT RULE BY FRANCE AND SPAIN..."
WORLD ALMANAC
HMM... "KING DOGBERT OF ANDORRA" HAS A NICE RING TO IT. NOW I JUST NEED SOME MERCENARIES.

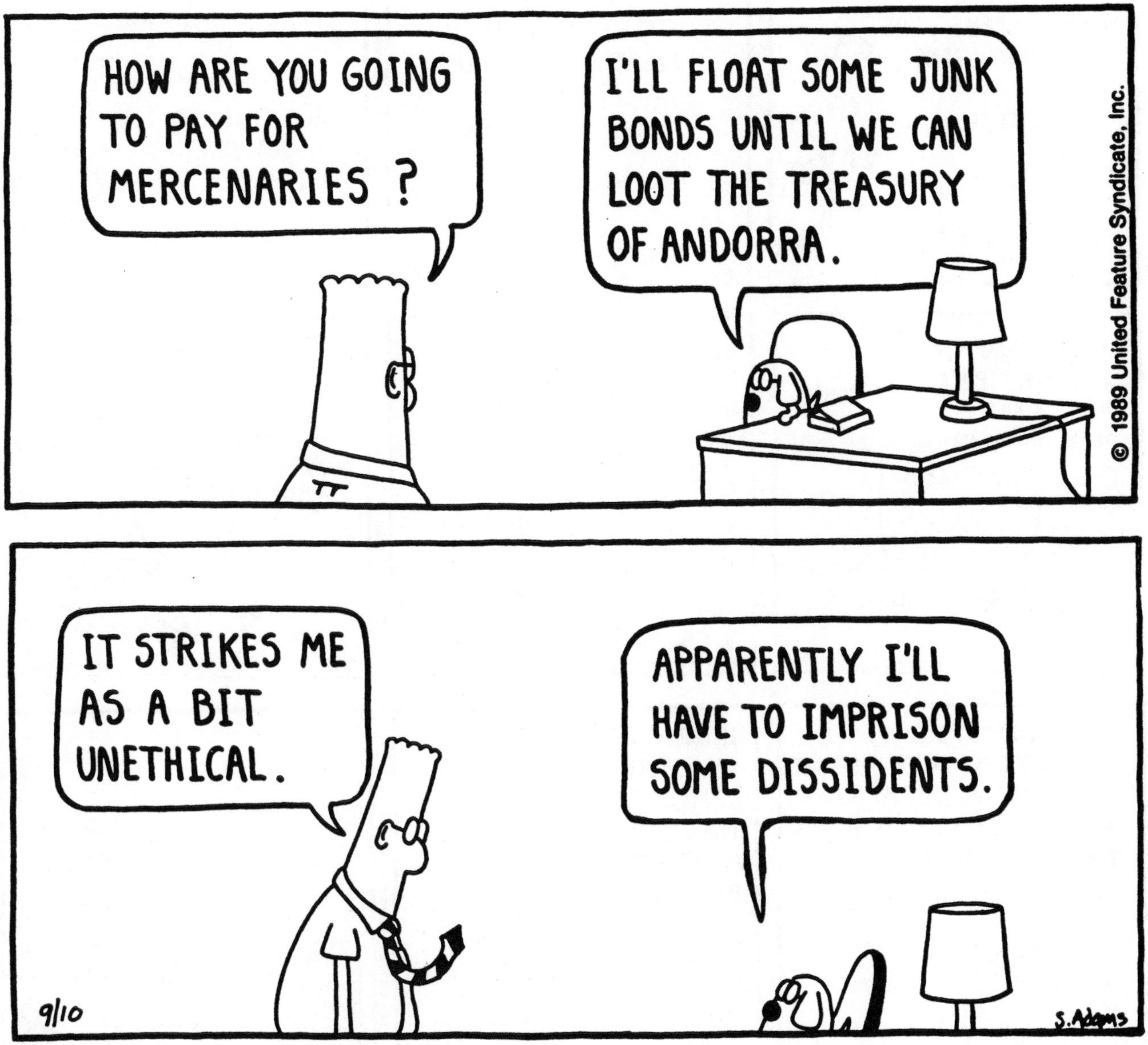
HOW ARE YOU GOING TO PAY FOR MERCENARIES ?
I'LL FLOAT SOME JUNK BONDS UNTIL WE CAN LOOT THE TREASURY OF ANDORRA.
© 1989 United Feature Syndicate, Inc.
IT STRIKES ME AS A BIT UNETHICAL.
APPARENTLY I'LL HAVE TO IMPRISON SOME DISSIDENTS.
9/10
S. Adams

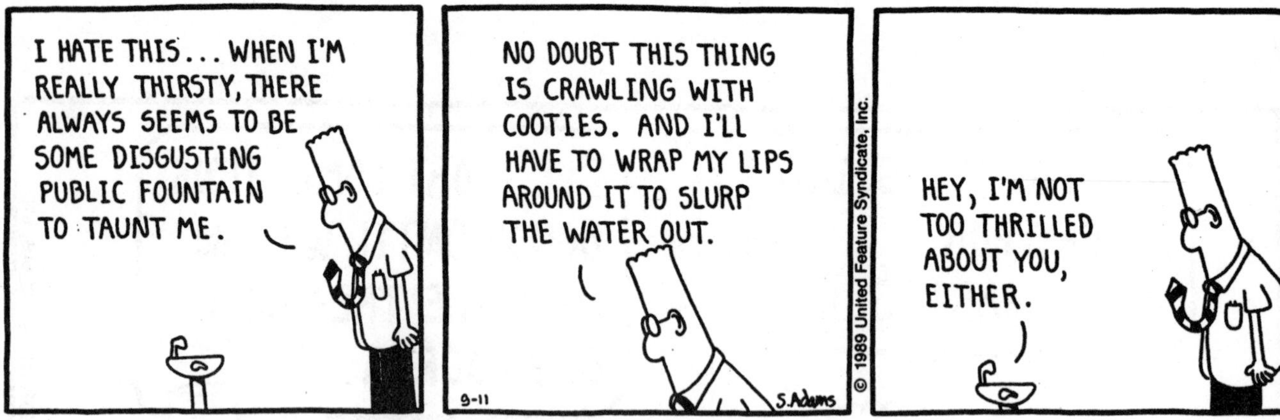
I HATE THIS... WHEN I'M REALLY THIRSTY, THERE ALWAYS SEEMS TO BE SOME DISGUSTING PUBLIC FOUNTAIN TO TAUNT ME.
NO DOUBT THIS THING IS CRAWLING WITH COOTIES. AND I'LL HAVE TO WRAP MY LIPS AROUND IT TO SLURP THE WATER OUT.
9-11
S. Adams
© 1989 United Feature Syndicate, Inc.
HEY, I'M NOT TOO THRILLED ABOUT YOU, EITHER.

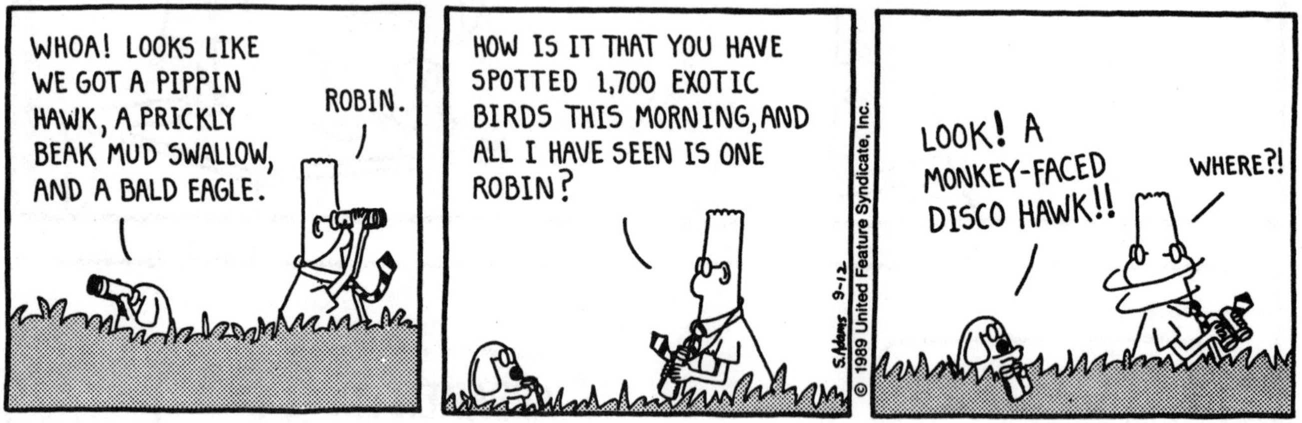
WHOA! LOOKS LIKE WE GOT A PIPPIN HAWK, A PRICKLY BEAK MUD SWALLOW, AND A BALD EAGLE.
ROBIN.
HOW IS IT THAT YOU HAVE SPOTTED 1,700 EXOTIC BIRDS THIS MORNING, AND ALL I HAVE SEEN IS ONE ROBIN?
S. Adams 9-12
© 1989 United Feature Syndicate, Inc.
LOOK! A MONKEY-FACED DISCO HAWK!!
WHERE?!

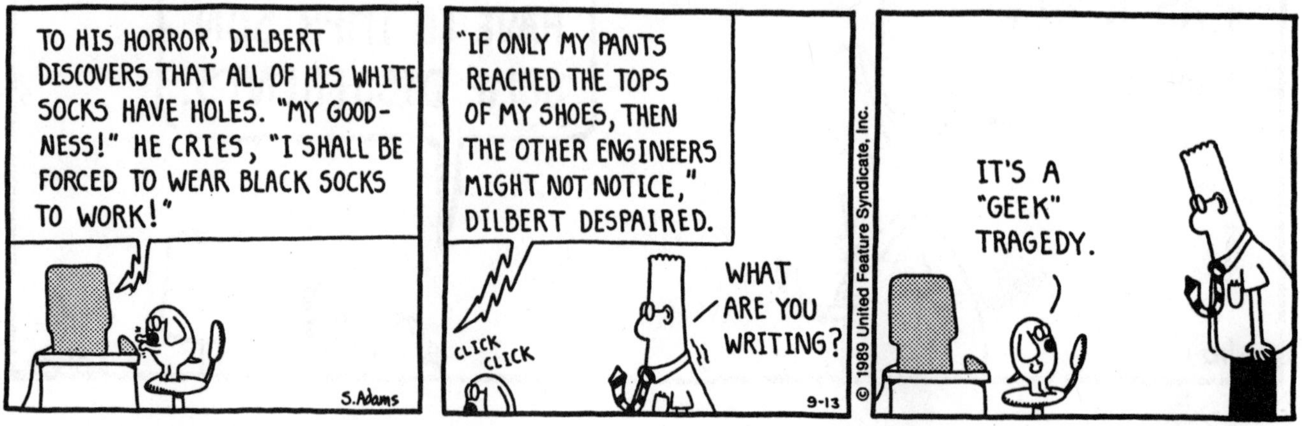
TO HIS HORROR, DILBERT DISCOVERS THAT ALL OF HIS WHITE SOCKS HAVE HOLES. "MY GOODNESS!" HE CRIES, "I SHALL BE FORCED TO WEAR BLACK SOCKS TO WORK!"
S. Adams
"IF ONLY MY PANTS REACHED THE TOPS OF MY SHOES, THEN THE OTHER ENGINEERS MIGHT NOT NOTICE," DILBERT DESPAIRED.
CLICK CLICK
WHAT ARE YOU WRITING?
9-13
© 1989 United Feature Syndicate, Inc.
IT'S A "GEEK" TRAGEDY.

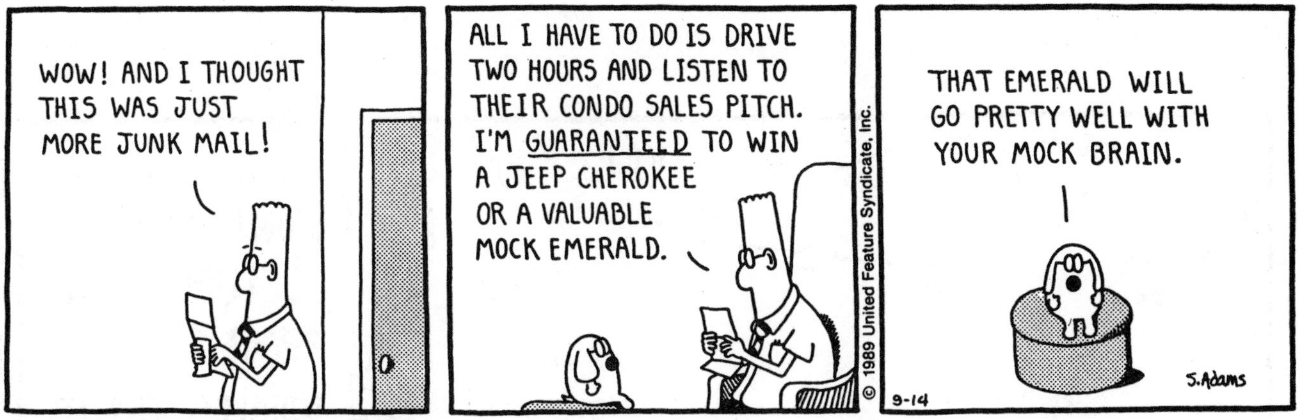
WOW! AND I THOUGHT THIS WAS JUST MORE JUNK MAIL!
ALL I HAVE TO DO IS DRIVE TWO HOURS AND LISTEN TO THEIR CONDO SALES PITCH. I'M GUARANTEED TO WIN A JEEP CHEROKEE OR A VALUABLE MOCK EMERALD.
© 1989 United Feature Syndicate, Inc.
9-14
THAT EMERALD WILL GO PRETTY WELL WITH YOUR MOCK BRAIN.
S. Adams

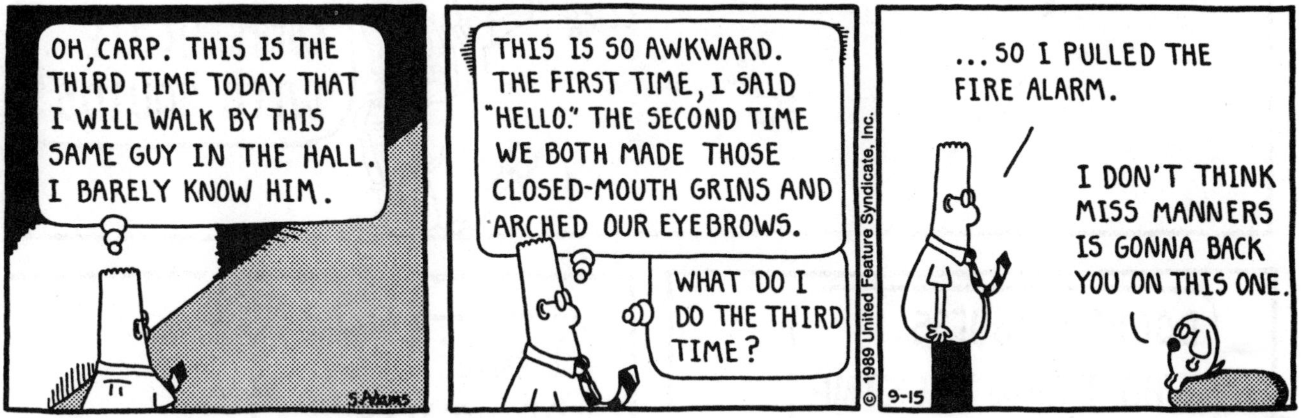
OH, CARP. THIS IS THE THIRD TIME TODAY THAT I WILL WALK BY THIS SAME GUY IN THE HALL. I BARELY KNOW HIM.
S. Adams
THIS IS SO AWKWARD. THE FIRST TIME, I SAID "HELLO." THE SECOND TIME WE BOTH MADE THOSE CLOSED-MOUTH GRINS AND ARCHED OUR EYEBROWS.
WHAT DO I DO THE THIRD TIME?
© 1989 United Feature Syndicate, Inc.
9-15
...SO I PULLED THE FIRE ALARM.
I DON'T THINK MISS MANNERS IS GONNA BACK YOU ON THIS ONE.

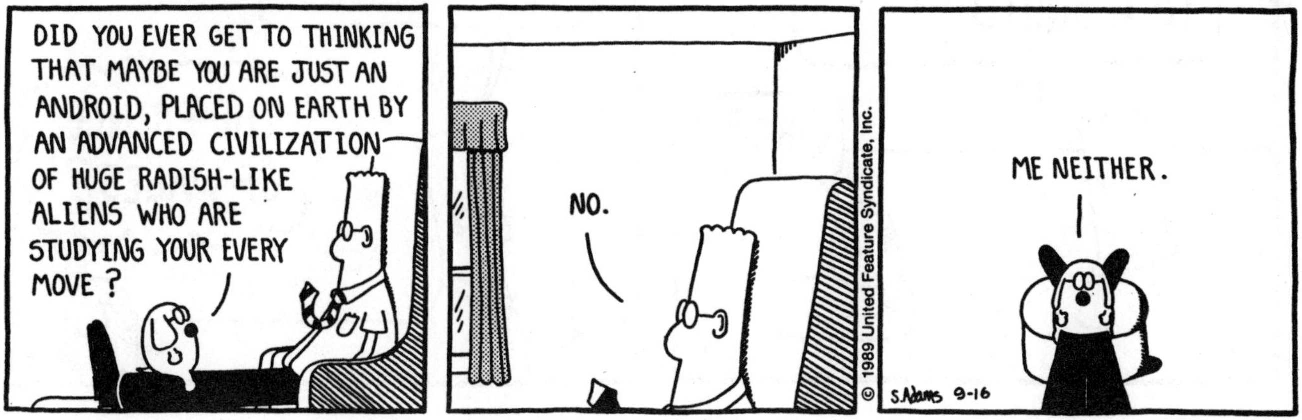
DID YOU EVER GET TO THINKING THAT MAYBE YOU ARE JUST AN ANDROID, PLACED ON EARTH BY AN ADVANCED CIVILIZATION OF HUGE RADISH-LIKE ALIENS WHO ARE STUDYING YOUR EVERY MOVE?
NO.
© 1989 United Feature Syndicate, Inc.
S. Adams 9-16
ME NEITHER.

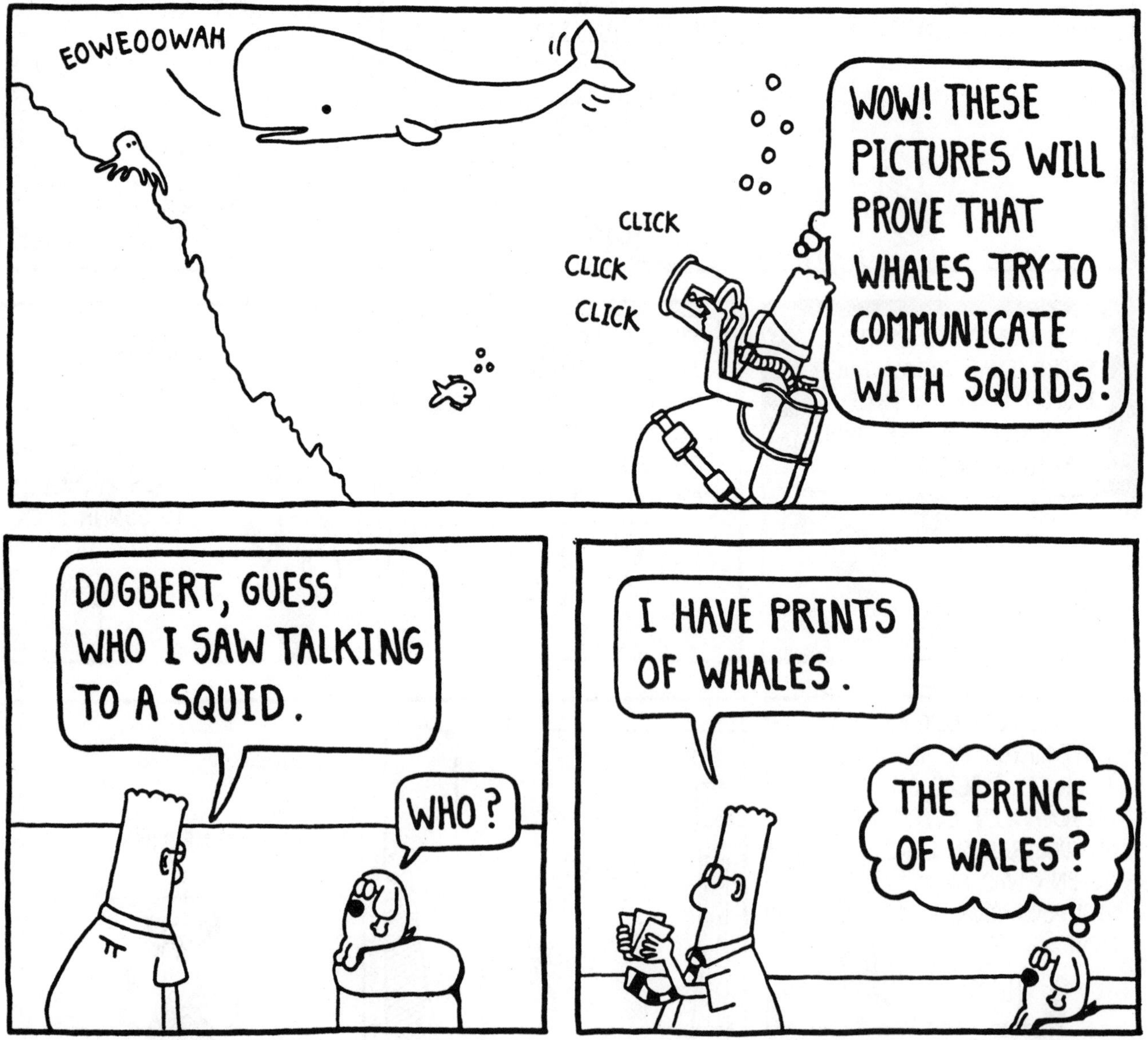
EOWEOOWAH
CLICK
CLICK
CLICK
WOW! THESE PICTURES WILL PROVE THAT WHALES TRY TO COMMUNICATE WITH SQUIDS!
DOGBERT, GUESS WHO I SAW TALKING TO A SQUID.
WHO?
I HAVE PRINTS OF WHALES.
THE PRINCE OF WALES?

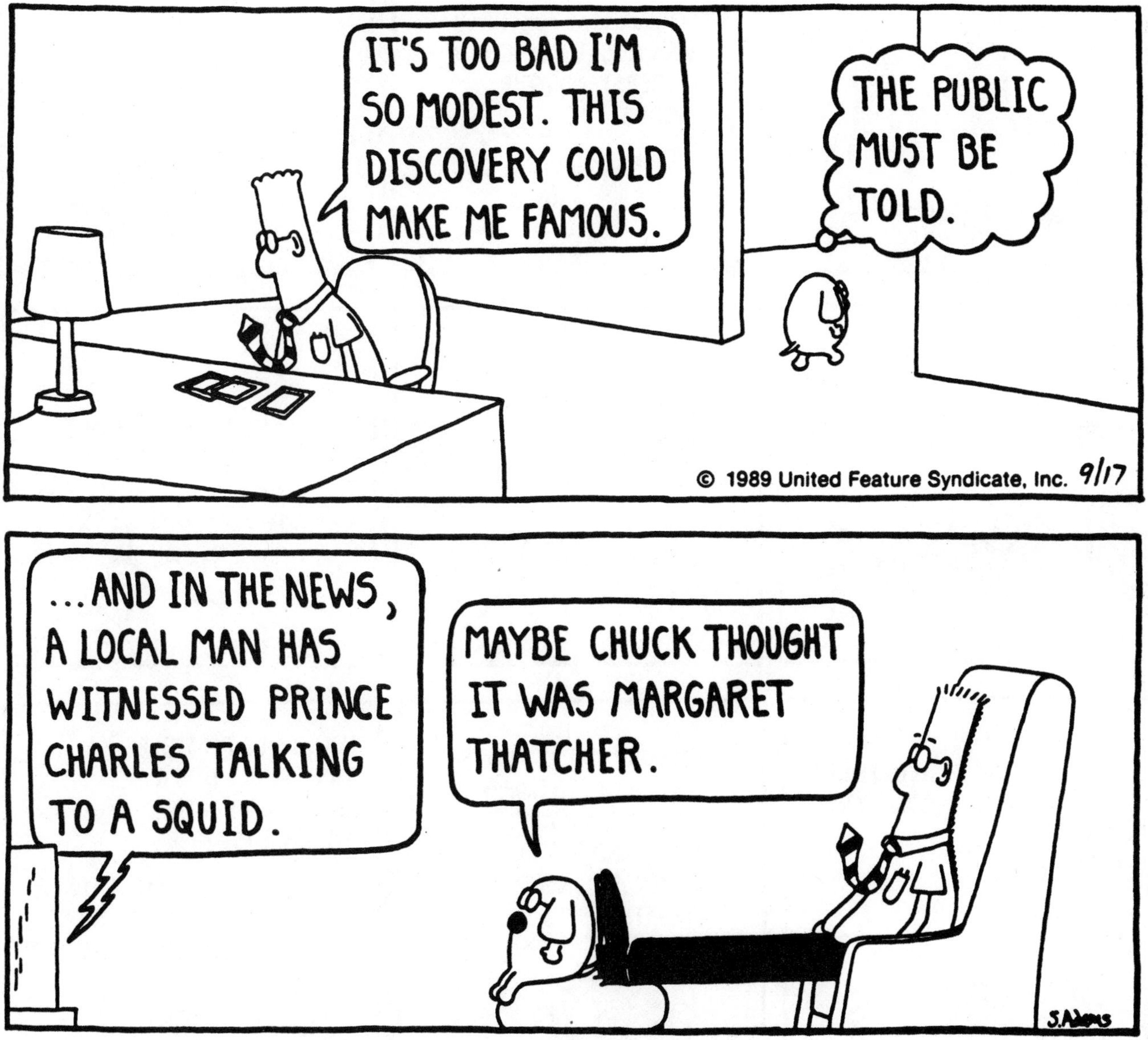
IT'S TOO BAD I'M SO MODEST. THIS DISCOVERY COULD MAKE ME FAMOUS.
THE PUBLIC MUST BE TOLD.
© 1989 United Feature Syndicate, Inc. 9/17
...AND IN THE NEWS, A LOCAL MAN HAS WITNESSED PRINCE CHARLES TALKING TO A SQUID.
MAYBE CHUCK THOUGHT IT WAS MARGARET THATCHER.
S.Adams

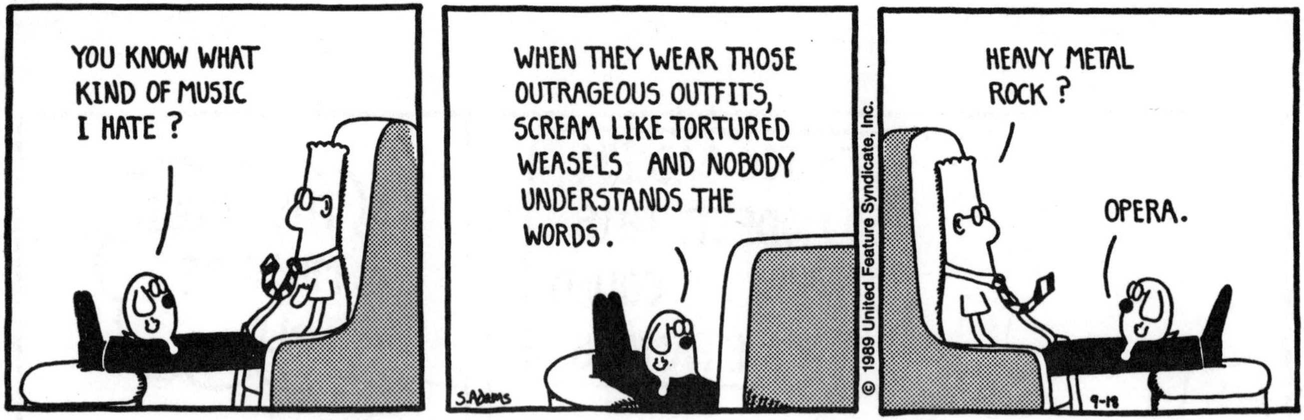
YOU KNOW WHAT KIND OF MUSIC I HATE ?
WHEN THEY WEAR THOSE OUTRAGEOUS OUTFITS, SCREAM LIKE TORTURED WEASELS AND NOBODY UNDERSTANDS THE WORDS.
S.Adams
© 1989 United Feature Syndicate, Inc.
HEAVY METAL ROCK ?
OPERA.
9-18

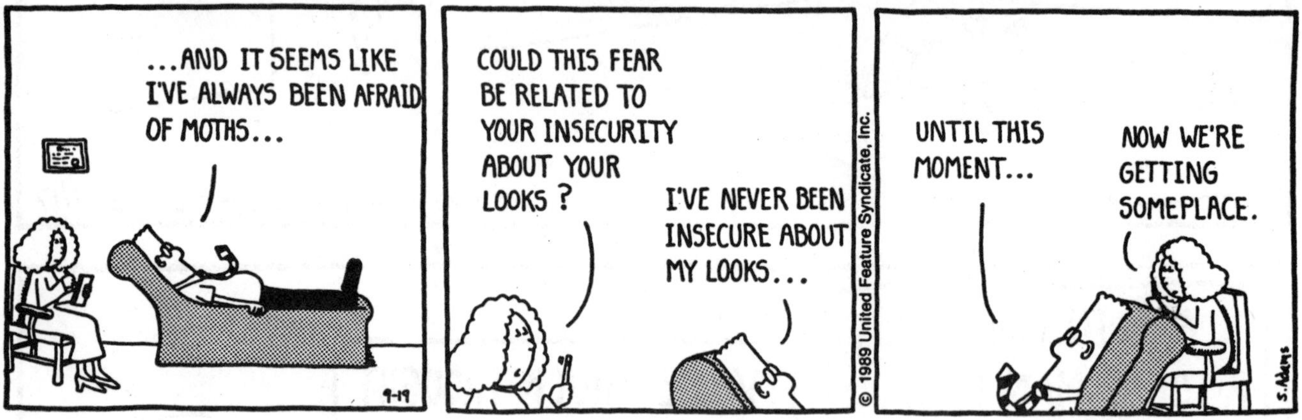
...AND IT SEEMS LIKE I'VE ALWAYS BEEN AFRAID OF MOTHS...
9-19
COULD THIS FEAR BE RELATED TO YOUR INSECURITY ABOUT YOUR LOOKS ?
I'VE NEVER BEEN INSECURE ABOUT MY LOOKS...
© 1989 United Feature Syndicate, Inc.
UNTIL THIS MOMENT...
NOW WE'RE GETTING SOMEPLACE.
S. Adams

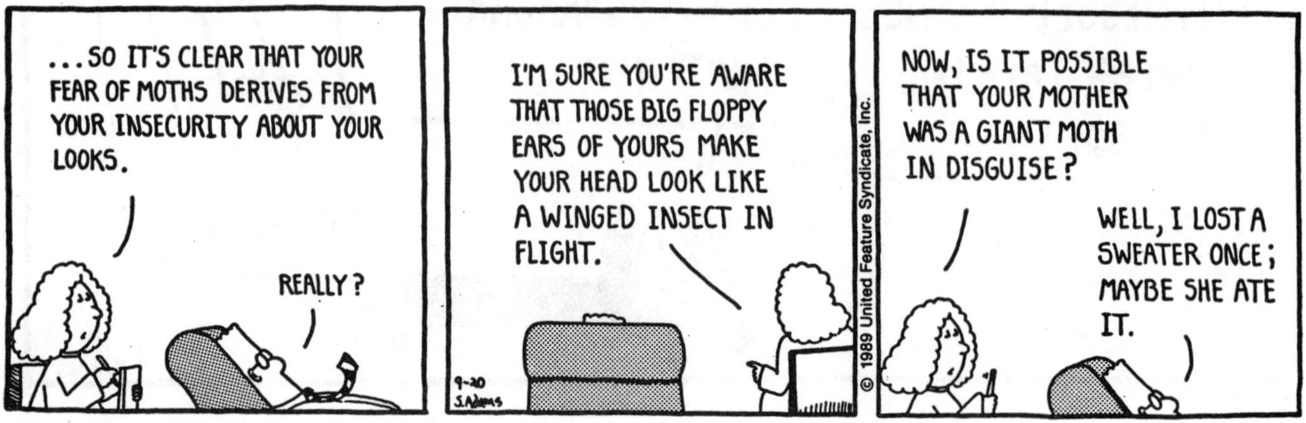
...SO IT'S CLEAR THAT YOUR FEAR OF MOTHS DERIVES FROM YOUR INSECURITY ABOUT YOUR LOOKS.
REALLY ?
I'M SURE YOU'RE AWARE THAT THOSE BIG FLOPPY EARS OF YOURS MAKE YOUR HEAD LOOK LIKE A WINGED INSECT IN FLIGHT.
9-20
S.Adams
© 1989 United Feature Syndicate, Inc.
NOW, IS IT POSSIBLE THAT YOUR MOTHER WAS A GIANT MOTH IN DISGUISE ?
WELL, I LOST A SWEATER ONCE; MAYBE SHE ATE IT.

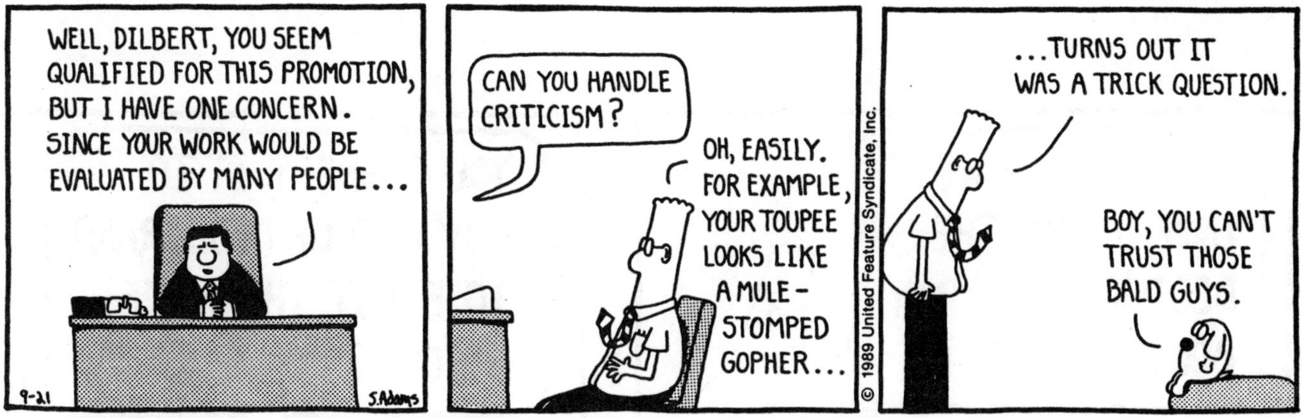
WELL, DILBERT, YOU SEEM QUALIFIED FOR THIS PROMOTION, BUT I HAVE ONE CONCERN. SINCE YOUR WORK WOULD BE EVALUATED BY MANY PEOPLE...
CAN YOU HANDLE CRITICISM?
OH, EASILY. FOR EXAMPLE, YOUR TOUPEE LOOKS LIKE A MULE-STOMPED GOPHER...
© 1989 United Feature Syndicate, Inc.
...TURNS OUT IT WAS A TRICK QUESTION.
BOY, YOU CAN'T TRUST THOSE BALD GUYS.

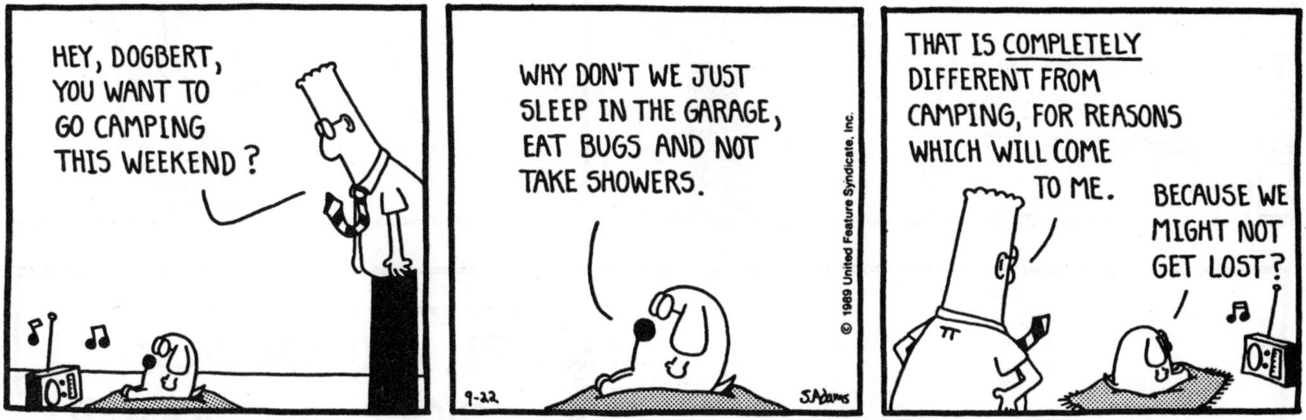
HEY, DOGBERT, YOU WANT TO GO CAMPING THIS WEEKEND?
WHY DON'T WE JUST SLEEP IN THE GARAGE, EAT BUGS AND NOT TAKE SHOWERS.
© 1989 United Feature Syndicate, Inc.
THAT IS COMPLETELY DIFFERENT FROM CAMPING, FOR REASONS WHICH WILL COME TO ME.
BECAUSE WE MIGHT NOT GET LOST?

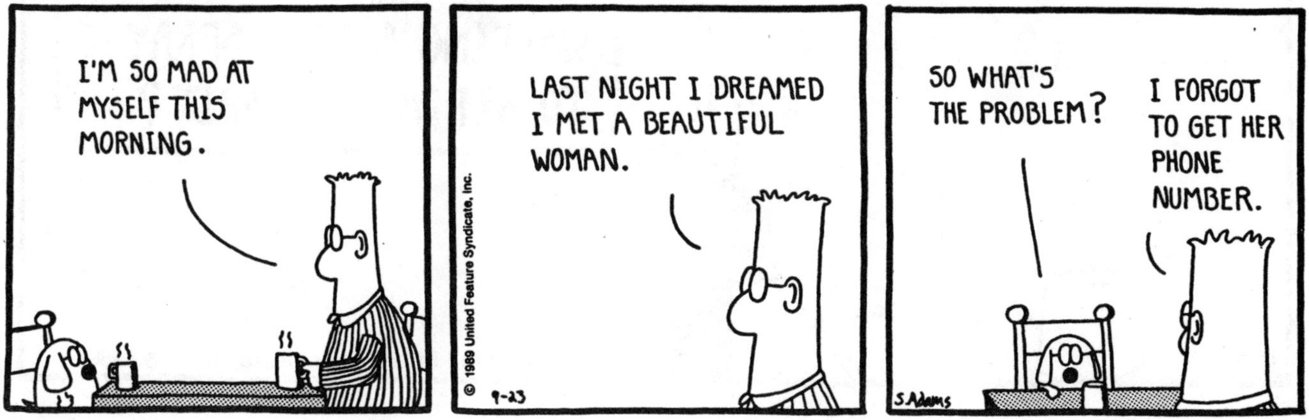
I'M SO MAD AT MYSELF THIS MORNING.
© 1989 United Feature Syndicate, Inc.
LAST NIGHT I DREAMED I MET A BEAUTIFUL WOMAN.
SO WHAT'S THE PROBLEM?
I FORGOT TO GET HER PHONE NUMBER.

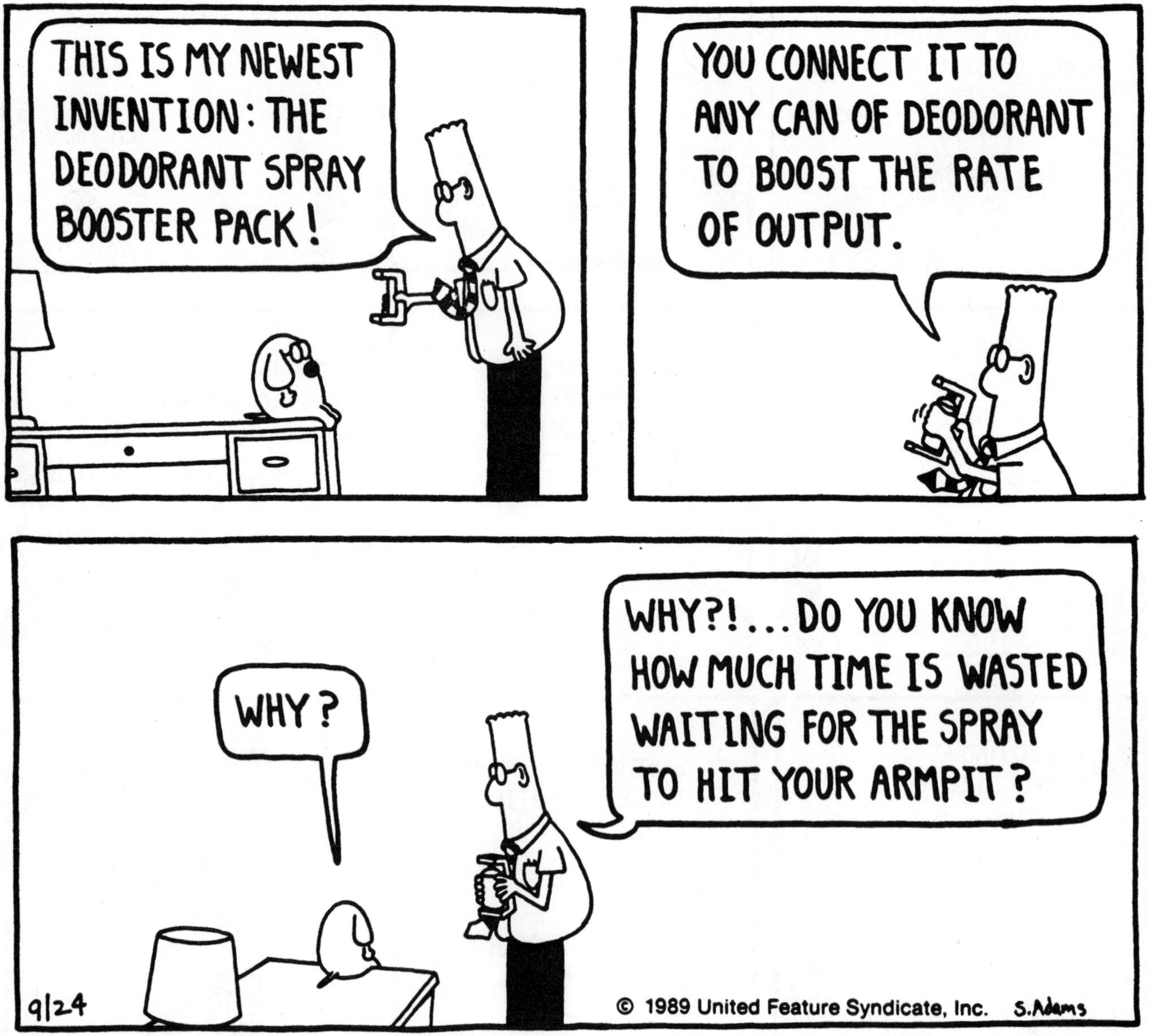
THIS IS MY NEWEST INVENTION: THE DEODORANT SPRAY BOOSTER PACK!
YOU CONNECT IT TO ANY CAN OF DEODORANT TO BOOST THE RATE OF OUTPUT.
WHY?
WHY?!... DO YOU KNOW HOW MUCH TIME IS WASTED WAITING FOR THE SPRAY TO HIT YOUR ARMPIT?
9/24
© 1989 United Feature Syndicate, Inc.
S.Adams

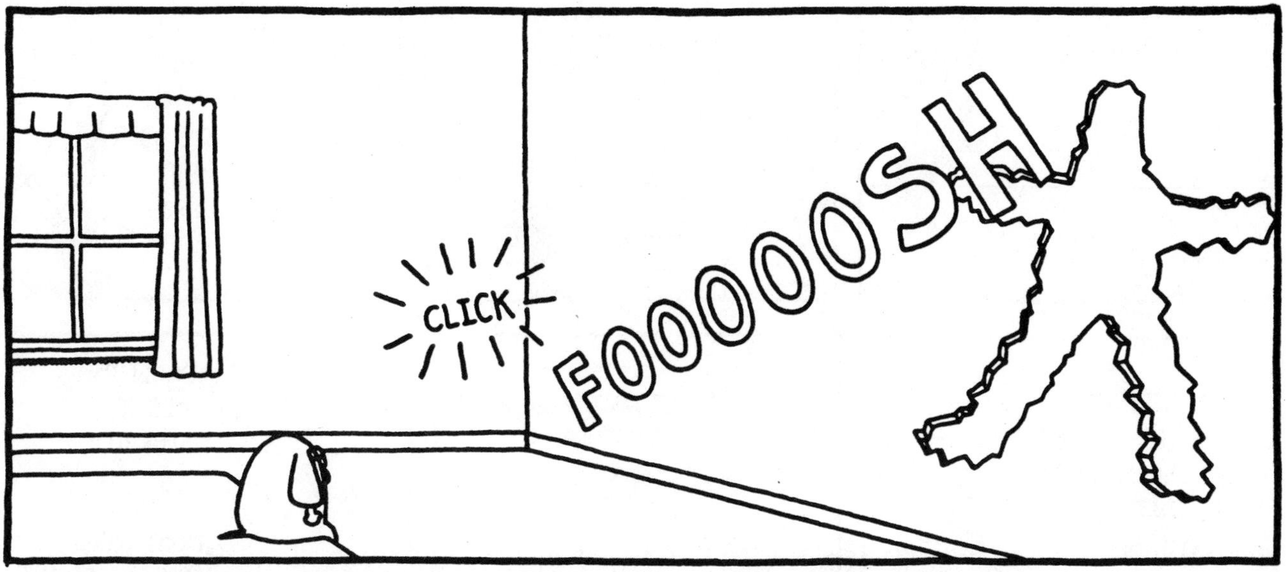
CLICK
FOOOOOSH

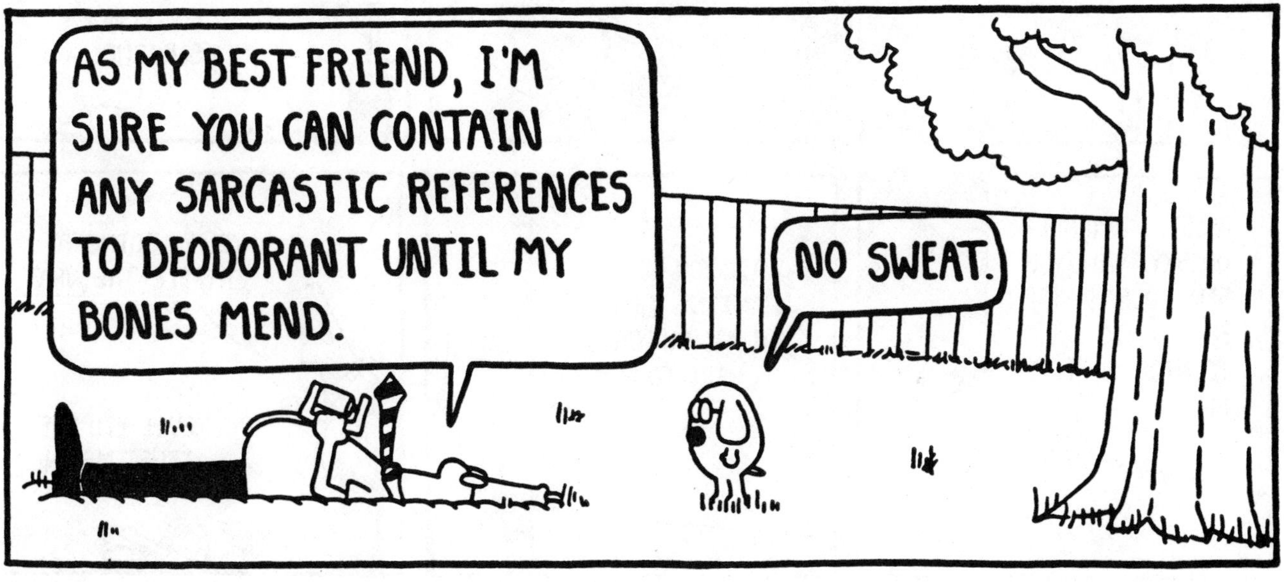
AS MY BEST FRIEND, I'M SURE YOU CAN CONTAIN ANY SARCASTIC REFERENCES TO DEODORANT UNTIL MY BONES MEND.
NO SWEAT.

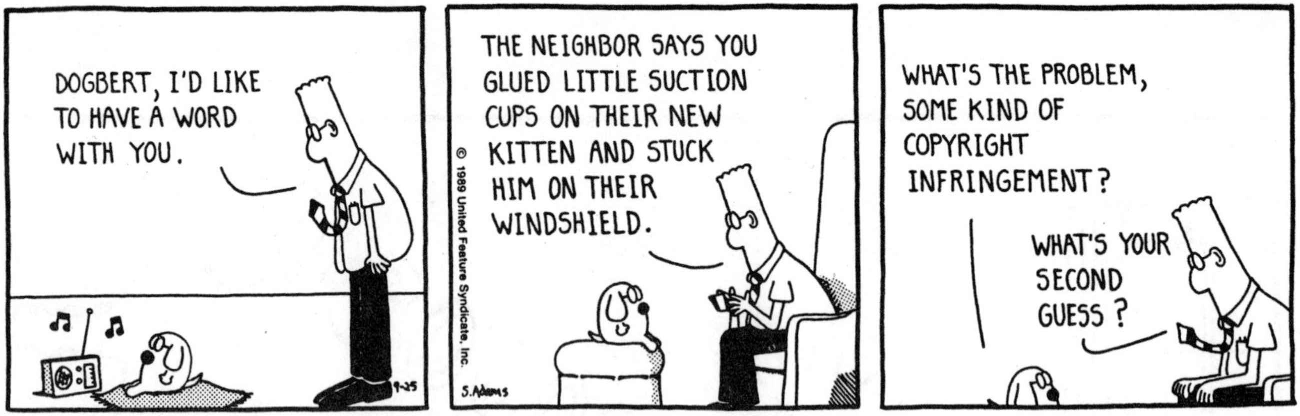
DOGBERT, I'D LIKE TO HAVE A WORD WITH YOU.
9-25
THE NEIGHBOR SAYS YOU GLUED LITTLE SUCTION CUPS ON THEIR NEW KITTEN AND STUCK HIM ON THEIR WINDSHIELD.
© 1989 United Feature Syndicate, Inc.
S.Adams
WHAT'S THE PROBLEM, SOME KIND OF COPYRIGHT INFRINGEMENT?
WHAT'S YOUR SECOND GUESS?

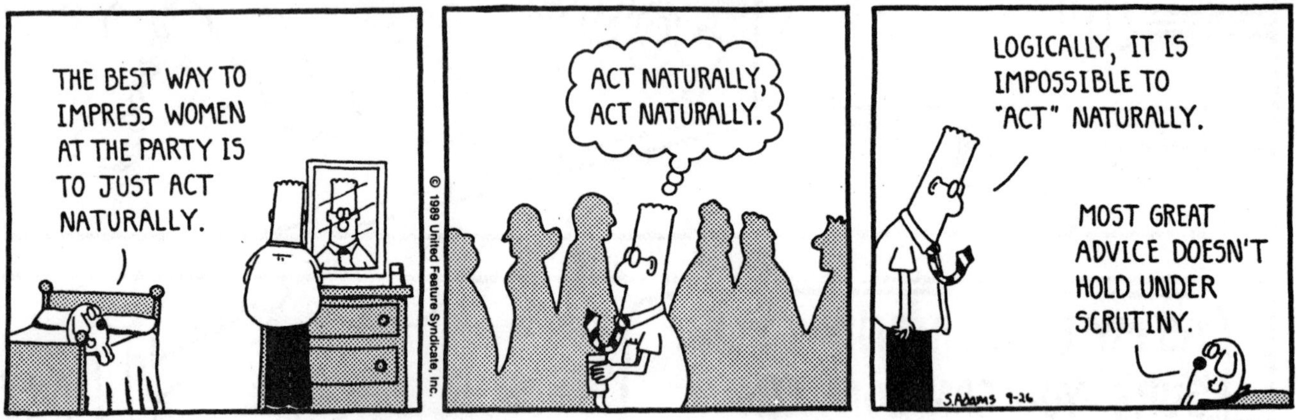
THE BEST WAY TO IMPRESS WOMEN AT THE PARTY IS TO JUST ACT NATURALLY.
© 1989 United Feature Syndicate, Inc.
ACT NATURALLY, ACT NATURALLY.
LOGICALLY, IT IS IMPOSSIBLE TO "ACT" NATURALLY.
MOST GREAT ADVICE DOESN'T HOLD UNDER SCRUTINY.
S.Adams 9-26

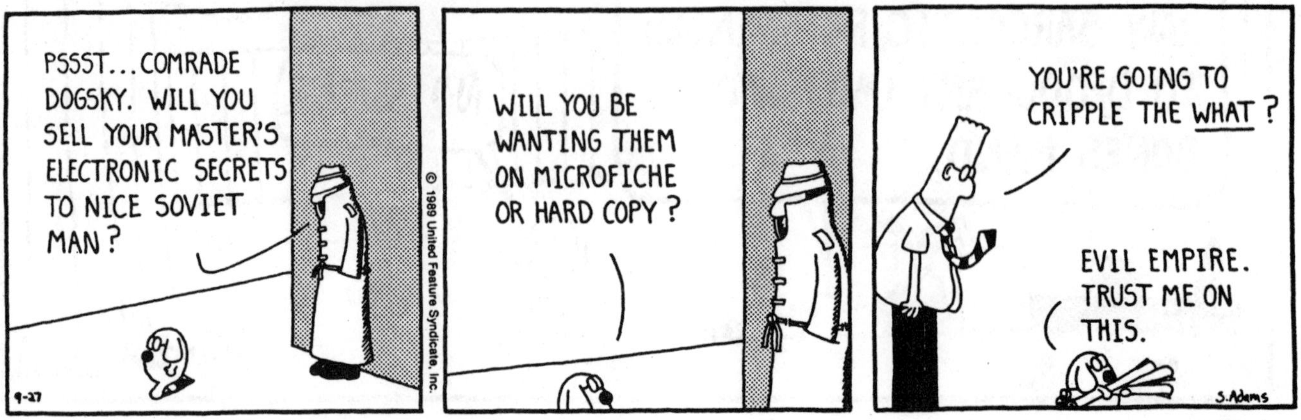
PSSST... COMRADE DOGSKY. WILL YOU SELL YOUR MASTER'S ELECTRONIC SECRETS TO NICE SOVIET MAN?
9-27
© 1989 United Feature Syndicate, Inc.
WILL YOU BE WANTING THEM ON MICROFICHE OR HARD COPY?
YOU'RE GOING TO CRIPPLE THE WHAT?
EVIL EMPIRE. TRUST ME ON THIS.
S.Adams

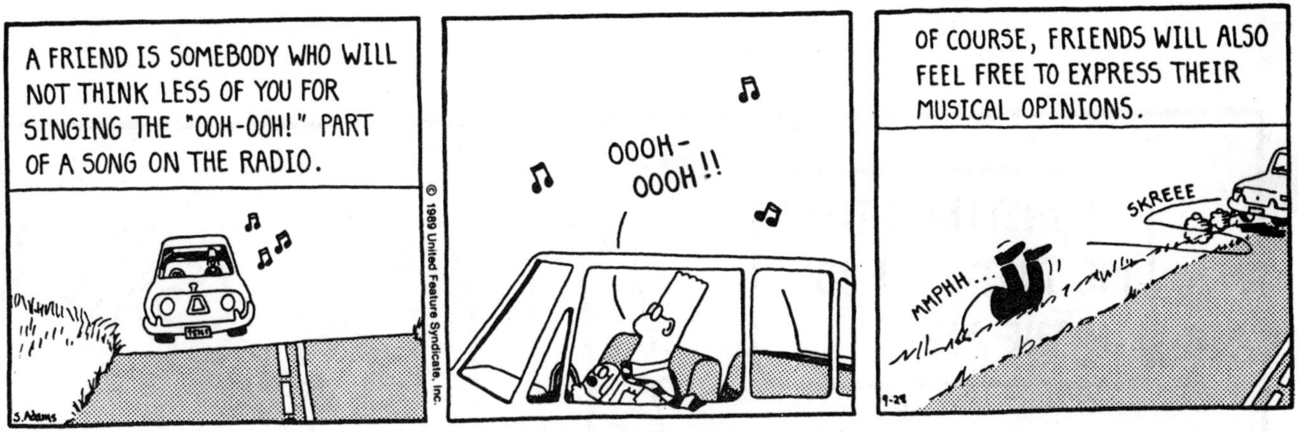
A FRIEND IS SOMEBODY WHO WILL NOT THINK LESS OF YOU FOR SINGING THE "OOH-OOH!" PART OF A SONG ON THE RADIO.
S. Adams
© 1989 United Feature Syndicate, Inc.
OOOH-OOOH!!
OF COURSE, FRIENDS WILL ALSO FEEL FREE TO EXPRESS THEIR MUSICAL OPINIONS.
SKREEE
MMPHH...
9-28

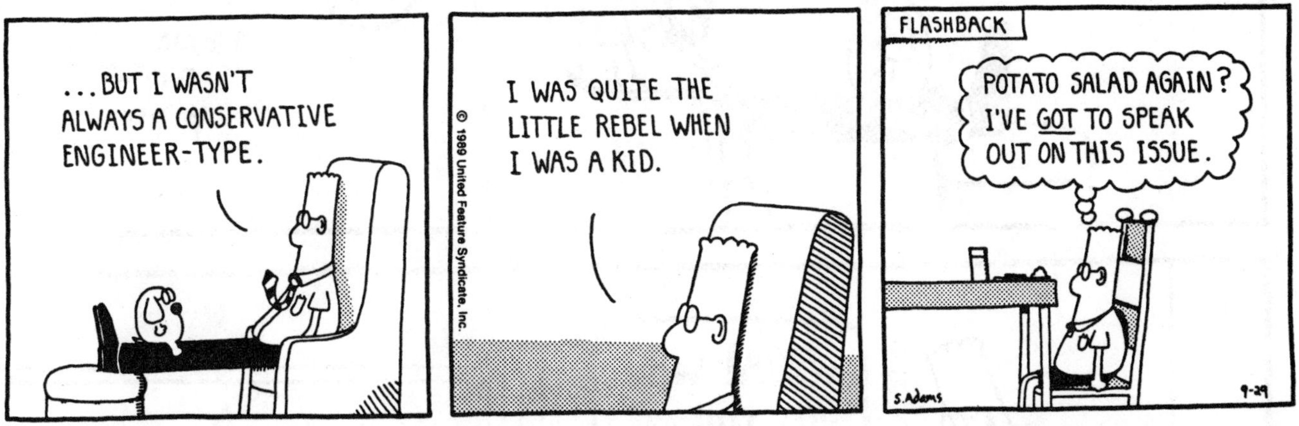
...BUT I WASN'T ALWAYS A CONSERVATIVE ENGINEER-TYPE.
© 1989 United Feature Syndicate, Inc.
I WAS QUITE THE LITTLE REBEL WHEN I WAS A KID.
FLASHBACK
POTATO SALAD AGAIN? I'VE GOT TO SPEAK OUT ON THIS ISSUE.
S. Adams
9-29

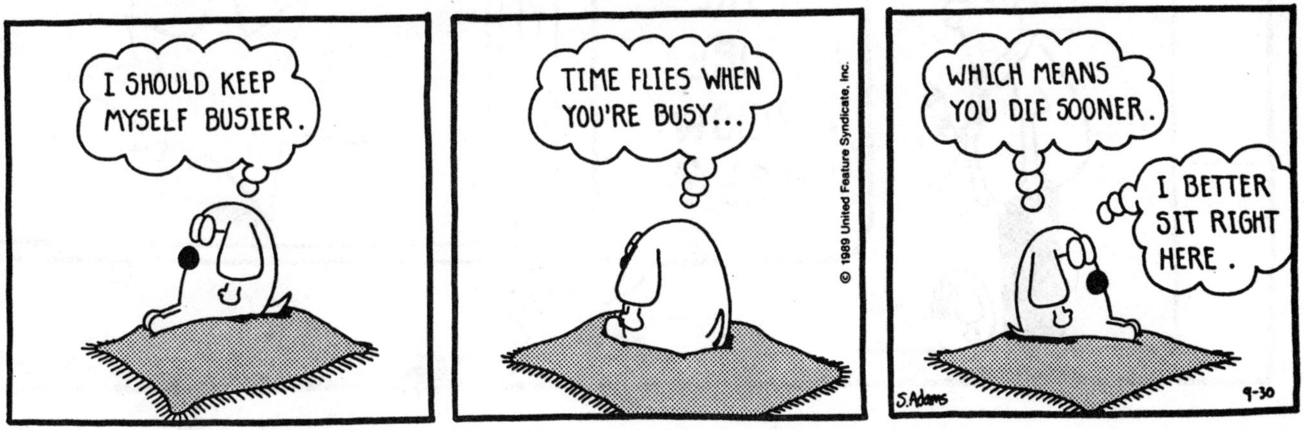
I SHOULD KEEP MYSELF BUSIER.
TIME FLIES WHEN YOU'RE BUSY...
© 1989 United Feature Syndicate, Inc.
WHICH MEANS YOU DIE SOONER.
I BETTER SIT RIGHT HERE.
S. Adams
9-30

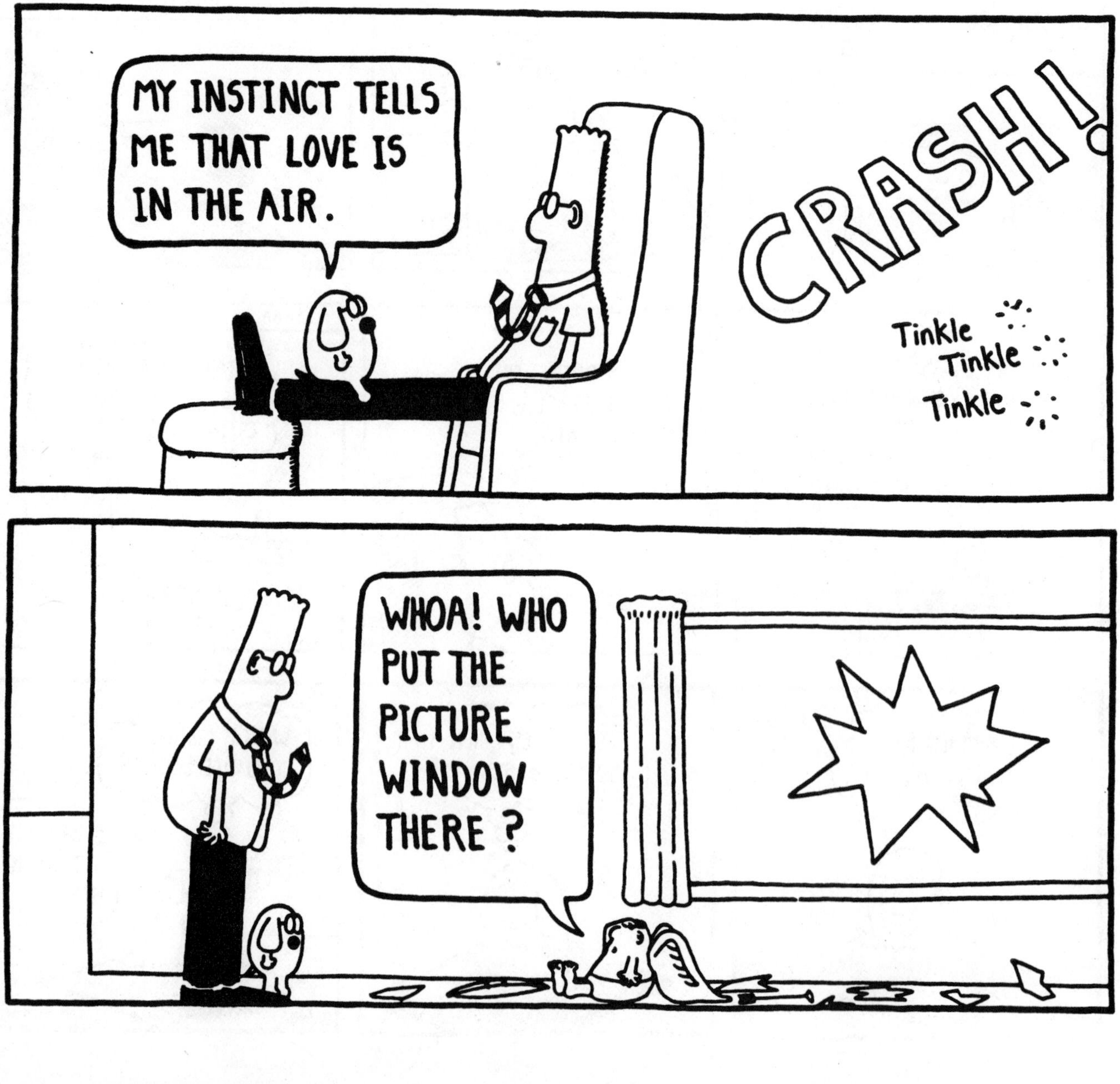
MY INSTINCT TELLS ME THAT LOVE IS IN THE AIR.
CRASH!
Tinkle Tinkle Tinkle
WHOA! WHO PUT THE PICTURE WINDOW THERE ?

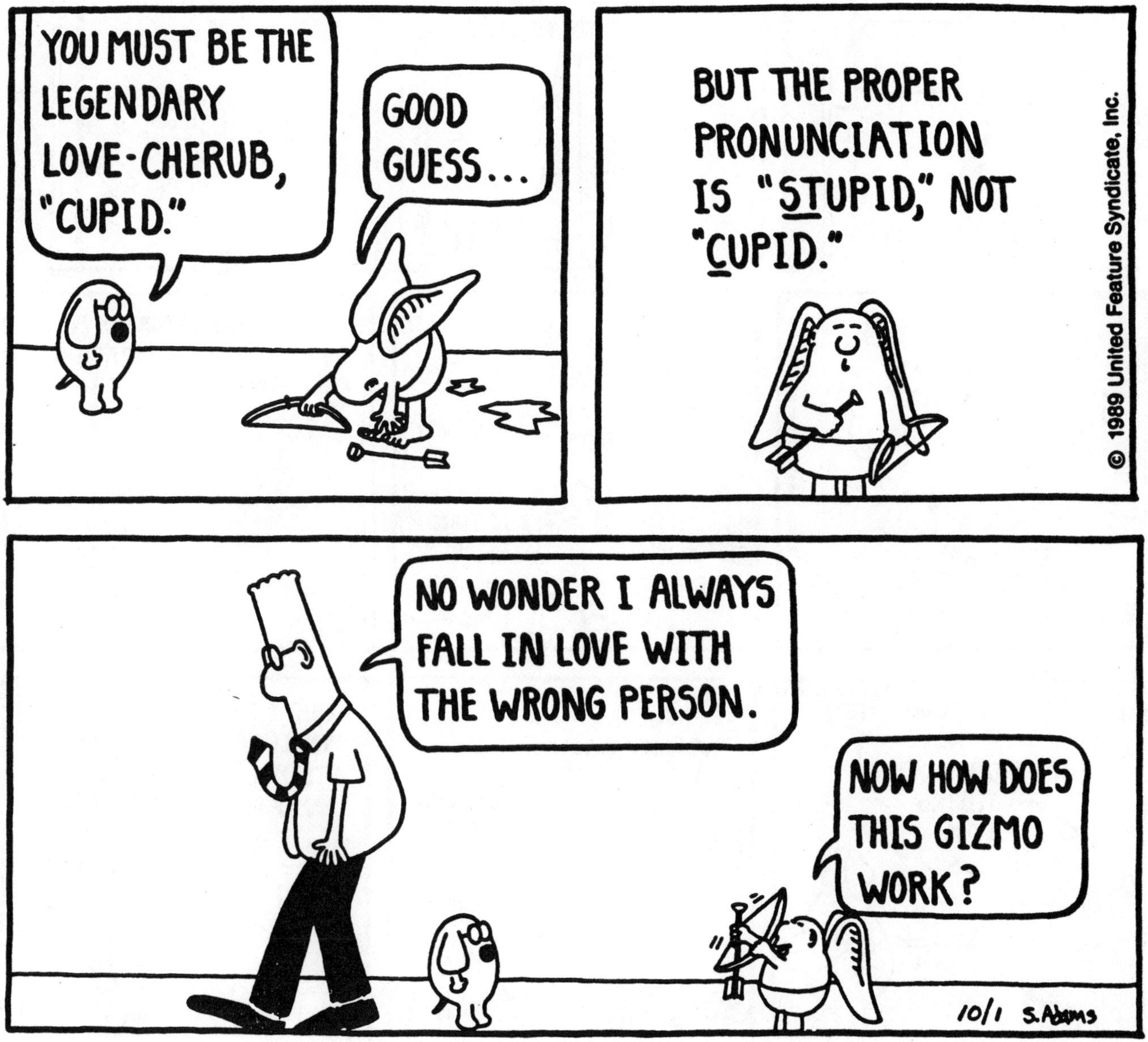
YOU MUST BE THE LEGENDARY LOVE-CHERUB, "CUPID."
GOOD GUESS...
BUT THE PROPER PRONUNCIATION IS "STUPID," NOT "CUPID."
© 1989 United Feature Syndicate, Inc.
NO WONDER I ALWAYS FALL IN LOVE WITH THE WRONG PERSON.
NOW HOW DOES THIS GIZMO WORK?
10/1 S.Adams

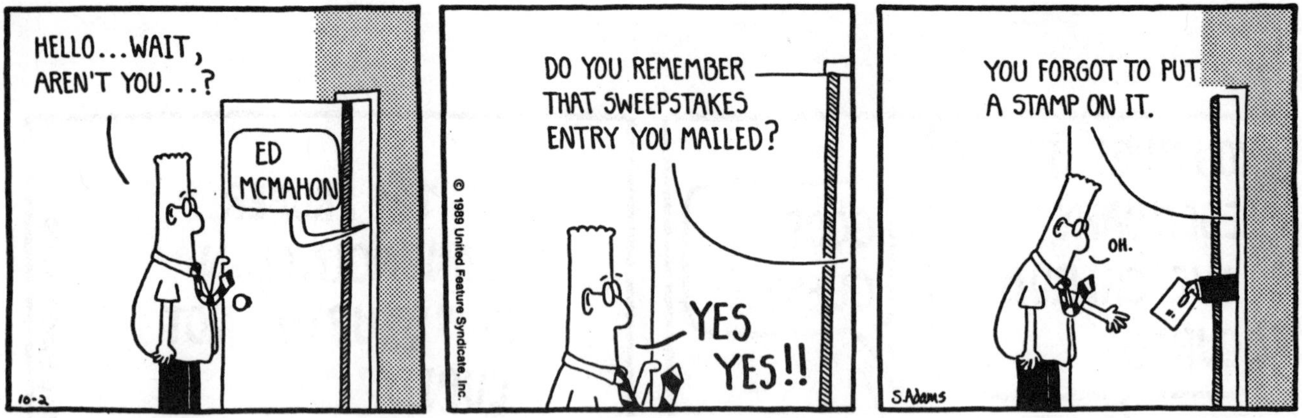
HELLO...WAIT, AREN'T YOU...?
ED MCMAHON
10-2
© 1989 United Feature Syndicate, Inc.
DO YOU REMEMBER THAT SWEEPSTAKES ENTRY YOU MAILED?
YES YES!!
YOU FORGOT TO PUT A STAMP ON IT.
OH.
S.Adams

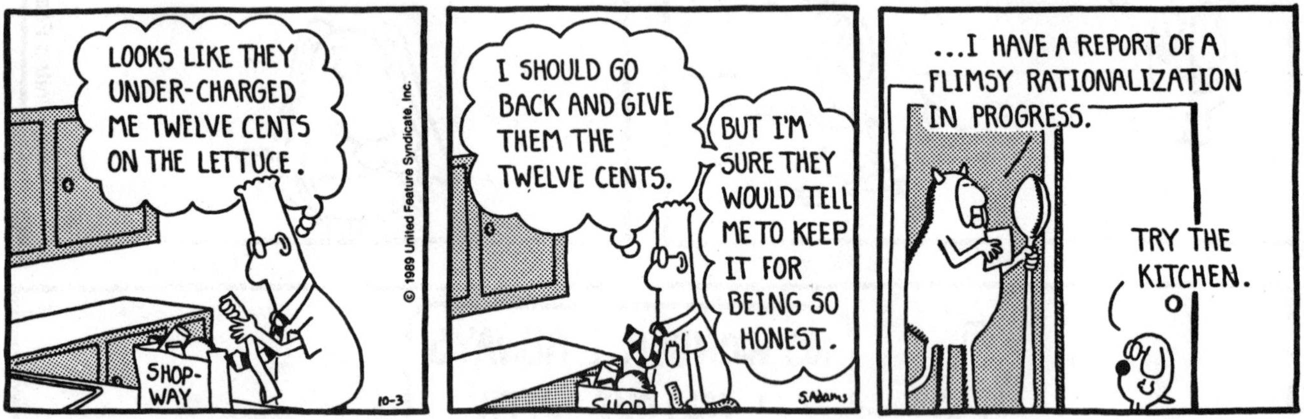
LOOKS LIKE THEY UNDER-CHARGED ME TWELVE CENTS ON THE LETTUCE.
SHOP-WAY
10-3
© 1989 United Feature Syndicate, Inc.
I SHOULD GO BACK AND GIVE THEM THE TWELVE CENTS.
BUT I'M SURE THEY WOULD TELL ME TO KEEP IT FOR BEING SO HONEST.
S.Adams
...I HAVE A REPORT OF A FLIMSY RATIONALIZATION IN PROGRESS.
TRY THE KITCHEN.

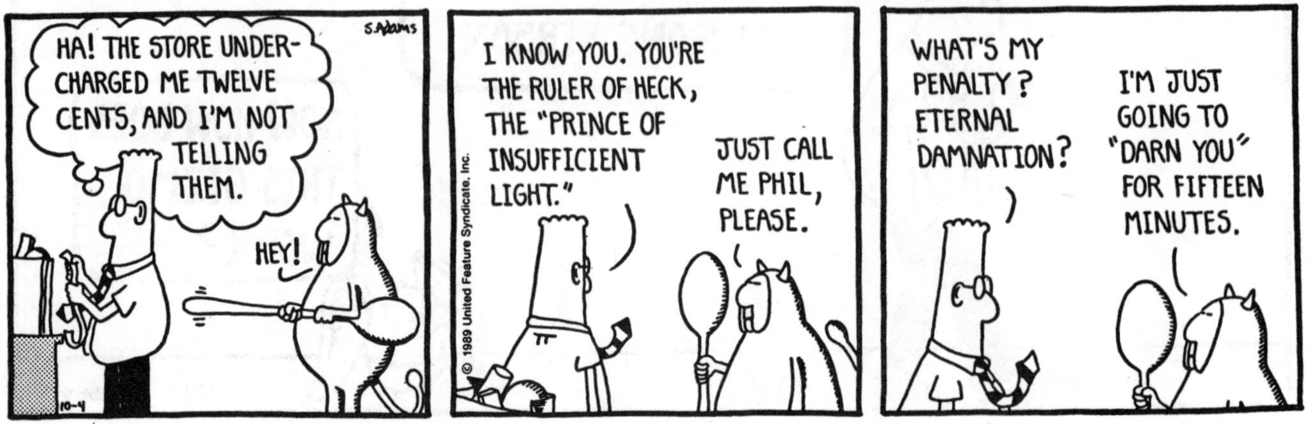
HA! THE STORE UNDER-CHARGED ME TWELVE CENTS, AND I'M NOT TELLING THEM.
S.Adams
HEY!
10-4
© 1989 United Feature Syndicate, Inc.
I KNOW YOU. YOU'RE THE RULER OF HECK, THE "PRINCE OF INSUFFICIENT LIGHT."
JUST CALL ME PHIL, PLEASE.
WHAT'S MY PENALTY? ETERNAL DAMNATION?
I'M JUST GOING TO "DARN YOU" FOR FIFTEEN MINUTES.

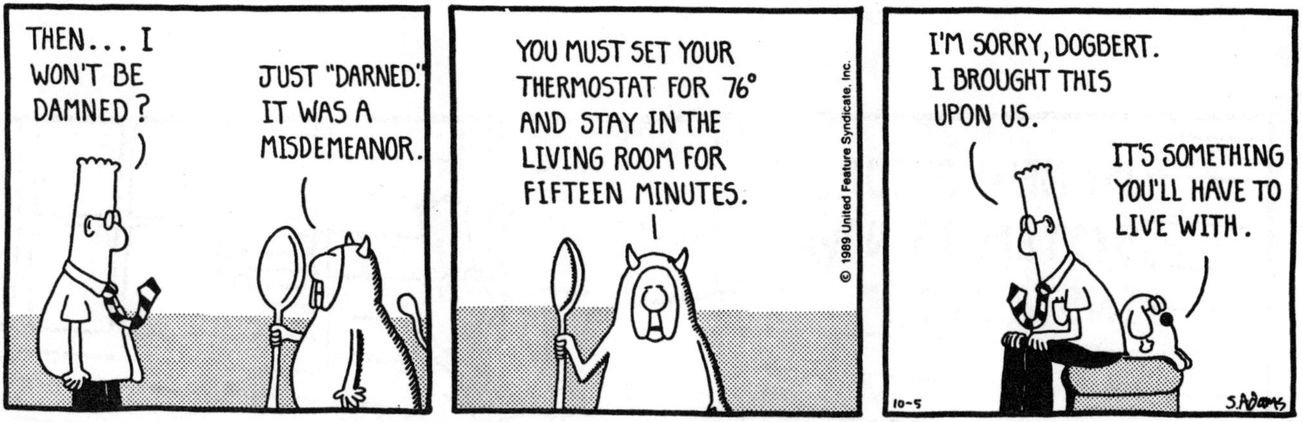
THEN... I WON'T BE DAMNED?
JUST "DARNED." IT WAS A MISDEMEANOR.
YOU MUST SET YOUR THERMOSTAT FOR 76° AND STAY IN THE LIVING ROOM FOR FIFTEEN MINUTES.
© 1989 United Feature Syndicate, Inc.
I'M SORRY, DOGBERT. I BROUGHT THIS UPON US.
IT'S SOMETHING YOU'LL HAVE TO LIVE WITH.
10-5
S. Adams

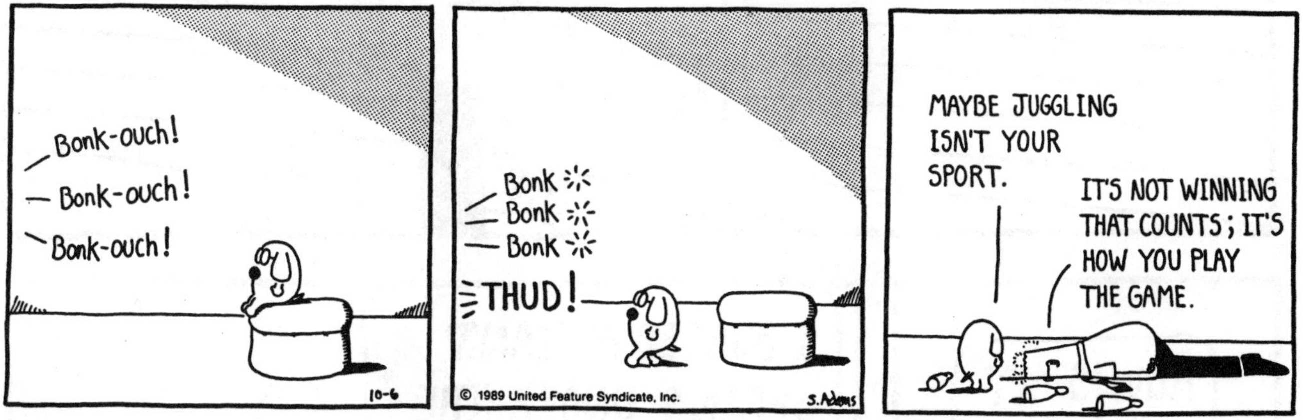
Bonk-ouch!
Bonk-ouch!
Bonk-ouch!
10-6
Bonk
Bonk
Bonk
THUD!
© 1989 United Feature Syndicate, Inc.
S. Adams
MAYBE JUGGLING ISN'T YOUR SPORT.
IT'S NOT WINNING THAT COUNTS; IT'S HOW YOU PLAY THE GAME.

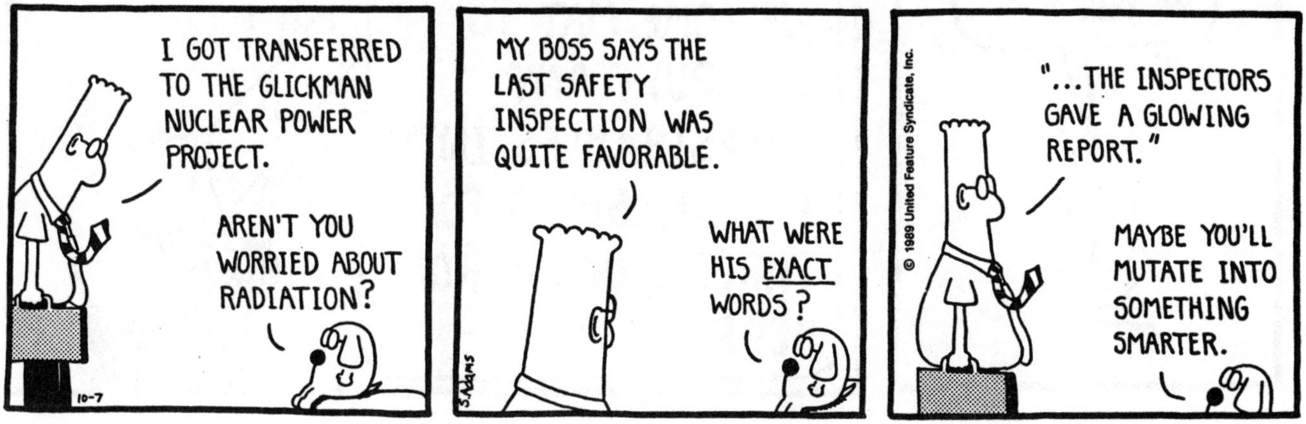
I GOT TRANSFERRED TO THE GLICKMAN NUCLEAR POWER PROJECT.
AREN'T YOU WORRIED ABOUT RADIATION?
10-7
MY BOSS SAYS THE LAST SAFETY INSPECTION WAS QUITE FAVORABLE.
WHAT WERE HIS EXACT WORDS?
S. Adams
© 1989 United Feature Syndicate, Inc.
"...THE INSPECTORS GAVE A GLOWING REPORT."
MAYBE YOU'LL MUTATE INTO SOMETHING SMARTER.

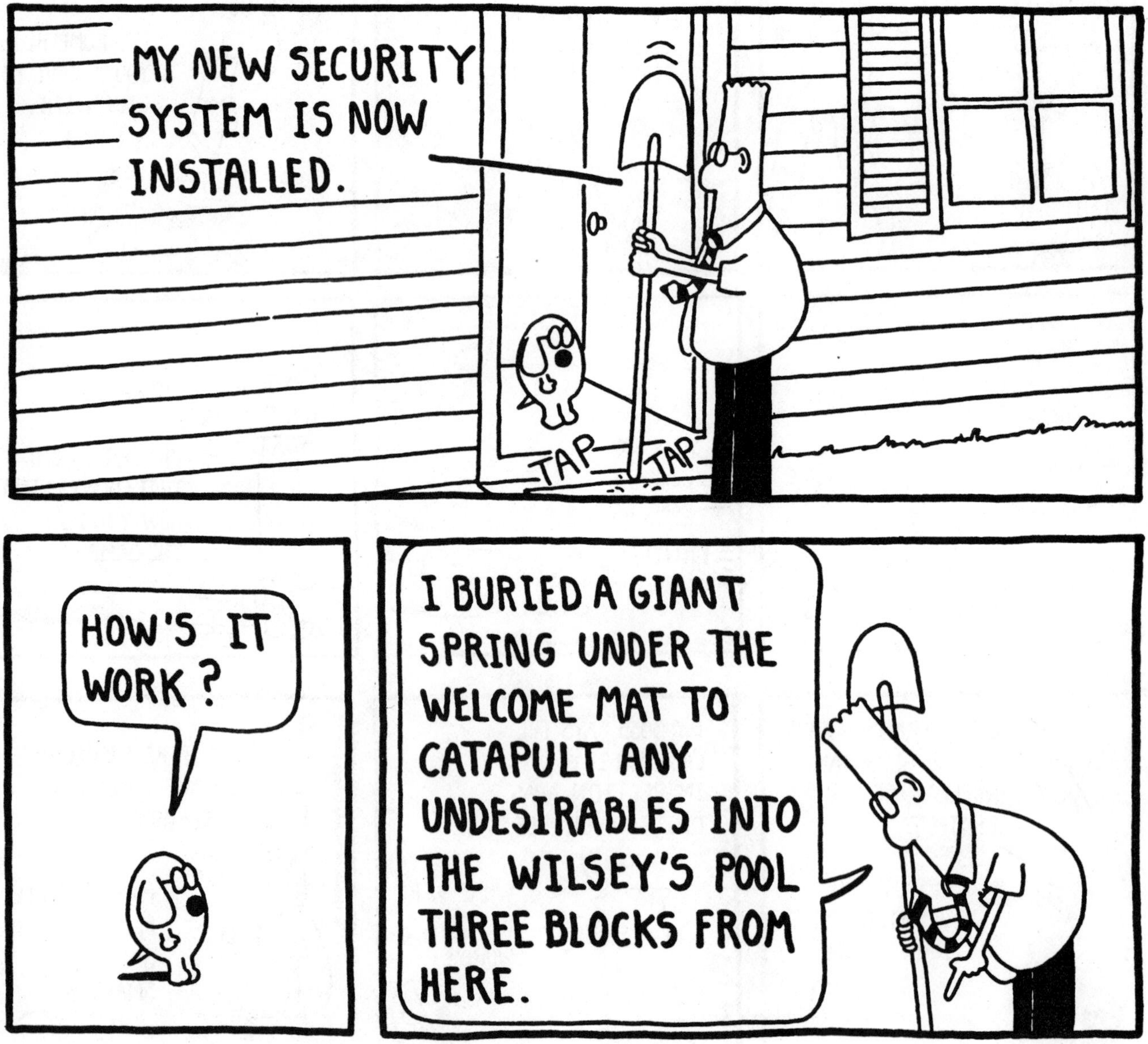
MY NEW SECURITY SYSTEM IS NOW INSTALLED.
TAP TAP
HOW'S IT WORK?
I BURIED A GIANT SPRING UNDER THE WELCOME MAT TO CATAPULT ANY UNDESIRABLES INTO THE WILSEY'S POOL THREE BLOCKS FROM HERE.

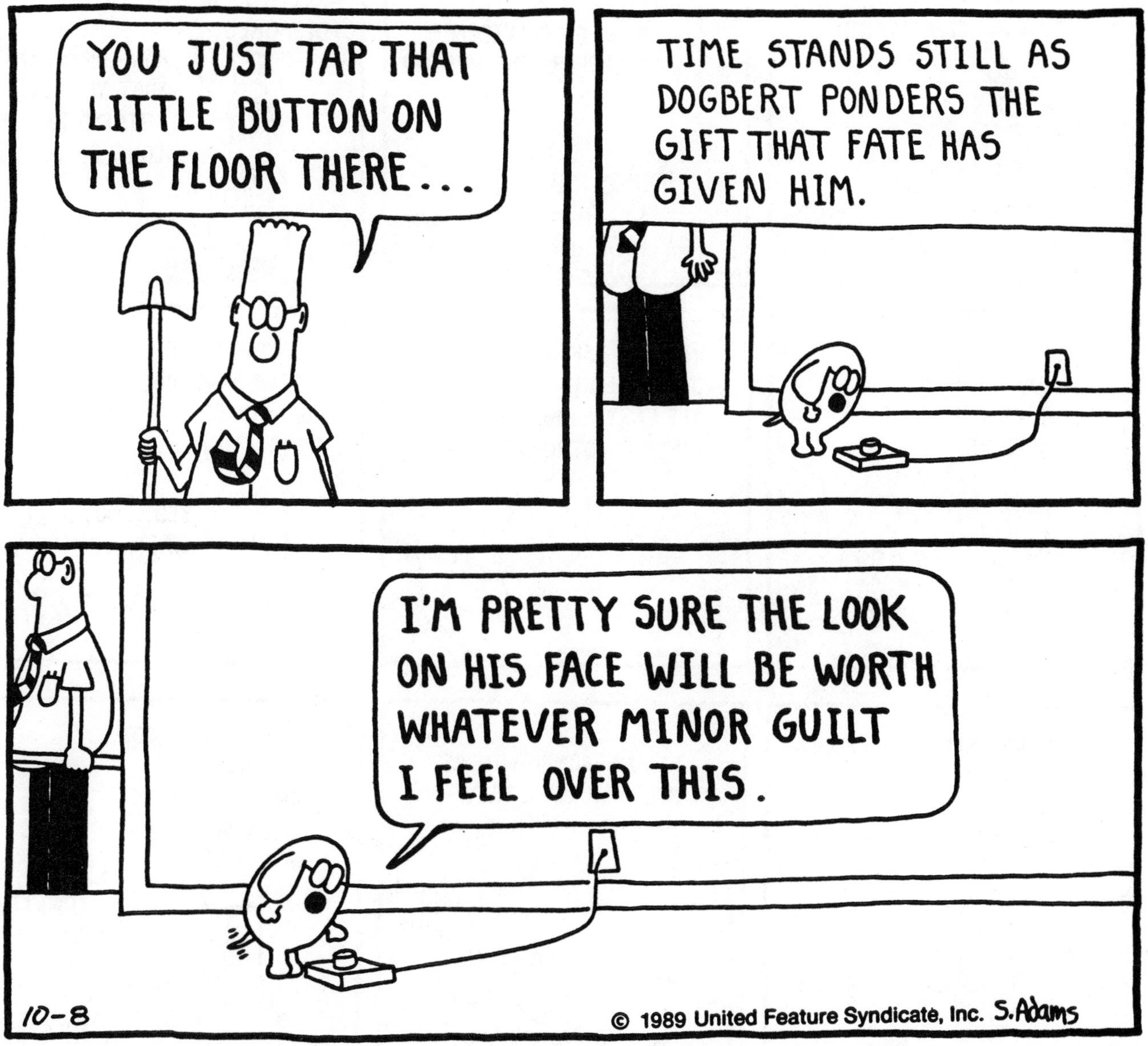
YOU JUST TAP THAT LITTLE BUTTON ON THE FLOOR THERE...
TIME STANDS STILL AS DOGBERT PONDERS THE GIFT THAT FATE HAS GIVEN HIM.
I'M PRETTY SURE THE LOOK ON HIS FACE WILL BE WORTH WHATEVER MINOR GUILT I FEEL OVER THIS.
10-8
© 1989 United Feature Syndicate, Inc. S.Adams

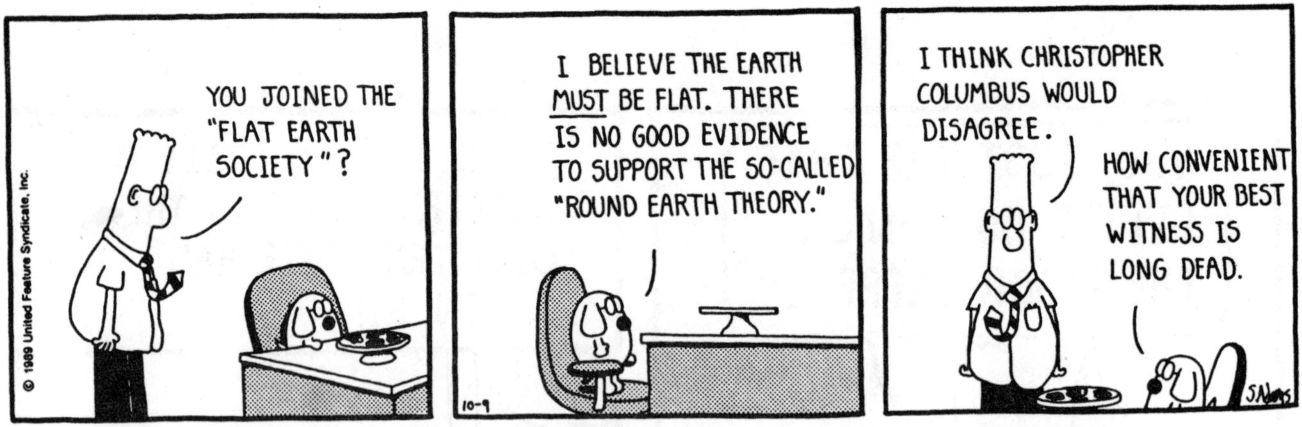
YOU JOINED THE "FLAT EARTH SOCIETY"?
© 1989 United Feature Syndicate, Inc.
I BELIEVE THE EARTH MUST BE FLAT. THERE IS NO GOOD EVIDENCE TO SUPPORT THE SO-CALLED "ROUND EARTH THEORY."
10-9
I THINK CHRISTOPHER COLUMBUS WOULD DISAGREE.
HOW CONVENIENT THAT YOUR BEST WITNESS IS LONG DEAD.
S.Adams

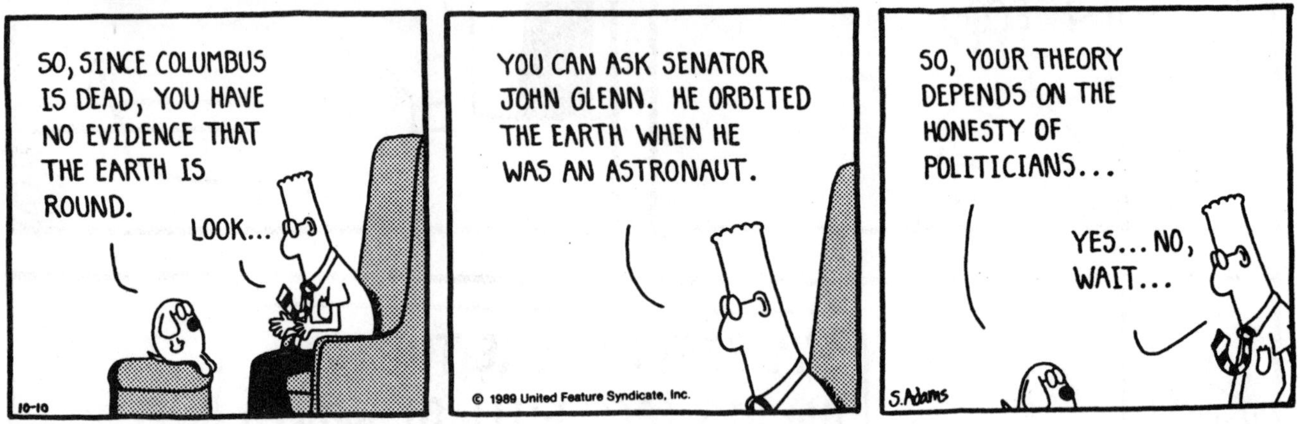
SO, SINCE COLUMBUS IS DEAD, YOU HAVE NO EVIDENCE THAT THE EARTH IS ROUND.
LOOK...
10-10
YOU CAN ASK SENATOR JOHN GLENN. HE ORBITED THE EARTH WHEN HE WAS AN ASTRONAUT.
© 1989 United Feature Syndicate, Inc.
SO, YOUR THEORY DEPENDS ON THE HONESTY OF POLITICIANS...
YES... NO, WAIT...
S.Adams

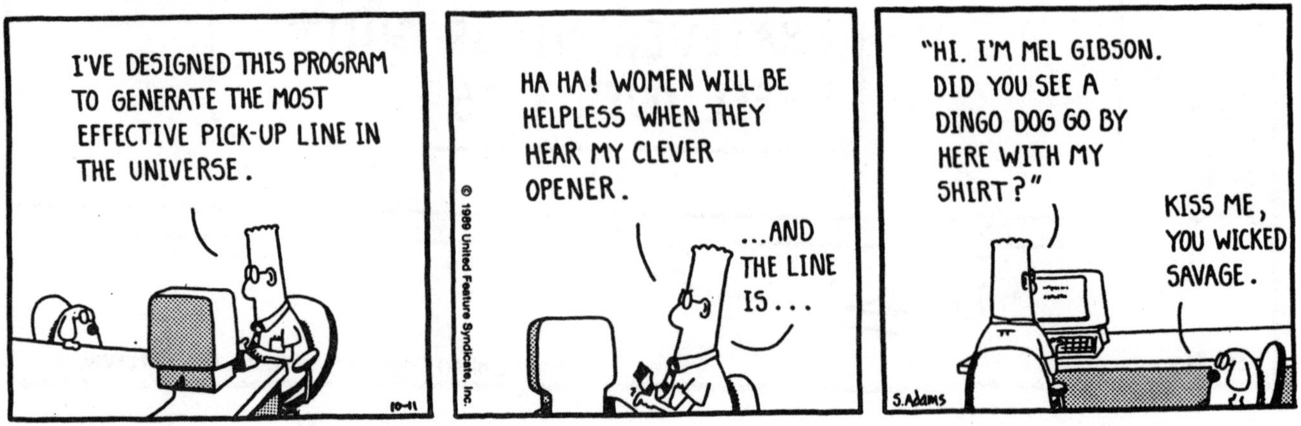
I'VE DESIGNED THIS PROGRAM TO GENERATE THE MOST EFFECTIVE PICK-UP LINE IN THE UNIVERSE.
10-11
© 1989 United Feature Syndicate, Inc.
HA HA! WOMEN WILL BE HELPLESS WHEN THEY HEAR MY CLEVER OPENER.
...AND THE LINE IS...
"HI. I'M MEL GIBSON. DID YOU SEE A DINGO DOG GO BY HERE WITH MY SHIRT?"
KISS ME, YOU WICKED SAVAGE.
S.Adams

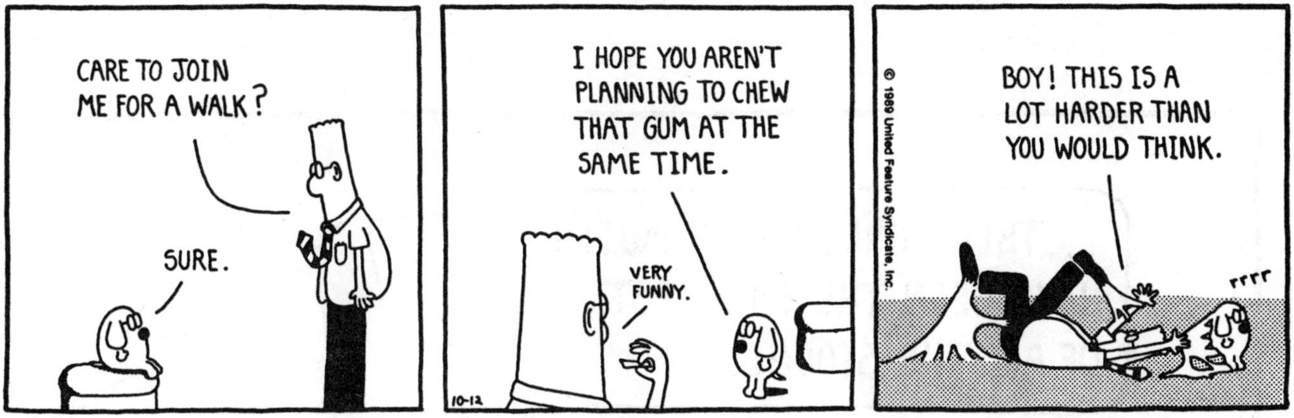
CARE TO JOIN ME FOR A WALK?
SURE.
I HOPE YOU AREN'T PLANNING TO CHEW THAT GUM AT THE SAME TIME.
VERY FUNNY.
10-12
© 1989 United Feature Syndicate, Inc.
BOY! THIS IS A LOT HARDER THAN YOU WOULD THINK.
rrrr

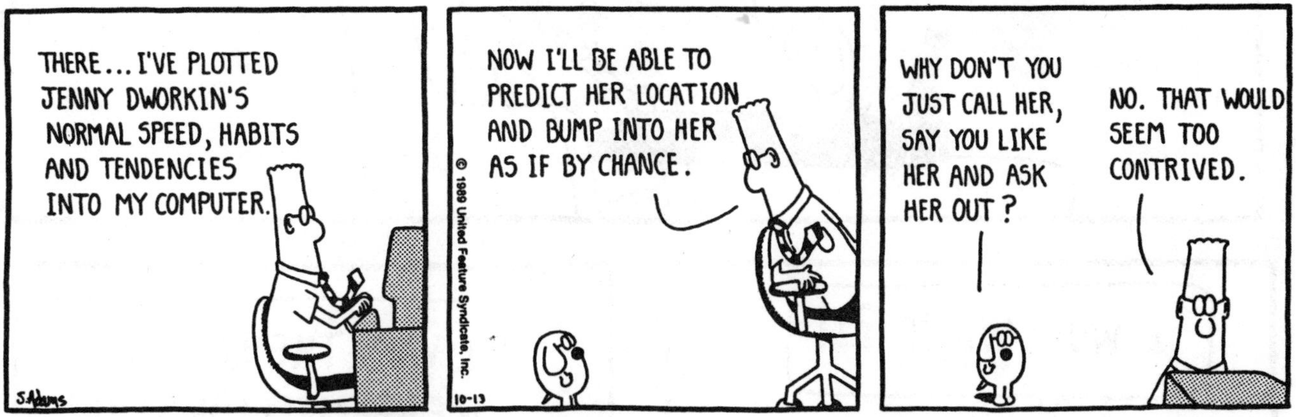
THERE... I'VE PLOTTED JENNY DWORKIN'S NORMAL SPEED, HABITS AND TENDENCIES INTO MY COMPUTER.
S.Adams
© 1989 United Feature Syndicate, Inc.
NOW I'LL BE ABLE TO PREDICT HER LOCATION AND BUMP INTO HER AS IF BY CHANCE.
10-13
WHY DON'T YOU JUST CALL HER, SAY YOU LIKE HER AND ASK HER OUT?
NO. THAT WOULD SEEM TOO CONTRIVED.

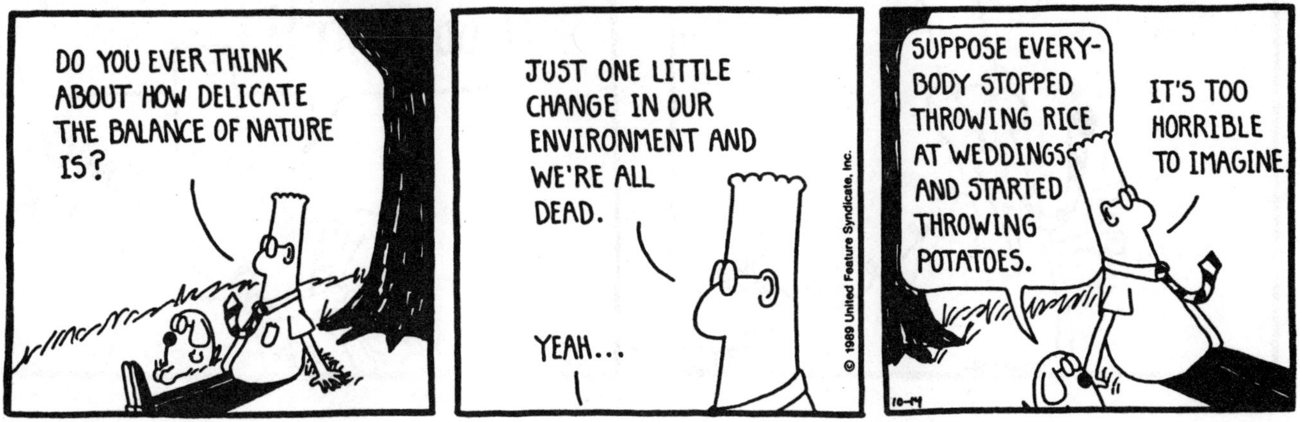
DO YOU EVER THINK ABOUT HOW DELICATE THE BALANCE OF NATURE IS?
JUST ONE LITTLE CHANGE IN OUR ENVIRONMENT AND WE'RE ALL DEAD.
YEAH...
© 1989 United Feature Syndicate, Inc.
SUPPOSE EVERY-BODY STOPPED THROWING RICE AT WEDDINGS AND STARTED THROWING POTATOES.
IT'S TOO HORRIBLE TO IMAGINE.
10-14

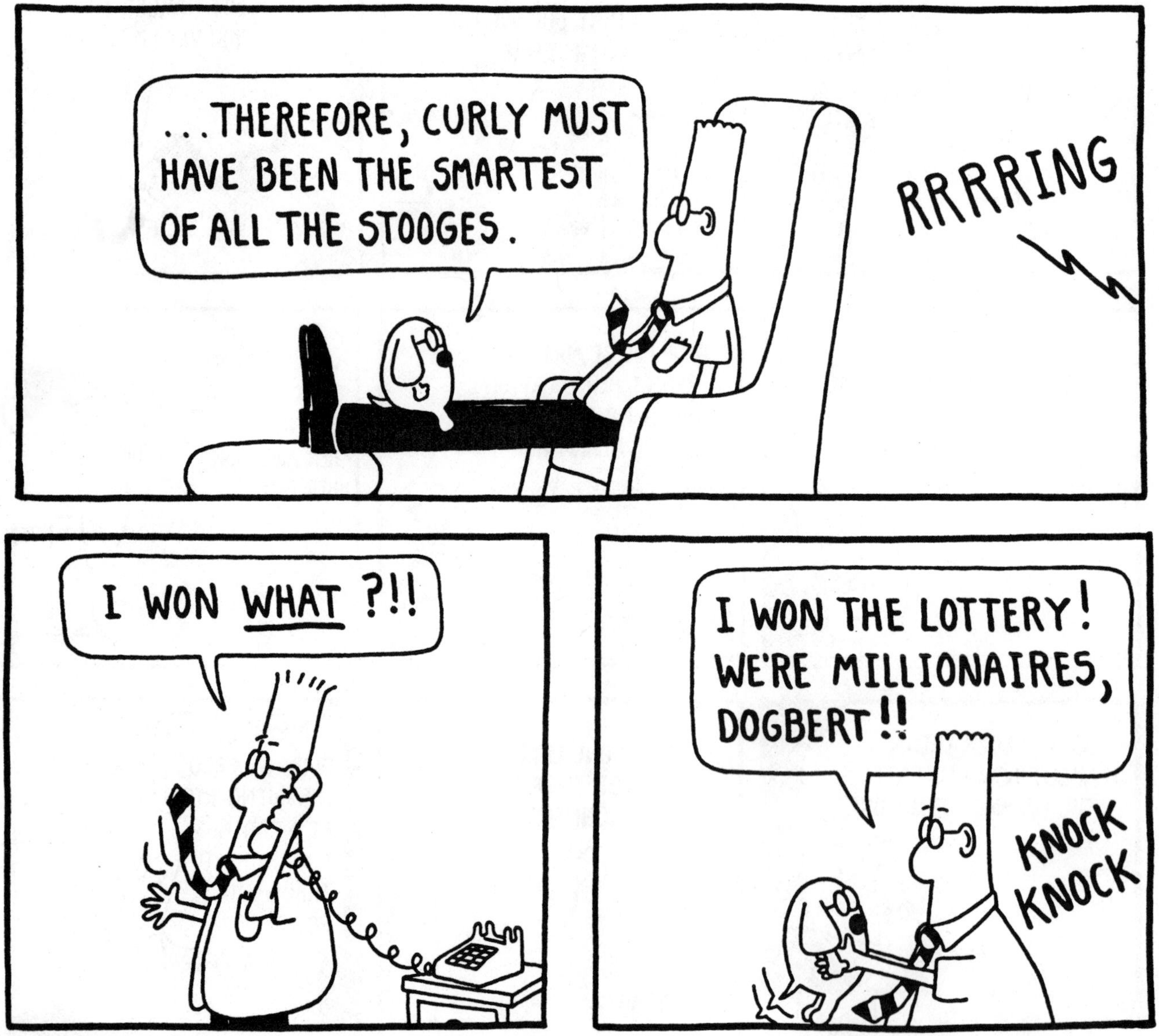
...THEREFORE, CURLY MUST HAVE BEEN THE SMARTEST OF ALL THE STOOGES.
RRRRING
I WON WHAT ?!!
I WON THE LOTTERY! WE'RE MILLIONAIRES, DOGBERT!!
KNOCK KNOCK

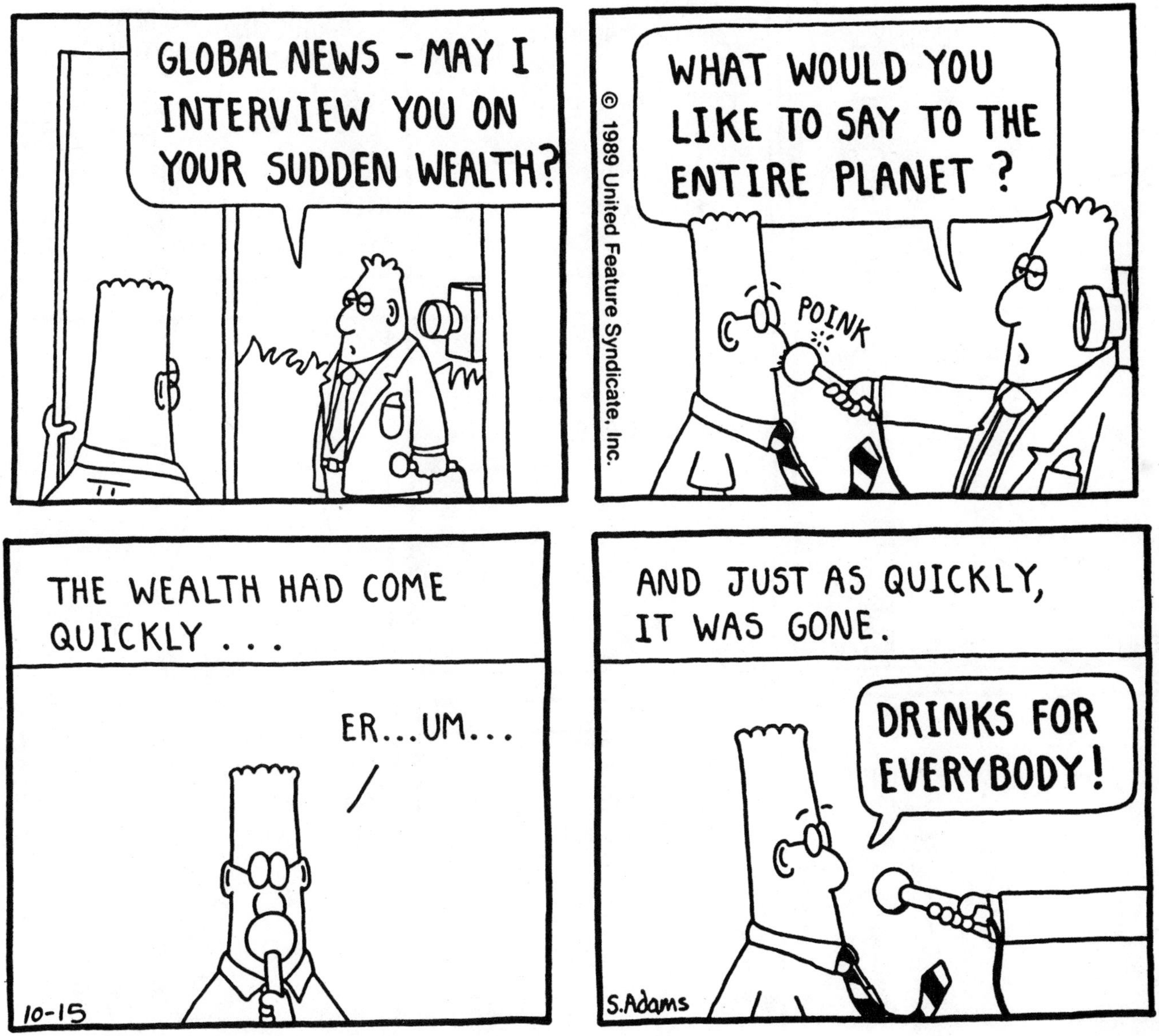
GLOBAL NEWS - MAY I INTERVIEW YOU ON YOUR SUDDEN WEALTH?
© 1989 United Feature Syndicate, Inc.
WHAT WOULD YOU LIKE TO SAY TO THE ENTIRE PLANET ?
POINK
THE WEALTH HAD COME QUICKLY . . .
ER...UM...
10-15
AND JUST AS QUICKLY, IT WAS GONE.
DRINKS FOR EVERYBODY!
S.Adams

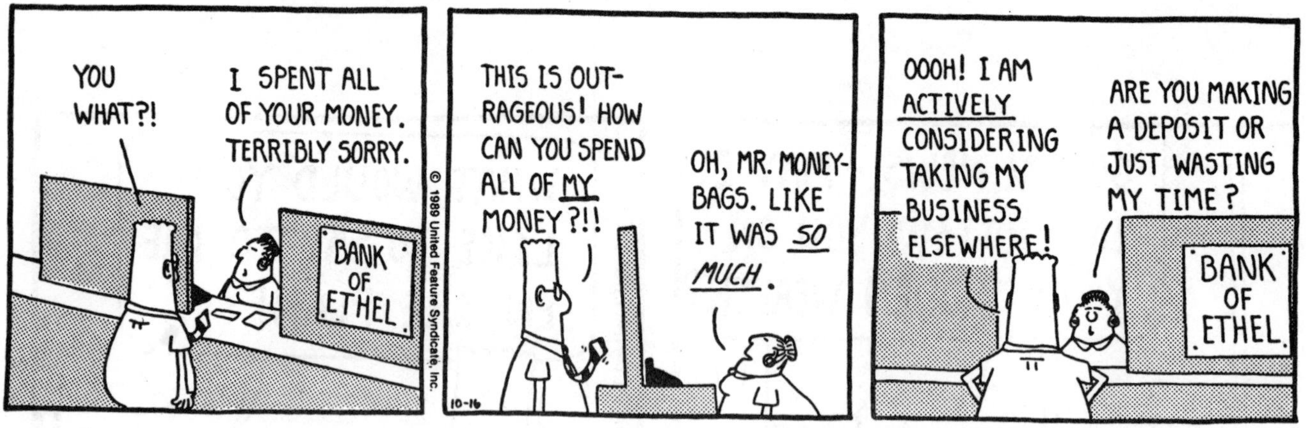
YOU WHAT?!
I SPENT ALL OF YOUR MONEY. TERRIBLY SORRY.
BANK OF ETHEL
© 1989 United Feature Syndicate, Inc.
THIS IS OUTRAGEOUS! HOW CAN YOU SPEND ALL OF MY MONEY?!!
OH, MR. MONEY-BAGS. LIKE IT WAS SO MUCH.
10-16
OOOH! I AM ACTIVELY CONSIDERING TAKING MY BUSINESS ELSEWHERE!
ARE YOU MAKING A DEPOSIT OR JUST WASTING MY TIME?
BANK OF ETHEL

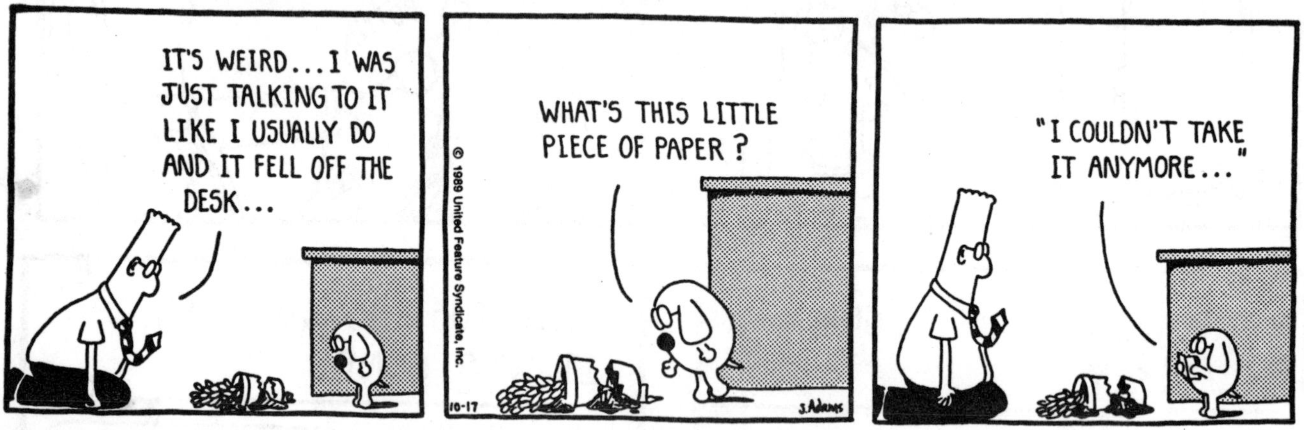
IT'S WEIRD... I WAS JUST TALKING TO IT LIKE I USUALLY DO AND IT FELL OFF THE DESK...
© 1989 United Feature Syndicate, Inc.
WHAT'S THIS LITTLE PIECE OF PAPER?
10-17
S. Adams
"I COULDN'T TAKE IT ANYMORE..."

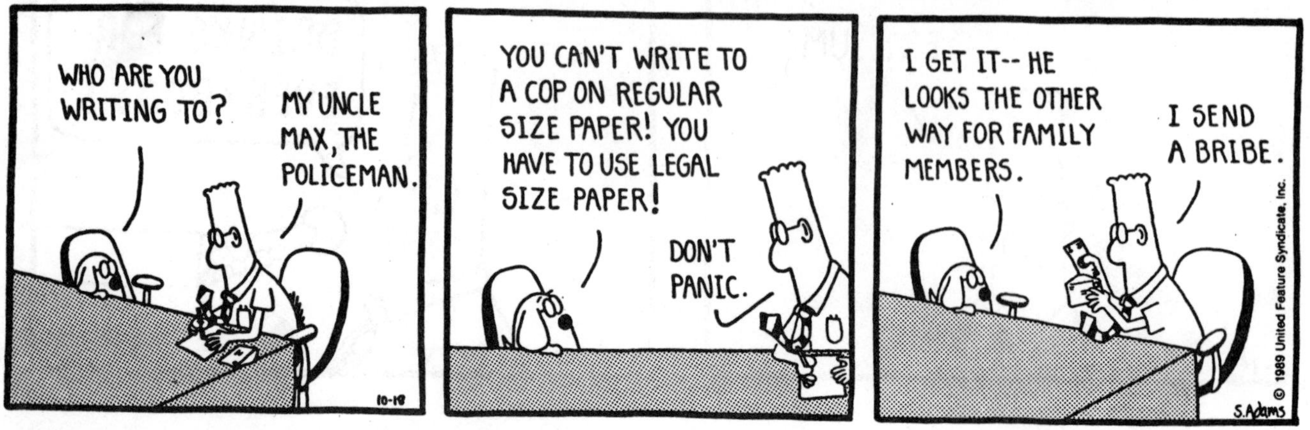
WHO ARE YOU WRITING TO?
MY UNCLE MAX, THE POLICEMAN.
10-18
YOU CAN'T WRITE TO A COP ON REGULAR SIZE PAPER! YOU HAVE TO USE LEGAL SIZE PAPER!
DON'T PANIC.
I GET IT-- HE LOOKS THE OTHER WAY FOR FAMILY MEMBERS.
I SEND A BRIBE.
© 1989 United Feature Syndicate, Inc.
S. Adams

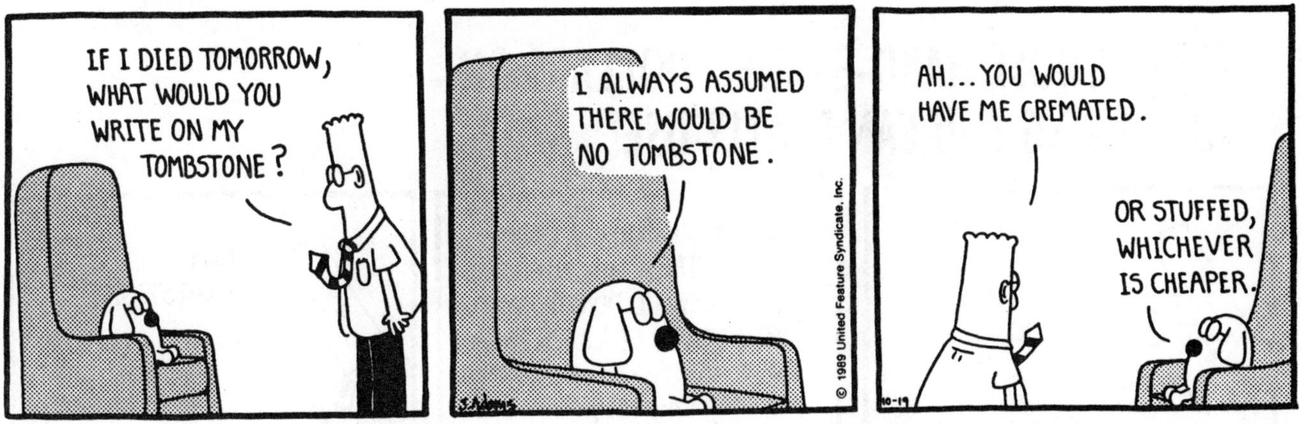
IF I DIED TOMORROW, WHAT WOULD YOU WRITE ON MY TOMBSTONE?
I ALWAYS ASSUMED THERE WOULD BE NO TOMBSTONE.
S.Adams
© 1989 United Feature Syndicate, Inc.
AH... YOU WOULD HAVE ME CREMATED.
OR STUFFED, WHICHEVER IS CHEAPER.
10-19

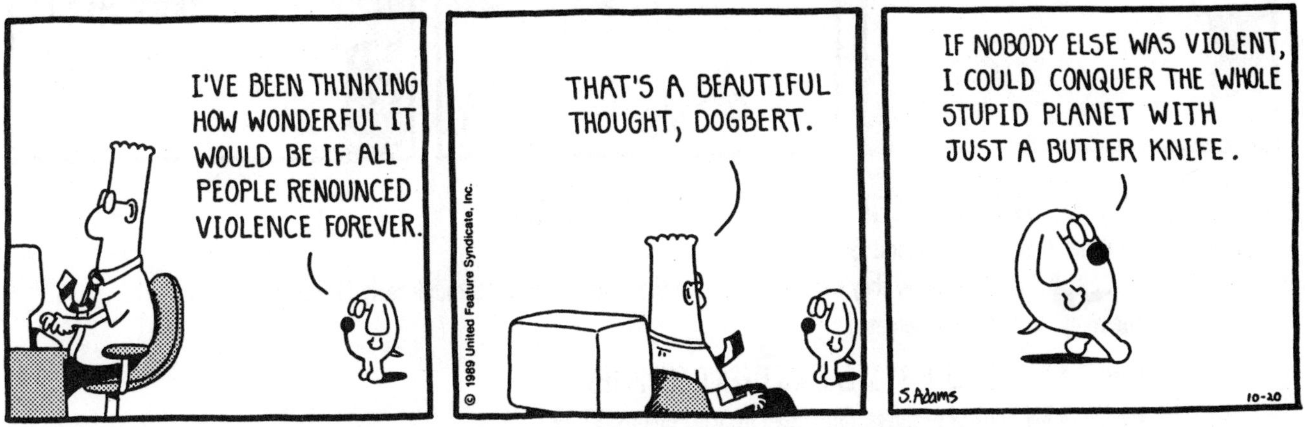
I'VE BEEN THINKING HOW WONDERFUL IT WOULD BE IF ALL PEOPLE RENOUNCED VIOLENCE FOREVER.
© 1989 United Feature Syndicate, Inc.
THAT'S A BEAUTIFUL THOUGHT, DOGBERT.
IF NOBODY ELSE WAS VIOLENT, I COULD CONQUER THE WHOLE STUPID PLANET WITH JUST A BUTTER KNIFE.
S.Adams
10-20

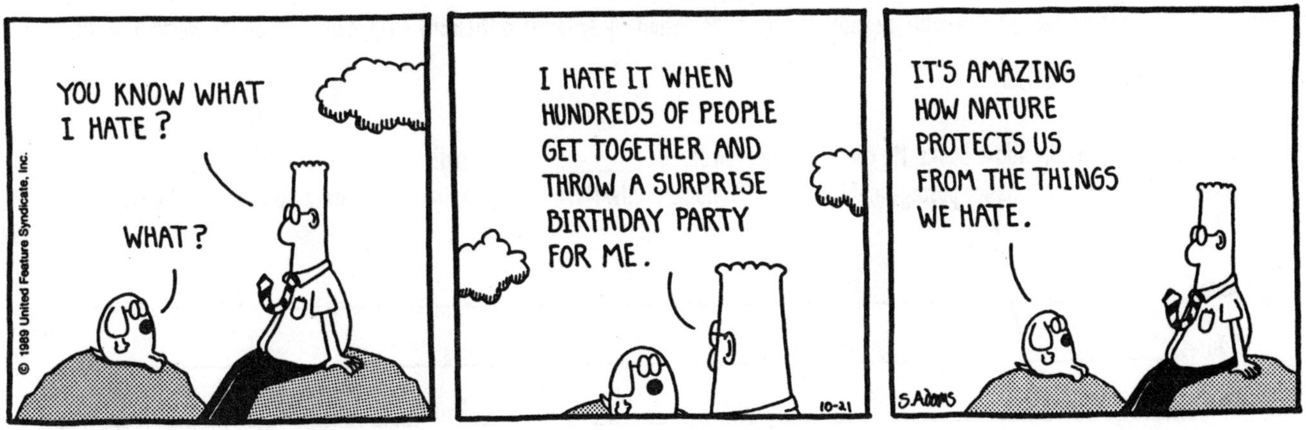
© 1989 United Feature Syndicate, Inc.
YOU KNOW WHAT I HATE?
WHAT?
I HATE IT WHEN HUNDREDS OF PEOPLE GET TOGETHER AND THROW A SURPRISE BIRTHDAY PARTY FOR ME.
10-21
IT'S AMAZING HOW NATURE PROTECTS US FROM THE THINGS WE HATE.
S.Adams

SPEND THOSE HARD-EARNED DOLLARS ON SOMETHING YOU CAN REALLY USE!

I'M THINKING OF GETTING A TATTOO.
ON MY SHOULDER... SOMETHING TASTEFUL YET TIMELESS. I DON'T WANT TO REGRET IT LATER.
S.Adams
© 1989 United Feature Syndicate, Inc.
ANY SUGGESTIONS?
HOW ABOUT "KICK ME"?
12-26

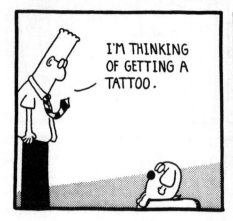

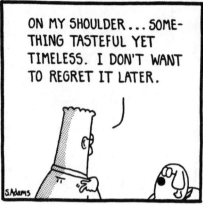

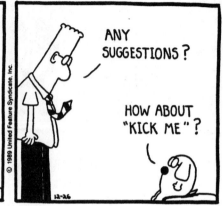

_____ **ALWAYS POSTPONE MEETINGS WITH TIME-WASTING MORONS**
A Dilbert Book by Scott Adams. $7.95
DILBERT strips, in the order they were created, from the strip's premiere through early 1990.
The complete collection, volume I.

_____ **BUILD A BETTER LIFE BY STEALING OFFICE SUPPLIES**
Dogbert's Big Book of Business. Illustrated by Scott Adams. $7.95
Dogbert, the entrepreneurial quadruped from the nationally syndicated DILBERT strip, expounds on the world of work.

_____ **TOTAL BOOKS**

Yes, please rush me the above books. My check or money order for ________ is enclosed!
(Please add $1.50 per book for postage and handling. US. dollars only. Make check or money order payable to Pharos Books.)

Name____

Address____

City_______________________________ State__________ Zip__________

Return to: Pharos Books, Sales Dept., 200 Park Ave., New York, NY 10166. Allow 4-6 weeks for delivery.